"In *The Fiction of our Lives*, Sandra Levy-Achtemeier beautifully balances her unique roles and talents as a neuroscientist, psychologist, and Episcopal cleric along with her skills as an excellent and engaging writer to offer a page-turning and compelling reflection on the narrative of our lives. This is a really good book and will be especially of interest for all those who are interested in reflecting on their own lives and stories as they enter their mid to later years. Book clubs will love this one!"

—THOMAS G. PLANTE

Augustin Cardinal Bea, SJ University Professor,
Director of the Spirituality and Health Institute, Santa Clara University

"I am part of the silent generation that has memories of World War II. I am not a North American Baby Boomer and have little knowledge of the songs that shaped Sandi's life. Some might therefore say that I lack the credentials to speak with authority on *The Fiction of our Lives*. But as I face turning eighty, I think I can say I know authenticity when I meet it; I recognize wisdom when it breaks unexpectedly into my life; and I can tell the difference between well and badly crafted books. *The Fiction of our Lives* pushes all these buttons. So thank you Sandi for including Isobel and me in your journey, and inviting us to share in the birthing of your book. Many others will also thank you for this passionate and skillful outpouring of heart and mind, marks of a genuine scientist and spiritual counselor."

—JOHN DE GRUCHY

Emeritus Professor, University of Cape Town

"In this affecting blend of memoir, cultural history, and popular science, Sandra Levy-Achtemeier captures the feelings and aspirations of American Baby Boomers, as we move inexorably into our later years. What kinds of stories will we now construct to make sense of our lives? Her book affirms hope and optimism in the face of uncertainty, while offering a profound meditation on the human condition and the unique experiences that define a generation."

—DAN P. MCADAMS
The Henry Wade Rogers Professor of Psychology, Northwestern University; Author of *The Art and Science of Personality Development*

"This is Sandra Levy-Achtemeier at the height of her craft—not only as a writer, but as a wise encourager who invites deep and meaningful reflection on life. Elegantly weaving together insights from such diverse sources as contemporary neuropsychology, hit songs from the 1960s and '70s, and scriptural meditation, she inspires us to mark our life journeys with integrity, faithfulness, and gratitude, to weave lives well-lived."

—JOEL B. GREEN, PHD
Provost, Dean of the School of Theology,
Professor of New Testament Interpretation, Fuller Theological Seminary

The Fiction of Our Lives

The Fiction of Our Lives

Creating Our Stories Over a Lifetime

~

SANDRA M. LEVY-ACHTEMEIER

CASCADE *Books* • Eugene, Oregon

THE FICTION OF OUR LIVES
Creating Our Stories Over a Lifetime

Copyright © 2016 Sandra M. Levy-Achtemeier. All rights reserved. Except for brief quotations in critical publications or reviews, no part of this book may be reproduced in any manner without prior written permission from the publisher. Write: Permissions, Wipf and Stock Publishers, 199 W. 8th Ave., Suite 3, Eugene, OR 97401.

Cascade Books
An Imprint of Wipf and Stock Publishers
199 W. 8th Ave., Suite 3
Eugene, OR 97401

www.wipfandstock.com

PAPERBACK ISBN: 978-1-4982-2512-0
HARDCOVER ISBN: 978-1-4982-2514-4
EBOOK ISBN: 978-1-4982-2513-7

Cataloguing-in-Publication data:

Names: Levy-Achtemeier, Sandra M.

Title: The fiction of our lives: creating our stories over a lifetime / Sandra M. Levy-Achtemeier.

Description: Eugene, OR: Cascade Books, 2016 | Includes bibliographical references.

Identifiers: ISBN 978-1-4982-2512-0 (paperback) | ISBN 978-1-4982-2514-4 (hardcover) | ISBN 978-1-4982-2513-7 (ebook)

Subjects: LCSH: 1. Narrative. | 2. Baby boom generation—United States. | 3. Rock music—social aspects. | 4. Neurosciences. | I. Title

Classification: BL2525 L46 2016 (paperback) | CALL NUMBER (ebook)

Manufactured in the U.S.A.   11/07/16

Until the day we die, we are living the story of our lives. And, like a novel in process, our life stories are always changing and evolving, being edited, re-written, and embellished by an unreliable narrator. We are, in large part, our personal stories. And those stories are more truthy than true.

—Jonathan Gottschall

We are all descended from ancestors who loved music and dance, storytelling, and spirituality. We are descended from ancestors who sealed mating rituals and wedding ceremonies with song, as we do now (or at least boomers like me) with "The Wedding Song" (There Is Love), The Carpenters' "Close to You," Nat King Cole's "Unforgettable," and Billy Joel's "Just the Way You Are." Songs like these remind us during life cycle events that we are part of a chain of continuing ceremony and ritual, participating as our ancestors did, binding our collective past to our personal future.

—Dan Levitin

The I becomes an autobiographical author; the Me becomes the story it tells. The internalized and evolving amalgam of self stories—what is now typically referred to as a narrative identity . . . aims to integrate the reconstructed past, experienced present, and imagined future.

—Dan McAdams

The Divine infiltrates our being and manifests, as it must, through the electrochemical processes of our brain.

—Bruce Cockburn

Faith is not easy. It is a daily struggle to affirm that there is purpose and meaning in life, that love does endure and ultimately conquers, that miracles do happen, and that there are signs of hope that keep budding like the fynbos after a fire.

—John deGruchy

Contents

Permissions | ix
Acknowledgments | xi
Introduction | xiii

1 Wired for Song and Story | 1

Section I—Wired for Friendship, Knowledge, and Joy: Building the Story

2 "If I Had a Hammer" | 37
   The Protest Generation and Idealism Writ Large

3 "Which Side Are You on, Boy?" | 72
   Education of the Moral Sense

4 "I'm on Fire" | 101
   The Celebration of Life

Section II—Wired for Religion, Comfort, and Love: Continuing the Story

5 "My Sweet Lord" | 139
   God's Lure and the Life Well-Lived

6 "Take Me Home, Country Roads" | 175
   The Comfort of the Familiar

7 "Imagine Me and You . . ." | 211
   The Many-Splendored Thing Called Love

Epilogue: The Story of Our Lives and the Future of Fiction | 245

Bibliography | 249

Permissions

Grateful acknowledgment is made to the following for permission to reprint:

"Sounds of Silence." Words and music by Paul Simon. Copyright 1964 by Paul Simon Music. All rights reserved. Used by permission, Paul Simon Music.

"America." Words and music by Paul Simon. Copyright 1968 by Paul Simon Music. All rights reserved. Used by permission, Paul Simon Music.

"If I Had a Rocket Launcher." Written by Bruce Cockburn. Copyright 1984 by Golden Mountain Music Corp (SOCAN). Used by permission of Rotten Kiddies Music, LLC.

"The Dangling Conversation." Words and music by Paul Simon. Copyright 1966 by Paul Simon Music. All rights reserved. Used by permission, Paul Simon Music.

"Young Girl." Words and music by Jerry Fuller. Copyright 1968 (renewed) Warner-Tamerlane Publishing Corp. All rights reserved. Used by permission of Alfred Music.

"Cecilia." Words and music by Paul Simon. Copyright 1969 by Paul Simon Music. All rights reserved. Used by permission, Paul Simon Music.

"If You Could Read My Mind." Words and music by Gordon Lightfoot, Copyright 1969/1970 (copyrights renewed) WB Music Corp. All rights reserved. Used by permission of Alfred Music.

Acknowledgments

During the four years or so that I spent writing this book, many friends, colleagues, family members, and professional contacts have added immeasurably to what you now hold in your hands. First—in addition to thanking James Stock and the entire editorial staff at Wipf and Stock for bringing this work to completion—I especially want to thank my editor, Rodney Clapp, for all of his encouragement and support in writing this work. He believed in me and in the concept for the project and I am profoundly grateful. Likewise, I offer great thanks to Connie Dowell, my local editor, for her patience and diligence in assisting in this book's completion—saving me from some embarrassment along the way. I also want to add thanks to Linda Fairtile, head music librarian at the University of Richmond, and Melanie Armstrong on her staff, who helped me track down the several music publishers who have granted permission to quote from various song lyrics in their copyright holdings.

I covered a lot of ground in this book involving several fields of scholarship. Thus, I turned to a number of colleagues and professional friends who read portions of this work—or whose writings contributed to the knowledge base for this project. Specifically, I offer my profound gratitude to South African theologian John deGruchy; biblical scholar and neuroscientist at Fuller, Joel Green; Cate Wallace, writer and friend in Chicago; Tom Plante, fellow psychologist at Santa Clara University; poet and scholar Jill Baumgartner at Wheaton College; and psychologist Howard Friedman, on the faculty at University of California-Riverside.

Very special thanks goes to Dan McAdams at Northwestern University, whose research is credited with being absolutely seminal to the whole field of narrative psychology. We have corresponded over the years and his writings provided a major anchor and inspiration for this current book. One of Dan's students, Will Dunlop—at the University of California-Riverside—was very helpful in my thinking through the future of story in the epilogue.

Finally, musician and neuroscientist Dan Levitin, at McGill University, has been both an inspiration to this writing and a generous correspondent when questions arose from my end.

Within these pages are several interludes containing interviews from early and late Boomers. And my gratitude is now extended to them, who gave their time so generously: Paul, "Beth," Patty, Dave, and Becky. But there were several others who were gracious in sitting with me while talking into a microphone about their childhoods and later years: Judge Roger Gregory, Chief Justice of the Fourth US Circuit Court of Appeals; Carol Wharton, retired sociology professor, University of Richmond; Karla Hunt, retired geologist; Ray Inscoe, retired chaplain, Westminster-Canterbury; historian Dave Crosson; and David Ekey, recently retired physician. To all of these folks who contributed to the richness of the current text, a hearty thank you for your generous gift of time.

Finally, my major supports for not only this work but my life as well, I end this section with my love and gratitude extended to my family—my two sons, Brian and Kevin, and my dearest sister/friend, Karen. Kevin—who also happens to be a professor at the University of California-Riverside—gave invaluable critique to the chapters as they unfolded; Brian—psychologist with an MBA and successful manager in his own right—as always supported me with enthusiasm for my work. And finally, Karen—fellow psychologist and friend—read every word of the entire manuscript, spending hours as she critiqued the pages that came her way.

In the end, it is impossible to give credit to all who deserve it when one reflects across a lifetime and searches for the source of what flows from one's pen—or in this case, the computer keys. One can only give thanks with gratitude for life itself and all those who have provided inspiration along the way.

Introduction

All men are mortal: they reflect upon this fact. A great many of them become old: almost none ever foresees this state before it is upon him . . . . In the old person that we must become, we refuse to recognize ourselves . . . . Old age looms ahead like a calamity: even among those who are thought well preserved, age brings with it a very obvious physical decline. When we look at the image of our own future provided by the old we do not believe it: an absurd inner voice whispers that that will never happen to us . . . . Until the moment it is upon us old age is something that only affects other people.[1]

****

These words were written by the French philosopher Simone de Beauvoir, in the introduction to her work *The Coming of Age*. I read the American edition of this book when I was twenty-nine. I remember reading this longish and scholarly tome with feelings of horror. At about this same time, Simon and Garfunkel's album *Old Friends* hit the market—it must have been a long-play album I suppose, before the days of CDs (which are now also obsolete). Their title song observed "How terribly strange to be seventy . . . ." I agreed: How terribly strange to be seventy. I was part of that generation that didn't trust anyone over thirty (although I was, after all, pushing that dividing line myself).

I picked the book up again recently. It is indeed a grim picture of aging in the Western industrial world. Of course, de Beauvoir was a Marxist, or at least had strong Marxist or socialist leanings. Her book was (and still is) an indictment of society's treatment of its elderly—economically and socially

---

1. de Beauvoir, *The Coming of Age*, 4–5.

marginalizing the frail and dependent aged who are no longer considered quite human since they have ceased being productive selves, capable of contributing to society as a whole. De Beauvoir examined minutely the social context of the elderly on both sides of the Atlantic, as well as the inner experience of these same poverty-ridden aged as they live out their own decrepitude.

As I leafed through de Beauvoir's book again, I wondered how dated her analysis was. I wondered what has changed in the decades that have passed, and what has changed very little since her writing. The reason, of course, why I'm intensely curious about this question is that I'm fast approaching that terribly strange year that Simon and Garfunkel mourned in song. You see, I'm on the leading edge of that bulging cohort known as Baby Boomers. My generation is now working its way toward retirement and beyond. We are heading into that next phase, shaping our life's story over the next decade or two.

So is the future for us inevitably grim . . . or not? Oliver Sacks, once professor of neurology at the New York University School of Medicine, wrote an opinion piece for *The New York Times* titled "The Joy of Old Age. (No Kidding.)." He ended his piece with this: "I do not think of old age as an ever grimmer time that one must somehow endure and make the best of, but as a time of leisure and freedom, freed from the factitious urgencies of earlier days, free to explore whatever I wish, and to bind the thoughts and feelings of a lifetime together. I am looking forward to being 80."[2]

Of course Sacks, as he approached age eighty, didn't technically qualify as a Boomer (more about that cohort in a moment). He was certainly part of a highly educated elite, those privileged who often age more gracefully and more easily than others. Even de Beauvoir recognized that those fortunate elderly with education and money enjoyed their last years in relative comfort. But Sacks also represented a very different view of growing old than what others have described. His counterpoint invites me to reflect on aging in contemporary society—invites me to raise questions and examine what might be the same and what might be different for my own cohort as we move into our own senior status.

Now a great deal has been written about Baby Boomers in recent years. In his *Great Expectations: America and the Baby Boom Generation*,[3] Landon Jones describes Boomers as those of us not having a personal memory of World War II but shaped by the postwar American optimistic high.[4]

---

2. Sacks, "The Joy of Old Age. (No Kidding)."
3. Jones, *Great Expectations*.
4. Often categorized into two groups, the early Boomers (1943–1955 or so) came of

According to William Strauss and Neil Howe in their book, *Generations*,[5] our generation—born between 1943 and 1960—is wedged between what they refer to as the Silent Generation, born between 1925–1942, and Generation X, born between 1961–1981 (my sons' generation).

According to these writers, we Boomers took time to reflect and explore being young between the innocence of childhood and the responsibility of burden-ladened adulthood. We were those youthful radicals who later became stockbrokers. (I remember the "professional graduate students" at Indiana University when I was a student there, those who strung out their education as a very comfortable way of life for years, living a lifestyle where they could be rebels with a cause—passionately arguing with each other at tables in the library cafeteria.) We were idealistic, politically active, antiestablishment dropouts from traditional religious practices; we did sit-ins, we went to Woodstock to "make love, not war." We were the "me" generation, spending lavishly on ourselves, individualistic, doing it all our way.

So here we are today, edging toward what is next. I return to the question raised by de Beauvoir's book. A recent Pew Survey provides some statistics that make me think perhaps her gloom is still relevant to our own coming experience. According to this report, today's Baby Boomers are a generally "glum" group, with 80 percent or so expressing dissatisfaction with how their lives are progressing. In fact, many expect both physical and financial decline in the years ahead, fitting nicely with de Beauvoir's portrayal. Of course, the recent and great recession, wiping out savings and causing widespread layoffs and job loss, has certainly contributed to this malaise.

But there are other notes to hear—that counterpoint voiced by Sacks as we stare down the seventh and eighth decades of our lives. Andrew Oswald and David Blanchflower have analyzed cross-cultural data drawn from eighty different countries over the past thirty-five years, showing that there is a U-shaped curve to levels of life satisfaction. That is, across the world, as folks age—interestingly, regardless of economic status—levels of anxiety and depression go up and satisfaction goes down until middle age (around mid-forties), when the trend becomes reversed (barring serious physical

---

age during the Vietnam War, experienced the Cuban Missile Crisis, the assassinations of JFK, Robert Kennedy, and Martin Luther King, political unrest, the first walk on the moon, antiwar protests, the women's movement, and Woodstock. The late Boomers—born between 1956–1964 or so—experienced Watergate, the Nixon resignation, the Cold War, the oil embargo, rising inflation, and the age of Ronald Reagan's morning in America.

5. Howe and Strauss, *Generations*.

disability).⁶ Other researchers have also found this trend. Carstensen and her colleagues report in their 2011 paper that "as people age and time horizons grow shorter, people invest in what is most important, typically meaningful relationships, and derive increasingly greater satisfaction from these investments."⁷ In other words, with age comes wisdom. We make better life decisions that bring greater satisfaction in the end.

The answer then to what lies ahead for us Boomers seems to be either/or, doesn't it. Some age well; some do not. And hence—since we are all aging one way or another—the reason for writing this book.

Let me just say up front that my first career was as a trained scientist—an academic psychologist specializing in the emerging field of psychoneuroimmunology (that is, looking at the connections between psychological factors, stress-related hormones, and immune function); and my second "career" was (and is) as an Episcopal priest. Thus, this dual training allows me to bring both science and spirituality to bear on the question of aging well.

I'm also going to explore aging in contemporary society in part through the lens of my own life. And I have traveled some interesting terrain with some major turning points in the road along the way. Many of the early turns were leaps into unknown territory because I was single-mindedly pursuing some goal, "come hell or high water" as they say. After all, I was part of the "me" generation and we pretty much all did it our way. In hindsight, of course, I was reinventing myself at each of these turning points, assuming another identity, rewriting my life's story into a coherent whole.

Now I have taken another turn down my life's road. I have assumed another massive shift in my identity—a shift not of my own making or choice but quite the opposite. Six months ago I became a widow for the second time in three years. In 2010, my husband of thirty-five years, Leon Levy, died of complications from Alzheimer's disease. But because of his crippling mental deterioration—traveling from brilliant academic scholar to someone who could no longer recognize one of his daughters or remember our shared past—I actually lost him years before his physical body finally gave out.

Later in that same year, I married again, joining my life to that of Paul Achtemeier's, a dear friend and colleague—and another internationally recognized scholar—who had lost his wife to cancer in 2002. Paul died last January, at age eighty-five, of the prostate cancer he had battled for nearly twenty years. The disease finally won, progressing with a vengeance the last few months of his life. So now I face my own Boomer's future as widow.

---

6. Discussed at length in Jonathan Rauch's article, "The Real Roots of Midlife Crisis."
7. Quoted in ibid., 93

But I am also other selves than just widow. I'm a devoted mother to two "boys" (who are now middle-aged men with families of their own!). I have gathered some lovely step-children along the way. I have accumulated some very dear friends here and there. I have my work: I serve as an associate clergy in a local, historical church (where Patrick Henry took his "give me liberty or give me death" stand); I also write nonfiction books such as this one. These pieces of me are very much alive. They are vital parts of my ongoing story, the parts that remain as stable aspects of my core identity.

The point I want to make here is that although there have been major turning points in my life where I've rewritten the story as it unfolded before me, this time as never before I am keenly aware that I have taken a seismic turn. I am facing for the first time in my adult life the fact of being alone, without a loving partner by my side. This is a scary landscape that I have ventured into, and yet ... and yet I am bidden by life itself to move into this new story plot and make new meaning out of what is left of my time. And that is true for all of us, is it not?

****

Oscar Wilde is supposed to have said something to the effect that "the books that you read when you don't have to, determine what you will be when you can't help it." This is a controlling theme of this book, but its truth is embedded in a larger truth about what it means to be human. The weight of both contemporary science and theology is that we are embodied selves, holistic beings, embodied souls endowed with marvelous brains that are wired for story in all its various forms—stories we sing, chant, read, write, and tell. There is a narrative shape to our lives that reflects the way our brain is neurologically wired to make sense of the world around us.

As a preview of coming attractions, let me give you a brief look at the chapters that lie ahead. In chapter 1, "Wired for Song and Story," I want to spend a little time (painlessly I hope) on the neurobiology of our evolved brain, examining how you and I are wired to tell stories—looking at how we sculpt our brains in becoming who we are when we can't help it. In the process, I'll describe a bit of recent psychology research concerning how we shape our lives especially through the power of fiction.

One of the neuroscientists whom I draw from in that first chapter is Daniel Levitin. In his *The World in Six Songs*,[8] the author lists six categories of music that can be found universally, six categories of songs whose lyrics are about the great human existential concerns of friendship, knowledge,

---

8. Levitin, *The World in Six Songs*.

joy, religion, comfort, and love. But beyond songs with lyrics, it occurred to me that those six categories really cover universal concerns of all stories, sung or otherwise. Reflecting back on de Beauvoir's book, in addition to her Marxist orientation, she was also a Freudian. And if you remember, Freud's classic description of mental health is the ability to work and to love. In broad strokes—drawing from both Levitin and Freud—this is how I have grouped the rest of the chapters that follow the science base I lay down in chapter 1.

The three chapters that comprise section I, "Wired for Friendship, Knowledge, and Joy: Building the Story," reflect the work (or *praxis*, if you want to get technical) of our cohort's early adult years, as well as our current lives. Chapter 2, "'If I Had a Hammer': The Protest Generation and Idealism Writ Large," will include a look at recent narrative psychology research on writing and rewriting one's story—both then and now. Chapter 3, "'Which Side Are You on, Boy': Education of the Moral Sense," and chapter 4, "'I'm on Fire': The Celebration of Life," will examine among other things the shaping power of autobiography and the current research on gratitude and happiness.

Firsthand accounts drawn from interviews with Boomers—those idealists from the "me" generation who are now at peak career points in their lives—will be interspersed throughout section I. I'll focus especially on the quality of our friendships and life satisfaction as we begin to entertain thoughts of retirement over the next decade—or have already made that leap—and muse on what might lie ahead in the next phase of our lives as we continue to write our life stories.

The three chapters that make up section II, "Wired for Religion, Comfort, and Love: Continuing the Story," reflect Freud's second component of health, the power to love. Specifically, chapter 5, "'My Sweet Lord': God's Lure and the Life Well Lived," will take a look at our cohort's search for community apart from traditional religion, and will include a discussion of recent research on acceptance, adaptation, forgiveness, and life satisfaction, as well as religion and health. We'll examine research on sources of comfort in the face of loss and sorrow, as well as acceptance of the self's needs along the way in chapter 6, "'Take Me Home, Country Road': The Comfort of the Familiar." And in chapter 7, "'Imagine Me and You': The Many-Splendored Thing Called Love," we'll look at some research on romantic versus mature love, the effects of living a grateful life, and the process of co-authoring our lives with friends and lovers.

Finally, in the epilogue, "The Story of Our Lives and the Future of Fiction," I'll consider the practice of fiction reading, music listening, and video playing as we re-create our own life stories, discussing the future of fiction[9] within a larger cultural context.

As in section I, throughout this second section I'll include excerpts from interviews with those who are now facing or have already moved into retirement from the main workforce. I'll especially consider the quality of their communal bonds, as well as the place of various spiritual practices that may enrich their lives. We'll look at the coherence of their life stories at this point (or lack of it, as the case may be) as they head into that terribly strange eighth decade.

The title of this book, *The Fiction of our Lives*, has two meanings, doesn't it? On the surface, the title suggests that we sort of make it up as we go along, living lies in the process, creating fictions we tell to others, fictional masks to hide behind and cover up the truth of our lives. But in the deepest sense meant here, we do create our lives and our stories because this is what it means to be human—from our genes to our culture. We create and we re-create and co-create our stories over the course of the years we are given in order to make something of ourselves. Some are more successful at this creative process than others. But all have the capacity to weave a life that has worth, integrity, and coherence. So let's travel this road together and see where the journey takes us in the pages ahead.

---

9. The premise here is that most if not all stories are fictional in the sense that when we call on our memories for words, metaphors, and images, and imagine an episode's closure—whether we're writing an autobiography, sharing last night's dream over lunch with a friend, or telling our spouse about the interaction with our boss this morning—we fill in the gaps as we weave the tale. Chapter 1 will consider the fictional character of stories in more detail.

I

Wired for Song and Story

It is the love of our existence that is the highest love of all, the love of humanity with all our flaws, all our destructiveness, all our petty fears, gossip, and rivalries. A love of the goodness that we sometimes show under the most difficult stresses, of the heroism of doing the right thing even when no one can see us doing it, of being honest when there is nothing to gain by it, of loving those whom others might find unlovable. It is all this, and our capacity to write about it—to celebrate it in song—that makes us human.[1]

****

A few years back, my husband and I flew down to Ft. Myers, Florida. We rented a car and drove to Ft. Myers Beach, where my brother and his wife have a condo so they can escape the winter snows of northern Indiana. We stayed at a motel along the strip of beach there, and one night, after we had gone out to dinner with them, we came back early to the motel. Because it was still an early hour, and because it seemed like a good idea to us to go have a night cap by the pool, that's where we found ourselves that evening. Us and about a hundred other folks shouted at one another over the sounds of a live band under a big outdoor awning protecting the bar from the elements. The noise level was pretty intense (for example, the bartender had to read our lips to figure out what we wanted for our libations), and the music

1. Levitin, *The World in Six Songs*, 289.

with its insistent beat was so loud that we could feel it all the way down to the soles of our feet.

We actually found a table just then being vacated. We grabbed it and sat down to sip and listen to songs—many or most were of the "oldies" genre, given the average age of the crowd jostling around the cramped spaces between tables and bar. Suddenly, some really groovy song was struck up by the band (I mean they were nothing if not loud!), and I and many others decided—or rather were drawn—to stand in place and clap and sway to the beat. (Not my husband, I should add.) I don't remember exactly what "oldie" they were playing, but it drove our rhythm movement, from feet to hands to head bobbing.

Maybe it was Buddy Holly's "That'll Be the Day." Or maybe it was Sonny and Cher's "The Beat Goes On." Or maybe it was the Cuff Link's "Tracy." Anyway, whatever the song was, it electrified the night, and most of us were on our feet swept up in a feeling of communal bonding, almost like one giant, swaying unit of humankind, sharing the moment that bordered on ecstasy.

****

It is likely that if you lived through the 50s, or the 60s, or the 70s, as you read the above song titles, you heard one or more of these songs in your head. You not only heard the lyrics, you actually heard the tune and the signature voices of Buddy Holly, Sonny and Cher, or the Cuff Links in your head. You may have caught yourself actually humming one or more of them, maybe moving rhythmically in your chair just a tiny bit, and maybe you felt good if the memory evoked positive feelings in your brain's memory and pleasure centers.

Now what does this little episode by that Florida poolside tell us about our brains, about us as communal creatures? What does it tell us about ourselves as storytellers as we remember and reflect on emotionally laden events in our lives? Well, it turns out that current science has quite a bit to tell us about the evolutionary and neurochemical roots of our everyday experience—how we see and feel the world about us, how we are drawn into the social bonds that unite us to one another. In the pages that lie ahead, I trace out some of the answers to these questions.

This book is also in part my story, the story I've made of my life so far, my uniqueness as I have moved through my adult years. Moreover, this book is, in some basic sense, your story, because of the humanity—our humanness, our commonality—that we share as fellow creatures. William

James once said something to the effect that after all, we are all pretty much alike. But he added that it's the small differences that make us unique and interesting to one another.

In fact, those small differences, those human qualities, extend all the way down to our genetic make-up. For the most part, you and I share a common human genome, a gene sequence programmed to produce some shade of human being and not any other creature resembling your pet canary or dog. But beyond that common human core program, our uniqueness develops from the ground up. You inherit half your particular genes (determining your eye color and your temperament, for example) from each parent—with perhaps a minor mutation or two thrown into the mix. Over your lifetime your culture and your personal experience shift and shape the expression of your unique subset of genes, developing you into James's singular self.

As I said in the introduction to this work, I have lived through some interesting times and have done some interesting things—at least to me and perhaps also to you. I have grown up as part of a cohort referred to by social scientists as Baby Boomers. So although this book will draw from my own life experiences, it will also be a study of our culture and its times, focusing on the books and songs that have played a role in shaping me into the person I became and am still becoming when I can't help it—to echo again Oscar Wilde's quote.

This book, then, will include a tour of those imaginative products—songs and stories—that have at least partially shaped me, as I have also shaped the person I am now and will be as I make my way toward my end in this world as we know it. More generally, this will be a story of aging in the twenty-first century, a story reflecting the coming of age in those of us born between the years of 1943 and 1960 or so. Thus, it is—beyond my narrative—a story we share as we grapple with the *What next?* of our own lives.

Let me say right up front—since this will be "memoirish" in part as I recall details of my life to flesh out the discussion at hand—that a memoir is a true story of a life as remembered. Thus, from time to time in the pages ahead, I will draw from my memory store episodes experienced as an embodied human creature, raised in a culture that has provided a menu of stories and songs from which I sampled and selected. Perhaps another way to approach the matter at hand is to say that this is in part a memoir—like all remembered past—that is more "truthy" than truth. That is, from both a subjective experiential, as well as neuronal or biological point of view, what we remember is mainly the gist of events in our past, as we fill in the contours of that past with our current experiences and future hopes. The answer then to Pilate's question, "What is truth?" is in fact a complicated one. But more on that later.

What I hope to accomplish in this first chapter is a fairly painless exploration of our common human brain[2]—specifically, our evolved brain structure wired for song and story. We'll consider our brain, from its most primitive core to its more highly refined conceptual apparatus—our miraculous brain that provides the neural network out of which consciousness arises, allowing us to be the human beings that we have become. I hope to make the case, along with several scholars from whom I draw, that it is our imaginative powers expressed in song and dance, in rituals and stories, that have allowed our *homo sapiens* line to not only survive and thrive, but to also reach for the highest heavens in our search for and creation of the deepest meanings of our lives.

Speaking of heaven, I will also say up front—as other scientists and artists have said before me—that in my blending of science and art, nothing of these products of human creation contradicts the notion that there exists some transcendent Being, a Creator beyond our limited time and conception, a Creator who can and does work through the process of evolution to call forth human beings as co-creators of our world and history. Along these lines, someone has noted that "to say that we should drop the idea of [objective] truth as out there waiting to be discovered is not to say that we have discovered that, out there, there is no Truth."[3] Although we will never know ultimate Truth in this limited life, I believe that Truth in the form of Divine and gracious Mystery is both real and engages humans who are open to such encounters.

In sum, this book is basically about fashioning your and my life story with the creative power our inherited brain structures allow—in the company of others, within a culture that provides a menu of options. We can tell

---

2. For my purpose here, I do not intend to address the particulars of the aging brain—that is, the changes that take place in the human brain as it develops over time as we approach senescence. A fairly recent summary of the latest neuroscience findings in this area concludes that current research favors continued plasticity and neural compensation for age-related losses, and neural recovery processes across the life span. In short, our brains—at least in the healthy old—continue to adapt and make up for neural losses over time. Reuter-Lorenz and Park summarize recent findings by stating that "brain-based approaches to aging suggest continuities across the life span whereby investments made earlier in life, in the form of intellectual, social, and physical enrichment, may increase neural reserve and potential for effective scaffolding as people meet increasing challenges in later life" ("Human Neuroscience," 412). I would thus argue that the cultural products and practices related to song and story—for which our brains are already wired—have positive and lasting effects as we sculpt our minds over our adult years. This is the matter taken up in this book.

3. Quotation by Richard Rorty found in Lehrer's *Proust was a Neuroscientist*, 190.

a good story of our life—not because good things necessarily happen to us, but because we have the power to create a good, meaningful, coherent life story across our days as we age. Our brain is wired for that—with a little help from our friends (as the Beatles sang). And I would also add with a little help from Divine grace.

That's the story you're going to see unfolding in the pages before you. The book's refrain is this: You have the inborn potential to create a good life story—no matter what. This book is meant to tell you how and why. With that, let's begin our voyage together through our wondrous human brain, the creator (or co-creator) of our embodied humanity.

****

"Thou shalt not" might reach the head, but it takes "once upon a time" to reach the heart.[4]

Good music, like good poetry [or novels] can elevate a story to give it a sense of the universal, of something larger than we or our own problems are. Art can move us so because it helps connect us to the higher truths, to a sense of being part of a global community—in short, to not being alone.[5]

****

I'm going to assume that most of us are at least familiar with the idea of our species' evolution from prehuman hominid lines of past millennia. Some of us might not be terribly comfortable with that generally accepted scientific fact—although as someone has pointed out somewhere (and I don't mean to demean individual sensibilities in this regard), that it all happened so very, very long ago, that we really needn't worry too much about it in any case. And I really don't want to get into all the counterarguments for the role of a Creator in all of this process, from intelligent design to a more nuanced theory of evolutionary theism endorsed by such scientific luminaries as Francis Collins, head of the Human Genome Project, and now head of the National Institutes of Health. But since Collins's position is also mine on the matter of human evolution and God the Creator's role in all of this

---

4. Boyd, *On the Origin of Stories*, 376.
5. Levitin, *The World in Six Songs*, 132.

process, I'll just briefly quote him right here and then leave the argument for another day and other writers:

> God, who is not limited in space or time, created the universe and established natural laws that govern it. Seeking to populate this otherwise sterile universe with living creatures, God chose the elegant mechanism of evolution to create microbes, plants and animals of all sorts. *Most remarkably, God intentionally chose the same mechanism to give rise to special creatures who would have intelligence, a knowledge of right and wrong, free will, and a desire to seek fellowship with Him (and one another).*[6]

Our modern understanding of human evolution began with Charles Darwin's descriptive scientific writings after his 1831 five-year voyage on the ship the *Beagle*. After his return to land at age twenty-nine, apparently he clearly grasped the idea of human evolution that would electrify the scientific world and the public at large some twenty-one years later. Simply put, "we are descended from a common stock of anatomically modern humans who migrated out of E. Africa as recently as 200,000 years ago and spread around the world."[7]

This is really the point in our human story where I want to begin because I'm primarily interested in our evolved human capacity for singing, dancing, and storytelling—unique to humans as our line has evolved to its current creative and imaginative capacity these past millennia. But perhaps I should back up just a bit and mention the genetic line we superseded, the Neanderthals. In that prehuman branch, we find the origins of song, dance, and rudimentary oral utterings that apparently communicated social meaning for our early ancestors who lived in caves.

Let me first mention what Darwin came to understand—the simple principle that lies at the base of evolutionary theory. Biological evolution occurs when a genetic mutation arises (as they do in each generation) that

---

6. Collins, *The Language of God*, 200–1, emphasis added.

7. McEwan, "Literature, Science, and Human Nature," 10. However, recent research reported in *Science* by a team of paleoanthropologists suggests that our human (or proto-human) line may extend unbroken from our earliest hominid ancestors, tracing our ancestral line back 1.8 million years. Based on the findings of a primitive skull found in a dig site in the country of Georgia, these investigators concluded that the shape of this relatively small brain case suggests a direct line from early and upright hominids (*H. Erectus*) migrating out of Africa much earlier than previously assumed, with that early line evolving from that proto-human ancestor to our present *H. Sapiens* species. Their conclusions have raised the usual scientific controversy, so I cite the study for information only. Their argument makes no substantive difference for our purpose here, in any case.

turns out to have adaptive, survival significance. That is, chance mutations[8] that give the creature and its offspring some survival advantage will tend to persist in the gene pool and be passed on to future generations. If the mutation enhances self-reproduction by, for example, allowing the bearer to find food more efficiently, or appear more attractive to the opposite sex, such mutations tend to get passed on as sexual fitness is enhanced—first to the small local group, and after 50,000 years or so, to the population at large. As someone recently noted, you should congratulate yourself on being the latest reproductive success of a genetic line extending back beyond memory, replete with a full complement of genes that have proven to have great survival value. So pat yourself on the back because you are a winner!

Beginning with our Neanderthal cousins, it turns out that around 1.8 million years ago these prehumans migrated into areas of the African savannah (and likely farther—see note six). Because this climate was quite hot and humid, apparently these individuals learned to stand upright in order to—seriously—catch the breeze. As Stephen Mithin states it in his delightful book, *The Singing Neanderthals*[9] they adapted to the geography as they learned to "stand tall, stay cool!" Interestingly—and very significantly for our own human destiny—as they developed what's referred to as "bipedalism," their skeletal frame began to shift. Among other things that shift allowed the larynx in the neck to elongate and move down lower in the throat, affording a greater range of vocalizations beyond what Mithin refers to as the "grunts and barks" of their predecessors. As I discussed in an earlier book,[10] their upright posture also required a larger brain to coordinate upright movement, "which became rhythmic in gait, allowing them to run long distance, to jump, and to dance."

Still living in small groups or tribes, these early ancestors had no need to develop complex, nuanced language communication. So they continued to express emotion and signal information holistically, using vocal and bodily gestures to greet, warn, appease, and so forth, manipulating others' responses in turn. They also expressed social meaning through rhythmic dance displays, vocalizing or singing rhythmically to sooth their young, and so on. Thus, the evolution of mental mechanisms to maintain rhythmic

---

8. We can debate how "chance" these mutations are, depending on where you stand regarding the "throw of the dice" versus Intelligent Design versus the evolutionary theist positions. Again, I don't want to get into that argument here beyond stating my position in concert with the latter argument. Later in these pages, we will take up the role of God or the Transcendent Other or Infinite Spirit in a discussion of our human flourishing through song and story.

9. Mithin, *The Singing Neanderthals*.

10. Levy-Achtemeier, *Flourishing Life*.

coordination of muscle groups contributed to the development of the human brain.[11]

The brain we inherited from our Neanderthal cousins when our *homo sapiens* line evolved about 200,000 years ago (with some intermingling of our two species before that based on findings from recently discovered traces of Neanderthal DNA in modern humans) already had the capacity for rhythm, dance, and humming song to sooth the young, as well as to utter sounds with social meaning. As I'll elaborate below, song and dance clearly preceded language as human adaptive skills that you and I have retained across widespread regions of our brain, even though the actual rhythm/dance connections have become somewhat attenuated through lack of exercise in our more sedate Western culture.

Our immediate, *homo sapiens* ancestors lived in larger social groupings than did our Neanderthal cousins, which had obvious survival value (after all, there's safety in numbers, more efficiency in gathering edibles, as well as the offering of a larger gene pool from which to select and generate additional novel and useful mutations). Our species thus needed more refined communication signals, and language developed. As our brain expanded to allow more sophisticated communication among larger tribes, our brains also developed the capacity to plan, to reorganize, and to develop rules for living in cooperative groups. Because of our complex, adaptive brain skills, our *homo sapiens* line won the evolutionary lottery, so to speak, and the Neanderthal line became extinct. But importantly for us, we retained their rhythm and song pathways that extend into all areas of your and my brain.

So let me now spend a few minutes on the structure and function of our evolved capacities for song, dance, and story.

THE WONDER OF OUR BRAIN: BUILT FOR SONG AND STORY

In his interesting little book *Keeping Together in Time*, William McNeill describes at length the social bonding effects of moving together in synchrony—whether marching, moving in ritual acts, singing, or dancing with others. "Moving our muscles rhythmically and giving voice consolidate group solidarity by altering human feelings."[12] Our species thrived in the beginning because some happy mutation produced offspring who were best able to elicit cooperation, group coordination, and social bonding by rhythmic movement and calling others to join in. And lo and behold, they all

---

11. Ibid., 42–43.
12. McNeill, *Keeping Together in Time*, viii.

became one group, discovering in the process that united we stand, divided we fall. "Humans need social linkages to make society work, and music is one of them."[13] In McNeill's own words:

> Human beings desperately need to belong to communities that give guidance and meaning to their lives; and moving rhythmically while giving voice together is the surest, most speedy, and efficacious way of creating and sustaining such communities that our species has ever hit upon. Words and ideals matter and are always involved; but keeping together in time arouses warm emotions of collective solidarity and erases personal frustrations as words, by themselves, cannot do. Large and complex human societies, in all probability, cannot long maintain themselves without such kinesthetic undergirding. Ideas and ideals are not enough. Feelings matter too, and feelings are inseparable from their gestural and muscular expression.[14]

****

"We are all descended from ancestors who loved music and dance, storytelling, and spirituality."[15] So states Daniel Levitin in his intriguing work *The World in Six Songs*. In his *On the Origin of Stories*, Brian Boyd also argues for the evolutionary roots of art, saying that "our impulse to engage in and respond to art, verbal, visual, musical, and kinetic, exists across human cultures and develops in all normal children without special teaching. And it depends on the [evolved] capacity of those around us to understand what we have done, even when we are absent or have devised something utterly new."[16] In other words, expression and response to art in all its forms is a bi-directional process, requiring both the creator of the song, dance, poem, or story, as well as the listener, viewer, or reader who grasps the significance of the product and co-creates meaning in the process.

Boyd also points out that since making art in whatever form requires time and energy, art-making was and is costly. As various art forms are found universally in our species, our capacity for music, dance, and storytelling must have had survival value or else these brain capacities would have been eliminated from our genetic pool. That is, these capacities would

---

13. Levitin, *This Is Your Brain on Music*, 258.
14. McNeill, *Keeping Together in Time*, 152.
15. Levitin, *The World in Six Songs*, 225.
16. Boyd, *On the Origin of Stories*, 11.

have been selected out if they had been costly in time and energy with no survival benefit.

Instead our ability to create art in its several forms evolved as evolutionary adaptations. As our brains grew in size and complexity, art forms likely arose as aspects of cognitive play. In fact, Boyd defines art as "cognitive play with pattern." Analogous to motor play in the young of many species including our own, play builds skilled movements and strengthens neural pathways that afford flexibility by anticipating the next moves of self and play partner. "Like play, art succeeds by engaging and rewarding attention, since the more frequent and intense our response, the more powerful the neural consequences."[17] Such consequences or neural effects are enhanced in part by the release of certain neurochemicals within the midbrain's pleasure centers in response to visual and musical patterned stimuli (for example, with increased social trust at the release of the brain-soothing hormone oxytocin). In short, we are evolved creatures, attracted to the cognitive play of pattern against the expected background of everyday routine stimulus—attracted by songs and stories as they surprise and delight us in our ordinary, taken-for-granted lives.

Humans are also "ultrasocial" creatures, and have evolved perceptual preferences where we especially watch each other. From the cradle to nearing the grave we pay special attention to faces—recognizing friends and lovers, finding comfort in the trusted familiar, and studying strangers to know their intentions. In short, we pay attention to what's new on our horizon, vigilant to detect threat, especially threat from strangers. We are also competitive even within our own communal group—seeking the esteem of others to be won through artistic display. If I sing well, others will applaud; if I dance a jig, others will admiringly watch; if I paint beautiful pictures or tell compelling stories, others will be attracted to me and my work, thus assuring the survival of my genes in offspring from my choice of suitors.

Researchers also make the point that in terms of evolution, our species' capacity for making music and moving rhythmically in ritual and dance—already developed in our Neanderthal cousins—preceded our language development within our *homo sapiens* line. To perhaps oversimplify, music evolved first, promoting intragroup cooperation (for example, by lowering testosterone levels affecting "fight" brain centers). Visual art likely appeared next in the form of body decorations as perhaps marks of affiliation leading to cooperation within the group, as well as attractions for sexual pairing. Lastly, language capacity arose as our brains developed the ability for

---

17. Ibid., 15.

rule-following,[18] and neural connections to midbrain memory and emotional centers gave rise to abstract thinking, planning, and problem-solving. In short, music-making paved the way for language—maybe because music promoted representational flexibility through play with pattern promoting the development of a bigger brain.

As we shall see, the evolutionary *functions* of music (attention-getting for purposes of cooperation, bonding, and sexual attraction) are the same as for storytelling. In fact, both music and language capacities are what is referred to as "generative"—in the sense that humans became able to combine and then recombine musical notes and words into creative products, making something new to catch others' attention. The development of language also allowed reflection about the world and then self-reflection about one's life as our consciousness expanded as a function of prefrontal cortex growth.

Given the evolutionary priority of music and likely dance (since the two art modes are neurologically linked in our human brains), let's consider our evolutionary and biological base for music-making first before considering the development of language and our evolved affinity for storytelling and listening.

****

Music, of course, is ubiquitous in our culture. According to Levitin, the average American hears music about five hours of every day. You can't get into an elevator, step into a grocery store, or shop in Nordstrom without having your ears assailed by musical sounds. Stores play Christmas carols before Thanksgiving to get us in the mood to shop early and grab bargains. And because of the development of our technology, the average fourteen-year-old today will apparently hear more music on their iPod in a month than their grandfather heard in his whole lifetime. I myself never take my walks around the neighborhood without my iPhone playing tunes in my ears—songs especially from the '60s and '70s, Bob Dylan and Mary Hopkins singing in my head.

Music affects our mood and our behavior by altering brain chemistry, and the neural pathways in our brain that respond to musical input are widely distributed throughout our brain tissue. As Levitin puts it, the power of music challenges the prediction centers in our prefrontal cortex, neurons that have learned the rules that govern both language and music

---

18. In fact, a common mode of pattern recognition through rule learning and following likely underlies both language and art.

display, and it causes us to pay attention when something unexpected occurs in our hearing. Music simultaneously stimulates emotional centers in the limbic system—the more "primitive" midbrain area lying beneath the cerebral cortex that also contains our memory centers—and activates motor systems in our basal ganglia and cerebellum (the most primitive areas of our brain lying in and near the brain stem area). "This widespread neural activation across the brain serves to tie an aesthetic knot around these different neurochemical states of our being, to unite our reptilian brain with our primate and human brain, to bind our thoughts to movement, memory, hopes, and desires."[19]

Now I don't want to bog us down with an overly detailed description of brain anatomy. In his *This is Your Brain on Music*,[20] Levitin does a nice job of detail. In this work he traces our neural pathways processing musical stimuli from the receptor hair cells of our inner ear through memory and emotion centers in the midbrain, into the "executive" prefrontal cortex that makes sense of it all by the rule-following, repetitive patterns that distinguish music from mere noise—sending signals to the motor regions of the brain and triggering our foot-tapping behavior to the beat. These multiple and widespread centers in the brain blend the music's pitch, timbre, contour, tone, and volume into an "organized sound" called music. If you recall my Florida swimming pool dance scene, these neural pathways were all activated, triggered, and enhanced by a flood of "feel-good" neurotransmitters (for example, oxytocin with its bonding, trust-inducing effects), chemical transmitters stimulating as well as inhibiting neural firings throughout my attention-focused brain.

Some years back Levitin wrote an op-ed piece that appeared in *The New York Times* describing the neural connections between hearing music and dancing in response—the music/movement connection. He ended the piece by suggesting (tongue in cheek, I guess) that the Lincoln Center should really rip up the seats and allow folks to dance to what they heard as they were intended to do by evolutionary programming.

Levitin has a point. It is true that as a result of the pleasurable tension that builds up in our bodies on hearing such organized sound we call music, triggering all that flood of neurotransmitters that light up our brain, we typically feel an excess of energy that we need to burn off in one way or another. Levitin says:

> Some of the energy we feel during music playing and listening is then expended in the increased mental activity (the visual

---

19. Levitin, *The World in Six Songs*, 226.
20. Levitin, *This Is Your Brain on Music*.

images that many people report accompanying musical activity, or other mental activity such as planning, ruminating, or simply aesthetic appreciation). Finger snapping, hand clapping, and foot tapping help us burn off the rest, unless of course we actually get up and dance, perhaps the most natural reaction, but one that has been socialized out of many western adults.[21]

Of course, there are individual differences, aren't there? Brains do differ from one another in both their structure (that is, their physical size as well as arrangement of key structures), the pathways that are available (because of the "use or lose" rule across our individual life span), and baseline levels of neurochemicals available for neural communication throughout the brain. (I was much more ready to get up and dance than my dear husband was at that poolside in Florida, but he was very indulgent about my need to move and perhaps he did clap a bit as he sat beside me!)

Ultimately we differ from one another in our temperaments, motivations, thought patterns, unconscious and preconscious perceptions of the world around us, in our imaginative capacities, our hopes, beliefs, and dreams. We are all unique creatures, from our inherited genes to the brains we have sculpted over a lifetime. Still, the mere observation of dance motor movements is catching for many of us—maybe all of us to a certain extent. Thinking back on that poolside episode, somehow the actual sight of others clapping and swaying to the music did entice me to join in. That is, there was sort of a group amplification effect in observation of others' responses to the music.

Maybe this is the place to just mention the mirror neurons we carry in our brains (as do some birds and other primates)—one of the most frequently cited discoveries in the neurosciences over the past twenty years. In short, these brain neurons fire both when *performing* an action and when *observing* an action being performed by a fellow creature. Thus, when you see someone dance a jig you have neurons in your brain that fire as if you were also joining in that dance. In terms of evolutionary adaptation, presumably this neural firing (perhaps first arising by chance mutation) had survival value because it helped our ancestors learn and prepare to perform actions that they had not done before—paving the way for their own actual performance in the future.

Since memory and emotion centers are closely neurally linked, such observational learning has emotional consequences. And emotions are the great motivating forces in our lives. They propel us into action. If you feel joy, you want to clap and jump and whoop and holler. If you're angry, you'd

---

21. Levitin, *The World in Six Songs*, 101.

like to punch the guy out . . . or at least "give him a piece of your mind!" "Emotion and motivation are thus intrinsically linked to each other, and to our motor centers. But the system can work in the other direction, because most neural pathways are bi-directional. In addition to emotions causing us to move, movement can make us feel emotional."[22]

As we have already seen, music and dance are powerful elicitors of emotional responses in us due to the rush of hormones and other neurotransmitters bathing our brain synapses. Since the amygdala, thought to be the seat of emotions in our midbrain region, is situated close to the hippocampus—the principal brain center for memory—if the music stirs up old memories, they will likely be accompanied by strong emotional associations. When I crank up my CD player and hear the song "MacArthur Park"—by the way, the greatest song ever recorded, in my opinion—I not only have to move to the beat once the song hits its high spot, but the memories of my graduate school days flood back, that '60s feeling, all those countercultural protests that were part of the antiwar *zeitgeist* of those days.[23]

Why does music move us so? Again, we can look to our brain wiring for our answer. As he points out in his *Proust Was a Neuroscientist*, Jonah Lehrer confirms what I have already noted: in response to song, neural pathways in our brain pass through our emotion centers directly—initially bypassing a need for interpretive ideas generated in higher cortical centers that would interfere with our immediate, emotional response to the music. He says this is why "all art aspires to the condition of music. The symphony gives us the thrill of uncertainty . . . without the risk of real life."[24]

Another little interesting fact about our memories is that when we revisit our remembered experience—in song or otherwise—we alter the memory trace at the level of synaptic connections, at the level of the dendritic net connecting cell to cell, thus coloring and altering the past memory with experience from our present lives. This is why the repeated hearing of our '60s favorites on satellite radio in part dulls the original memory and its context, watering down the power of our emotional response to the stimuli.

---

22. Ibid, 54.

23. Songs are not the only elicitor of emotion-colored memories. Our sense of smell and taste are powerful in this regard—they are "uniquely sentimental," states Jonah Lehrer in his *Proust Was a Neuroscientist* (80). There is a neurological explanation for this phenomenon. Both smell and taste are senses directly connected by neural pathways to the hippocampus—the center of long-term memory. (To this day, the smell of cigars bring back memories of my dad coming in the front hallway on a winter evening and my clinging to his tweed coat smelling of tobacco leaf.) Apparently signals from all of our other senses first pass through the thalamus, the neural base for language and the "front door" to consciousness.

24. Ibid., 133.

> Each neuron has dendritic branches and it's in this sprawling canopy that specific memories are preserved.... Every time we conjure up our past, the branches of our recollections become malleable again ... dendritic details are always being altered, shuttling between poles of remembering and forgetting. The past is at once perpetual and ephemeral.[25]

This is also why when we hear a song for the first time in years that was associated with an emotionally laden past episode, that original, emotion-charged memory comes flooding back, hitting us—triggering a nostalgic response as we relive the memory of the original event.

In his *The World in Six Songs*, Levitin's six categories pretty much cover the entire waterfront of music: songs of friendship, joy (expressing our exuberance at being alive), comfort (soothing songs with the message that "things will be all right in the end"), knowledge (songs that help us remember facts necessary for survival or cultural preservation), religion (songs bound to ritual in honor of the gods or God), and love. Common to all of them is a linkage to other human beings, links to others of our own kind. Just to highlight here his first and last categories—friendship songs and love songs—let's reawaken a few memories of our own as we move on in the pages ahead to a discussion of narrative.

According to Levitin, friendship songs are those that bind us as a self-conscious group in cooperation and good fellow feeling. Within this category that we'll examine more closely in chapter 2, the author includes social and political bonding, facilitated by protest and countercultural songs, often shared by subgroups living on the margins of society at large. As I write this, songs like Arlo Guthrie's "Alice's Restaurant," Peter, Paul and Mary's "Blowin' in the Wind," and the rock opera *Hair* come to mind. You can fill in your own favorites occupying your personal memory. For me, these songs defined who we were as students in that social roiling time (as well as influenced how we became in subsequent decades)—as the marginal, antiestablishment groupies who were going to make love and not war, who were going to save the world by dropping out at Woodstock. Remember?

Levitin's last category, love songs, evolved as originally adaptive as our ancestors bonded in monogamous pairs to raise their helpless young, essential for the maintenance of human society as we know it. In its broadest definition, under all the manifestations of human love—romantic love, mature love, love of parents and children for each other, love of God, love of country, love of liberty and life—underneath it all lies an intense caring about someone or something beyond oneself. Given this, clearly the opposite of

---

25. Ibid., 94.

love is not hate, but indifference. In essence, this many-splendored thing called love is what finally makes us human.

I suppose when we think of love songs, we think of romantic love. Since I have been paying attention to these song categories these days, it has seemed to me that about 90 percent of the songs they play on satellite radio are love songs of this type. Think of the love songs dear to your own heart. There are so many that come to my mind. "Someone to Watch over Me," "Love is Here to Stay," and closer to my own generation, the Turtles' "Happy Together,"[26] Tommy Roe's "Dizzy," the Kingston Trio's "Scotch and Soda," B. J. Thomas's "Hooked on a Feelin'." The oxytocin flows, eliciting trust beyond reason in the loved one, experientially dissolving the boundary between me and my beloved.

I think this may be a good place to begin to segue into our discussion of narrative and the evolutionary roots of story. Because if you think about the songs I just mentioned, or reflect on the ones you also brought to mind out of your own life's experience, you'll see that these songs with lyrics tell a story. Now of course you don't need lyrics to hear a "story" in music, but words do help clarify and convey meaning less ambiguously. "Victory at Sea" and "The Great Gates of Kiev" (from the larger work "Pictures at an Exhibition") don't have lyrics. Nevertheless, these musical pieces create some kind of story in your mind and mine. But our stories will likely be very different in kind and meaning.

If there are lyrics linked to the tune, then the meaning is much less ambiguous. Still, musical language expressed in lyrical form is compressed in the sense that the meaning of the words are still more ambiguous than if I were to spell out the story in prose. If you're the music listener you have to engage with the song and fill in the blanks, so to speak. For example, I mentioned the song "MacArthur Park" previously. Do you remember the refrain? It goes "Someone left the cake out in the rain / and I don't think I can take it / 'cause it took so long to bake it / and I'll never have that recipe again . . . oh nooooooo."[27]

Now what in the heck does that mean? Well it means something to me. There's a story in there for me, because whenever I hear it sung, tears invariably come to my eyes. For me, it's a story of irreversible loss . . . of a time . . . of youth . . . of love. Fold in all the losses of your own lifetime and maybe you can see what I mean. And it has a narrative shape of sorts. On hearing it, and dancing to it, I get lost in my story, in the memories of my life.

---

26. The Turtles, "Happy Together."

27. Written by Jimmy Webb, performed by Richard Harris. Copyright 1968 by Universal Polygram International Publishing Inc.

Our memories allow us to live in time, to reach back into the past, to fill in blanks, to recombine the bits and pieces of our past life into the meaning that we shape now, and the future that we expect. We tell a story that has a first this and then a that and then a next thing. Our brains are wired for story as well as music. Let's look.

THE WONDER OF OUR BRAIN: BUILT FOR STORY

Have you ever had the experience of being riveted to a story—particularly a fictional one unfolding in the pages of a book you are now immersed in—so immersed in fact that the room you're sitting in, your spouse in the chair beside you, the fight you had with your best friend on the phone last night, the appointment that you are going to be late for in about a half hour . . . all these mundane facts of your life have fallen away? Fallen away because you are transported to another world, the world of the story before you?

When I answer that question for myself, the book that comes to mind is one by Ken Follett titled *Hornet Flight*. I read this historical novel some years back and I remember it being a real, as they say, page-turner. If you haven't read it, I don't want to spoil it for you. But the last few pages were so tension-filled—involving two teens' flight of a patched together old Hornet Moth biplane to escape Nazi-controlled Denmark—that I was nearly white-knuckled while reading them.

Skipping the details of the plot, what I do remember is that as I reached the climax of the story, my heart was pounding, my breathing was coming somewhat faster, I held my breath, and my palms were sweaty until the plane landed safely on Britain's shore. At that point the release of my bodily tension was palpable—almost as if I had been on that biplane myself.

In recalling my reading and my response to the tale, I have also described certain essentials of narrative engagement, especially *fictional* engagement, that are important elements of story structure and reader response that I'll describe in a bit more detail in the pages ahead.

****

[Fiction] helps us to understand ourselves, to think—emotionally, imaginatively, reflectively—about human behavior, and to step outside the immediate pressures and the automatic reactions of the moment. From pretend play and jokes to Homer,

Murasaki, or James Joyce, fiction taps into the swift efficiency of our understanding of agents and actions. Old and new stories and characters open up and populate possibility space. All these fictions make us the one species not restricted to the here and now, even if that must be where we act and feel—and imagine.[28]

In his *The Storytelling Animal,* Jonathan Gottschall labels our species as *Homo Fictus,* as fiction man, as the "great ape with the story-telling mind." Indeed he makes the case that we humans are addicted to stories. Awake or asleep, daytime or nighttime, we weave our tales. We talk to ourselves and tell ourselves stories as we sip our coffee and gaze off into the distance, for example creating a narrative about what we could have said, should have said to that guy yesterday; as we arrive home in the evening and greet our spouse with the words, "Do I have a story to tell you. You wouldn't believe what the guy at the next desk said to me during break..."; as we meet a good friend for lunch and launch into our latest gripe about the dentist we saw this morning who promised it wouldn't hurt... but then it did! And so on. And as bizarre as our dreams are at night, nevertheless, they do have a story form, an order of sorts, a this leading to a that. Our daydreams and our night dreams, our gossip about others and the telling of our life events all have a temporal shape to them, a temporal movement that makes them story. Sportscasters tell stories, dramatic, suspenseful stories about sports plays; our trial lawyers tell great, dramatic stories to sway jurors' thinking. (As I write this the George Zimmerman trial for the murder of Trayvon Martin has just ended. If you watched the defense and the prosecution lawyers tell their version of events, you will have seen the weaving of powerful tales. It turned out that Zimmerman's lawyer's version was the more persuasive one in the jurors' judgment.)

As Gottschall puts it, our "brain circuitry shapes the chaos of our lives into story,"[29] creating a sense of self-coherence, ultimately weaving together our sense of present, past, and future. According to Gottschall and others, our storytelling mind allows us to experience our lives as a whole, in an orderly and meaningful way—making life more than a confusing, buzzing series of disconnected nows.

As is true for all human perception, whether creating or viewing art of all kinds—including of course music—or reading prose or fiction, we humans are pattern detectors. That is, we are wired to attend to repetitive patterns and to pay special attention to what appears to us as novel and thus worthy of scrutiny. Trying to understand the world around us, below

---

28. Gottschall, *The Storytelling Animal,* 208.
29. Ibid., xvii.

the level of consciousness, our brains process and make sense of incoming stimuli to anticipate and ward off surprises. But we are also—being playful creatures—delighted by surprising patterns that attract and stir the emotions that in turn motivate our overt or covert responses.

But why are we attracted to fiction? Why have we become *Homo Fictus*?

In his *On the Origin of Stories*, Brian Boyd's main argument is that story (especially fiction) like other forms of art such as music, is an adaptation that has become hardwired in our human brains as they evolved over past millennia. Fiction, as a form of linguistic play, increases the mind's flexibility. As we'll explore in more depth in the next chapter, fiction helps us explore future possibilities as well as real actualities. This experiential exploration costs us comparatively little effort—after all, I wasn't actually in danger escaping the Nazi killers in that taped-together biplane in Follett's *Hornet Flight* (more likely I was tucked into my favorite chair with perhaps a nice glass of Cabernet beside me)—allowing me in the safety of my chair to experience the thrill of danger and the relief of rescue at the story's end.

As I tried to say in telling that little story, I was quite unable to suppress my response to that well-told novel. I was sucked in, I was seduced, I was transported. In the process, I was exposed to a unique problem and its solution. I was confronted with evil in the form of Nazi racial hatred, and I experienced again the triumph of good over evil, justice over tyranny. In short, my mind was richly rewarded for turning the pages until the end of that work.

In arguing for the biological base of fiction preference, Boyd makes clear—as others have—that in order to claim an evolutionary base for some capacity, the evolved adaptation has to be designed for some biological function or purpose. He then goes on to list likely functions of fiction. He argues that reading fiction increases the "range of vicarious experience and behavioral options," and "improves our capacity to interpret events." By increasing our understanding of possible options, fiction "hooks our attention (thus increasing the social status of the storyteller), rouses emotion, and amplifies memory," since we tend to remember what moves us. All of this provides a broader basis for our thinking and problem solving—without requiring belief that the actual fictional events are true. After all, I was aware that Follett's novel was a made-up story, even though it was based on actual historical events. In neural terms, fiction "provides important nourishment for brain growth, it actually helps rewire the brain, increasing the connections between neurons in the cerebral cortex."[30]

---

30. Boyd, *On the Origin of Stories*, 191.

Boyd emphasizes the playful quality of both fiction telling and fiction enjoyment—even as he points out that fiction and myth and stories of various kinds can be harnessed for serious purpose. For example, religions of various stripes have always used song and stories to serve their own teaching and worship purposes. Nevertheless, despite serious purpose, like all art fiction is basically a creation of our brain's capacity to play with patterns (here linguistic) for our human delight.

All art has cost of course, cost in terms of time and energy both to create and to pay attention to the products, benefitting those who make and those who consume the products in one way or another. To repeat a central point here, there have to be species benefits, or our story-creating powers would long ago have been weeded out and eliminated from our species' repertoire.

Boyd lists as *low* cost *high* benefit stories captured in proverbs, fables, and parables—providing "moral rules of thumb." He cites stories in the form of jokes as having *low* cost and *high* immediate benefit for both teller and audience, "being brief, portable, and steeped in the pleasures of surprise ... like social play." On the other hand, stories of *high* cost and *high immediate* benefit include screen and print fiction (it usually takes years to write a novel), but produce pleasurable, short-lived entertainment—the best stories conveying some moral or real-life truth within them. And finally Boyd cites stories of *high* cost and *high, long-lasting* benefit to include serious stories "that provoke us to reconsider what it is to be human"[31]—perhaps an example being *Night*, Elie Wiesel's autobiographical account of his and his father's time in a Nazi death camp.

Gotschall argues that "when we experience fiction, our minds are firing and wiring, honing the neural pathways that regulate our responses to real-life experiences."[32] Citing Keith Oakley and his colleagues' work that showed that fiction readers had better social skills than those who mainly read nonfiction, Gotschall concludes that reading fiction is good for you because living in society is enormously challenging and we humans need all the help we can get. Recent research that we'll revisit in due course has shown that reading high quality, literary fiction in particular has long-lasting and positive interpersonal consequences for the reader. In short, reading fiction is an enriched and pain-free way to expand our understanding of other humans who occupy our real world, allowing us to interpret others who are different from us, to understand their motives as they can grasp

---

31. Boyd, *On the Origin of Stories*, 207–8.
32. Gotschall, *The Storytelling Animal*, 65.

ours, to anticipate their behaviors, and to solve problems that may arise in future new situations and encounters.

As we'll also discuss in a bit more detail in the pages ahead, from early childhood on, humans begin to develop what's referred to in child development studies as a theory of mind (or ToM for short). Early on, we begin to understand other minds, grasping them in terms of goal-seeking, intentional purpose, and desires. Our minds develop in ways that make us pretty good at reading one another, at taking the role of the other, or empathizing, and predicting others' actions as a function of their own beliefs and intentions. We also come to understand that they too are good at reading us. "Trying to understand why others do what they do matters so much in both human life and literature . . . . Higher intelligence emerged primarily as social intelligence . . . to understand conspecifics and to reveal or conceal from others our beliefs, desires, and intentions."[33] In evolutionary terms, humans developed such social intelligence as a result of neural connections in an expanded frontal neocortex, and this intuitive ability to read others' motives and predict their behavior led to greater group cooperation and safety—thus again enhancing survival.

To the point here, this power of cognitive-emotional perception that we carry around in our own theories of mind is enhanced by the reading of fiction, expanding our experience beyond the concrete particulars of our everyday life. Both fiction and autobiography provide enriched opportunities to exercise our ability to read others in flexible ways.

Additionally, reading both poetry and prose—fiction or otherwise—provides opportunity for meeting of the minds, the mind of the author and the mind of the reader, creating new meaning in the process. "What drives the creative process is our hankering for mind-making and mind-reading . . . [allowing us] to navigate our social world and also structure that world"[34] as we make our way through it.

At the beginning of this chapter, I talked about our memory as actually pretty faulty in terms of remembering exactly the actual past events that we have experienced. In fact, memories can be classified into semantic versus episodic ones. *Semantic memories* involve memories of fact. For example, we learn and then remember that September has thirty days and the Dow Jones Industrial Average is the average value of publicly traded stocks of thirty major industries. *Episodic memories* are memories of past events that we have experienced over our lifetimes. The "failure" of our episodic memories to recall precise replicas of our own experience is likely not a failure

---

33. Boyd, *On the Origin of Stories*, 141.
34. Zunshine, *Why We Read Fiction*, 160–62.

at all (and think of the horror if we remembered every minute of our past experience, never shaking a single detail of it over time). No, this weakness of our episodic memory may also be another evolutionary adaptation facilitating our retrieval of aspects of memories and recombining them in order to imagine simulations of future experience.

In other words, because our memories "fill in" details of past experience, we are able to imagine and create new meaning from past experience. We thus expand cognitive flexibility at the neural and experiential level at relatively low cost in the process. Taking that biplane ride of Follett's fiction in my imagination cost me minimal actual pain other than the tension that built during the reading. I gained not only new information about our culture's historical past, but also reinforcement of neural pathways undergirding my moral expectations regarding social justice.

In short, we are meaning-generating creatures; we realize by the mistakes that we make that our memories can be faulty—we can forget or "lose" someone's name, we can misremember by coloring the past that never actually occurred, we can be mistaken about "facts" we are certain about. We know this, but we persist in filling in the blanks as best we can. You and I desire to know, to know more, to predict, to not remain in the dark about our ultimate future even beyond the grave. We develop stories and myths (some true perhaps) to answer the ultimate questions of life. We coo songs and tell stories from the crib to the grave (so to speak). Let's spend a bit of time looking at our individual development in this regard across our own life span.

THE EMBODIED MIND: THE DEVELOPMENT OF OUR NARRATIVE MINDS OVER THE COURSE OF A LIFETIME

****

Fiction is even more central to human life than we feel from the moment we first engage in pretend play to the moment we finish our last story[35]

---

35. Boyd, *On the Origin of Stories*, 384.

****

When I was about four or five my parents took me across the Ohio River from our home in downtown Louisville to my Aunt Vi's house outside New Albany, Indiana. By that time my Grandma and Grandpa Shelton (my mom's parents) had moved in with Aunt Vi after her husband died; and so the three of them grew old together in this big old farm house on the edge of town.

I have this memory of sitting on the couch in Aunt Vi's living room and someone . . . maybe my mom . . . maybe my grandma . . . was reading to me out of a child's fairy-tale book. The particular story had a repetitive refrain at the bottom of every page that went "The goblins are gonna get you if you don't watch out!" Now I don't remember the tale at all but I do remember that refrain to this day. I also remember—some six decades or so later—that I didn't like the story, that I felt a shiver of fear every time we came to that line. Both the line and the fear, the rhythmic language and the negative emotion, became wired in my brain's memory center and pretty much remained buried there until I started thinking about the function of stories for children as they develop across their childhood years. This writing triggered that memory that had remained dormant until now.

****

In a lovely essay by the writer Ian McEwan (see note thirty-six), he distinguishes between what he refers to as the "standard social science model" of human nature and the "universal people" model. Drawing primarily from social science literature, McEwan traces the former model's popular preeminence to the rise of behaviorism in psychology found in the early to mid-twentieth century research and writing of such behavioral luminaries as John Watson and B. F. Skinner. In its extreme forms adherents of such an orientation conceived of human nature as a blank slate, infinitely malleable from birth onward. Nurture almost completely trumped nature in this view. Humans as such were not born with an essential human nature but were shaped, molded, and conditioned to think and act, to perceive and conceive as a strict function of environmental reinforcements, both primary (such as food or sex) and secondary or learned rewards such as money or professional advancement.

McEwan traces the modern form of the second model, the universal people model, to the work of Paul Ekman, who in the 1950s carried out cross-cultural research, studying the recognition of facial expression in photographs shown to the natives of New Guinea who had had little or no contact with the outside world before his study. Results showed that these natives had an uncanny ability not only to recognize the meaning of the facial expression, but they could also create stories appropriate to what they were seeing in the pictures. Ekman concluded that facial expressions revealing emotional states are a universal component of human being (and as we shall see, also influenced by the kind of fiction read). But the *display* of these inborn and universal states, that is, the conditions under which they are allowed to be displayed, are governed by social rules developed within particular cultures.

For example, you are much less likely to observe exuberant and extroverted behavioral displays such as glad-handing and backslapping among the Japanese than you are to observe such behaviors at a college frat party in this country. McEwan concludes that "social experience influences attitudes about emotion, creates display and feeling rules, develops and tunes the particular occasions which will most rapidly call forth an emotion." However, the *expression* of our emotions once aroused, the particular configurations of muscular movements that make up a grimace, a frown, or a look of emotional disgust or anger appear to be fixed—enabling understanding across generations, across cultures, and within cultures between strangers as well as intimates.[36]

After Ekman's work, a flood of cross-cultural studies in anthropology, sociology, and psychology followed. In 1991, Donald Brown reviewed much of the data drawn from early anthropological work such as that carried out by Margaret Mead and her contemporaries. Brown published a book titled *Human Universals*,[37] and in it, he provided a list of what he found to be common across human individuals, as well as across societies. Ranging from tool-making to gift-giving; from the role of gossip as social control to conceptions of justice in society; from the development of language components (e.g., nouns, verbs, possessives) to the rules for proper arrangement of them in sentence structure; from ritual and language as symbol to the making of world myths conveying ultimate meaning—all these human categories are found cross-culturally, from East to West, supporting Brown's conclusion regarding a universal human nature.[38]

The take-away point that we can conclude from all these research findings, and as has been a constant theme throughout this science-based chapter, is this: for both our species' development and our individual

---

36. McEwan, "Literature, Science, and Human Nature," 16–17.
37. Brown, *Human Universals*.
38. McEwan, "Literature, Science, and Human Nature," 17.

development over our lifetime, the consensus among scientists is that it is not a question of one model over the other—no longer a question of universal human essence or nature versus the nurture model of the blank slate writ large—but a question of both/and from cradle to grave. As newborns we arrive with a complete set of genes inherited and programmed to produce an infant who becomes an adult of a certain shape and size, a certain skin color and temperament (for example, with introvert or extrovert tendencies from the get-go). We inherit to a greater or lesser degree the creative capacities for art, language, and story, an ability to reason, anticipate, and plan, a capacity to self-reflect and self-transcend and reach out beyond ourselves to embrace others, nature, and God.

But beyond these biological givens, nurture then trumps nature by providing a context and culture within which we learn, choose, engage with literature and art, bond with others and open ourselves to new experience, molding our preferences, shaping our motives and goals—all the while molding and sculpting our brains as we move through our days, creating ourselves in the process.

My main interest here is in the power of music and story to shape ourselves into who we have become, as well as who we can yet be. This process of course does begin in the cradle. In fact, by the age of two, humans are able to engage in pretend play, enacting simple dramas with Legos and blocks. By the age of three or four, all children who are not severely deprived of environmental stimuli in the form of songs and stories and opportunities for play tend to inhabit—at least a good part of the time—the land of make-believe.

Gotschall calls children "creatures of the story." Although there tend to be inborn gender differences in boy versus girl play—boys gravitate toward blocks, girls gravitate toward dolls—the fact that all children express rich story imaginations is universal. Very young children tell simple stories in play before they can actually articulate in words the meaning of their actions. But they enact the story bodily, they rock the dolly in rhythm, they sooth the dolly's troubles with humming songs, they rhythmically march their toy soldiers to the rhythm of drumbeats in their heads. Later, they jump rope to the rhythmic beat of the rope's turns. Additionally, by age three children tend to create imaginary companions. Paul Harris and other psychologists trace a child's grasp of God as divine agent as likely stemming from this capacity to imagine what is not seen as nevertheless real.[39]

---

39. Harris, *The Work of the Imagination*; Rosengren et al., eds, *Imagining the Impossible*.

My central concern here is with the role of story, especially fiction, in our developing lives from childhood onward. In any consideration of story—whether in song or poetry or prose—we need to consider the role of trouble at the heart of the matter. The vivid stories that children tell in the nursery or kindergarten grab others' attention by the pitch of their voices adding spice and heightening drama as they enact stories about lions and tigers, about boogeymen, about witches and other such threats to be reckoned with. While initially children's pretend play lacks a clear story line with temporal continuity—a beginning, middle, and satisfactory ending—nevertheless the simple episodes they tell and enact are usually about trouble, about facing the bad and somehow overcoming it.

For all children, both singing and story enactment are forms of play—that adaptive and pleasurable mastering of skills in living, building the brain's synaptic connections in the process. As we saw earlier, repetitiveness lies at the heart of play, allowing time to sculpt bodies and brains and thus minds.[40] Repetitive play builds brain strength by "overlearning" actions and enhancing perceptual flexibility in planning for and dealing with real life. And a central part of real life for children and adults alike is the experience of trouble in the form of loss, pain, dangerous threat from forces that lurk in the dark, so to speak.

As children's Theories of Mind develop by mid to later childhood, their brains can link an understanding of the other's intentions, feelings, and belief to another's goal-directed behavior. Thus stories begin to take on a more coherent, temporal whole from a beginning to an ending, with causes and consequences laid out in logical fashion. But the overarching theme to these later stories is still trouble being confronted and mastered.

From early age then, stories work because they grab our attention. A good story catches us by surprise. And stories about the bad, the disaster, are the most compelling, attention-getting of all. Why?

The assumption here is that such story content simply helps prepare a child for future life. Hence children's stories, myths, and nursery rhymes are often about threat. "The Goblin's gonna get you if you don't watch out." Of course, as Gotschall points out, today the bad is more usually confronted on the cartoon TV network and in video games. But nevertheless, trouble is there at the heart of all of our stories.

You could say then that there is a gap between what we humans want, that is, peace and joy and pleasure, and what we desire to read or hear or sing about. In fact, if the film or novel doesn't have a horrendous problem to be solved somewhere along the line (such as escaping the Nazis in a flimsy

---

40. Boyd, *On the Origin of Stories*.

biplane) then we think it is superficial and boring—in fact like so much of our everyday lives. Even "lighter" fiction has a problem to be solved at its base. Gentle novels that have meant something to me—like Gail Godwin's *Father Melancholy's Daughter* or Annie Tyler's *Patchwork Planet* or Marilyn Robinson's *Gilead*—still deal with the problems of depression, love's loss, jealousy, aging, and dying.

No, from the age of two or three we need trouble in our pretend play to grab and keep our attention. This fact likely provides one basic answer for story's role in our species' evolution. We tell one another stories in order to normalize the unusual that happens to us—to fit it in and make some coherent sense of our experience. But we also need to sing and read about trouble not only because is it interesting, riveting us, getting our attention. But also so we can learn vicariously the strategies necessary for coping with life's losses.

In sum, despite our lives being boring for most of their mundane everydayness, every life has trouble, big time. Your life has or will have trouble across its days in the form of loss, sickness, and ultimately death. And the adaptive role of story is to allow us to imagine coping with trouble of all kinds, rehearsing and building flexible options for future coping strategies. While experiencing tension in the process of reading or hearing a good narrative, nevertheless, the experience itself—being vicarious—is painless. Stories, beginning in the nursery, thus focus on the great predicaments of human life: "Sex, love, suffering, death, power and weakness."[41] Stories in the form of songs, poetry, and fiction help prepare us by vicarious rehearsal for meeting those limits in our own lives when they befall us.

There likely is a central role here for those mirror neurons we carry around in our brains. If you recall, such neurons in part give rise to our emotional knowledge, allowing us to learn motor movements and be emotionally moved by the observation of feeling displays from others in our environment. We learn by mere watching; we experience like emotions when engaging with others. And when we hear a story, or read a novel, or hear a song with lyrics that convey a story line, our brains are busy responding vicariously to the story's plot. We can run "fictional simulations in our heads," experiencing the stories as if they were real. And we not only add to our store of flexible future options for coping with trouble, but—as I've said repeatedly throughout this chapter—we rewire our brains in the process.

Now the solutions that some fictions provide for life's big problems are not always good ones in the real world of possible actions. Think of some of the novels you've read that include life stories gone awry, wrong turns in

---

41. Gotschall, *The Storytelling Animal*, 56.

the road taken. Nevertheless the more we experience vicariously through story, the richer the base of options we develop over a lifetime of storytelling and hearing. "When you share a smile or laugh with someone face to face, a discernible synchrony emerges between you, as your gestures and biochemistries, even your respective neural firings, come to mirror each other."[42] I would say that is also true as you engage with the storytellers, meeting them in their song or narrative creations. And this meeting between humans, this learning from one another registered even at the level of neural synapse, begins in our earliest childhoods and doesn't end until our own life stories are done.

CULTURAL EVOLUTION: SONG AND STORY IN OUR TIME

I bought a new car this year, fresh off the lot, just delivered from the auto distributor the morning before I arrived to snap the beauty up. I was prepared to go all out. I wanted not only a navigation system with a built-in GPS, but also a satellite radio installed by the factory to be in place when I signed the deal. Then of course I discovered that I had to learn how to work the mysterious knobs on my dashboard. (Actually they weren't on the dashboard, but were accessed by a kind-of mouse operated like one on a computer.) Once I discovered how to switch from FM to satellite, however, I did not returned to my favorite NPR station. No, I have moved back and forth from the 1940s to the 1960s hit music. Actually the '40s were a bit before my time—or at least before I was much into pop songs—but they remind me of my parents and my childhood home, and therefore, bring back a good feeling when I hear "Begin the Beguine" or "In the Mood." In contrast, when I have occasionally wandered into the '80s Heavy Metal or Today's Hip Hop, I quickly turn it off because "That's not music!" and off I go in search of the familiar comfort given by the Beach Boys as they harmonize about "California Girls," or relish that '60s feeling of Don McLean's "American Pie"—some of the music we might have heard at that Ft. Myers Beach bar.

****

Human culture has always evolved over time, being the product of human minds that have evolved the creative capacity to make something new. As an ultra-social species, we are equipped to learn from one another

---

42. Frederickson, "Your Phone vs. Your Heart."

and cooperate within social networks to conduct scientific investigations and fashion art in order to expand beyond the known to discover and explore what lies beyond our everyday given. In mimicking the gods or in co-creating with the one God of our Western tradition, we have continuously explored and experimented beyond the edges of the known, to make what is new, and to revel in the making.

But it is possible—and I'm certainly not the first to suggest this—that we are witnessing today an aesthetic revolution in the creation and dissemination of song and story. Stories in lyrical form have always been sung in order to bond with others—to comfort, to protest, to praise, to worship, to express joyful exuberance and love. These deep human matters have been expressed in the form of psalms sung, rhythms chanted to the accompaniment of drums, choruses and quartets sung in harmony, hymns and liturgies sung by monks' choirs. But today, beginning with the invention of recording in the nineteenth century, this cultural evolution is undergoing a steep growth curve. The Internet, personal computers, ear phones, iPods and iPads and iPhones—all the various instruments of social media are allowing access to music of all kinds, and the choice for listening and mixing to our taste is almost unlimited. Today, new forms of musical art are being created, music like hip hop and rap that strain at least some of our brains to find the patterns that identify these aesthetic expressions as art and not just noise.

So too have the forms evolved for storytelling. The novel first appeared on the scene during the eighteenth century. Now we still voraciously read fiction (how many books did J. K. Rowling and her *Harry Potter* series sell?), but we also follow stories on TV reality shows and in video games, and we can participate as players and co-creators within virtual reality Internet technologies. The forms have changed, but the omnipresence of songs and stories remain.

In his *Proust was a Neuroscientist*, Lehrer defines music as that "sliver of sound that we have learned how to hear."[43] In a colorful description of audience response the first time they were exposed to Stravinsky's "The Rite of Spring" the author painted a scene of chaos. On first hearing what they apparently took as mere hideous noise, members of the audience erupted in emotional rage, even resorting to physical blows when their brains could no longer tolerate the sound assault on their ears.

Of course as Lehrer points out, now "The Rite of Spring" no longer surprises us. We have learned to hear the pattern in the sounds and our brains have come to understand these patterned sounds as indeed familiar

---

43. Lehrer, *Proust was a Neuroscientist*, 123.

music. "Our sense of sound is a work in progress. Neurons in the auditory cortex are constantly being altered by the songs and symphonies we listen to. Nothing is difficult forever."[44] The author makes the point that music only excites us when the auditory cortex has to struggle to make sense out of incoming musical stimuli. Our brains are driven to make order out of chaos. If the order is too obvious, the music bores us (think some church or elevator music); if the brain cannot discover any pattern to the incoming notes, then the tension becomes unbearable. The "music" is dismissed as nothing but random sound without the release of emotional tension that comes from the discovery of pattern (think my response to rap or the audience's response upon hearing Stravinsky's masterpiece for the first time).

As Lehrer traces it, Stravinsky's work was actually part of a wave of an aesthetic revolt that took place in both music and fiction writing during the early twentieth century. In striving to create something new, composers such as Stravinsky and Arnold Schoenberg (whose atonal experimentation inspired Stravinsky's work), and writers such as James Joyce, Virginia Woolf, and Gertrude Stein began to explore new expressions that went beyond the mere abstract—after all, music and prose by their very nature were abstract and symbolic. Lehrer describes how these artistic creators experimented with writing in streams of consciousness such as those found in Joyce's *Ulysses*, Faulkner's *The Sound and the Fury*, and Woolf's *To the Lighthouse*.

In a sense both music and prose fiction have divided into two streams in our contemporary culture: the popular stream consumed by us ordinary folk and appreciated by the masses, and the elite stream confined to the university department and conservatory. As Lehrer points out, works that followed from last century's aesthetic revolt mainly have penetrated only the second stream. Today no one reads Joyce except the academic crowd. Stories that are widely read—the stories found in movies, TV, and videos—tend to have understandable plots, stories with some suspense and resolution of sorts in the end.

On the other hand, although our brains do prefer the familiar, we don't want to be bored, do we? The paradox is that we want both the familiar and the new embedded within it. We do want tension aroused by surprise as we scan for patterns. We engage emotionally with tunes and fictional narrative that pull us into their story line of character plus predicament plus some escape and solution.

If we get caught up in the story line then one of the characters may well become ourselves. After all, this is the nature of engagement with both story and song. Being transported by a plot and emotionally embroiled in

---

44. Ibid., 125.

its movement, you and I are always part of the character structure in one way or another. Whether the goblin's gonna get me or whether I'm in the biplane cockpit along with the kids flying the plane or with Richard Harris in MacArthur Park, lamenting the loss of his cake—I'm part of that story and my brain thrives on the experience.

I suppose one lesson here—and underscored in Lehrer's work—is that it is crucially important in our lives that we remain open to new experience. Despite the fact that we find comfort in the familiar, we are called to grow and thrive and flourish to the end. The only way to do that is to be open to new things, new types of music, new stories and songs that feed our neural networks—all those dendrites forming and reforming canopies around emotional and memory centers in our brains. So yes, I should pay attention to the rap music on the street, and yes I should try to learn about abstract art and atonal music. Bob Dylan supposedly said something to the effect that one who is not busy being born (that is, growing experientially) is busy dying. So here's to life!

SCIENCE, ART, AND RELIGION

Antonio Damasio, Michael Gazzaniga, Jonah Lehrer, as well as many other neuroscientists, are very clear about the limits of their investigative methods. While we can with some precision map brain areas that are active in the perceptual and conceptual flow when we process incoming stimuli and select out patterns to attend to and make something of, we will never explain the origin of that attention, itself—that mystery of a self from which our conscious, emergent properties arise from no single, measurable source. Science cannot reduce all of reality to fit its tools. "Any explanation of our experience solely in terms of our neurons will never explain our experience, because we don't experience our neurons."[45] Ultimately, as I said at the beginning of this work, the origin of the sense of self—that which executes that executive power to select, attend, choose, and direct, that center out of which the sense of a whole self emerges is ultimately a mystery.

And where there is mystery, there is room for art. Noam Chomsky, the great twentieth-century linguist, is reported to have said, "It is quite possible—overwhelmingly probable, one might guess—that we will always learn more about human life and personality from novels than from scientific psychology."[46] I would also argue that there is room and a place for theology in striving to catch a more complete picture of the whole of the universe.

45. Lehrer, *Proust was a Neuroscientist*, 187.
46. Quoted in ibid., 187–88.

Both novels and autobiographies (as I said earlier, both more or less fiction genres) have been shown to be powerful influences in shaping our understanding of human nature, and function as models for the developing self. As a case in point, just this morning at the breakfast table I was reading my latest issue of the journal *Image*. And in it was an essay by Peggy Rosenthal—a poet and essayist who focuses on Christian spirituality. In her piece, titled "An Apprenticeship in Affliction: Waiting with Simone Weil," she describes the impact that Weil's writing titled "Human Personality" had on her life. Rosenthal says, "I gasped at the uncanny aptness to my personal crisis, and knew with gratitude that God would be addressing me directly through Weil's words.... Weil's prose had a quality which I'd call poetic—in its concision and its grasp of the single sharp image as insight's wedge into our souls."

Rosenthal goes on to describe her response to reading Weil's essay. She took to copying out longhand many of the author's words, making her reading experience indeed an embodied one. She says, "I felt compelled to copy its lines into my journal so as to pass them through my body, making sure their points dug in.... All my confidence had been in my intelligence, as the faculty to show me the truth about any subject, yet here was Weil: 'A mind enclosed in language is in prison ... the intelligent man who is proud of his intelligence is like a condemned man who is proud of his large cell.'"[47]

Truth often lies beneath and beyond what words can say. In the saying, of course, we express what we see. But the glimpse of reality penetrates deeper than the prose that expresses it.

There is much lip service today about the complementary nature of science and art, but woefully little actual collaboration as equals in our common search for truth. As Lehrer points out, the scientists who pride themselves on recognizing their own method's limits and who express a desire to go beyond empiricism in the process of discovery, have usually wound up simply translating their own empirical work into understandable public consumption. Instead of open and respectful collaboration with the poets, visual artists, and fiction writers who are somehow able to capture the universal in the particular image (as we saw above in Rosenthal's account), or theologians who address ultimate questions of why and to what end, these scientists refer to the mystery of self as the "neural correlate of consciousness" and proceed to "measure" consciousness with their tools of brain imagery. But those images in themselves are not reflections of conscious selves embedded in and engaged with a world of meaning that we co-create as it creates us in turn.

---

47. Rosenthal, "An Apprenticeship in Affliction," 83.

I think it is obvious that the public more easily grasps literature than scientific research with its technical jargon and findings. But beyond ease of mental grasp, the universal insights captured in the particular symbols and metaphors of the arts do convey, as Chomsky noted, aspects of human life that we could discover no other way. Thus art is useful in describing and helping us understand our experience of self and world. But I would also argue that beyond art, or perhaps through aesthetics of various kinds, theology also has a role to play in understanding human life—why we are here and where we are going. As art is not reducible to physics, neither is theology or the study of God's engagement with humankind reducible to art.

All of these disciplines—science, art, and theology—are in search of truth. None of them has a monopoly on that. All are human endeavors, worthy in their own right, but complementary human endeavors that have over the millennia tried to break through the wall of ignorance and reveal what is real, and mark the true (as we are able) from the false—generating knowledge in the process. Lehrer concludes thusly: "All knowledge . . . is mixed with our errors, our prejudices, our dreams, and our hopes; [and] all we can do is grope for truth even though it is beyond our reach." Neither is there any authority "beyond the reach of criticism."[48]

As an infinitely social species, we are embedded in human community, embedded in something larger than our own isolated selves. Witness the fact that almost all of our emotions are social in nature. Love, pride, ambition, mercy, anger, pity, and so on—all only have meaning as related to other people. We take into account others' motives and intentions based on our understanding of ourselves with wills of our own. We are tied to one another from our evolutionary roots to today's Internet community.

But we are also embedded in a larger mystery that goes beyond our social community. The neuroscientist Ramachandran concludes *The Tell-Tale Brain* with these words: "As human beings we have to accept with humility that the question of ultimate origins will always remain with us, no matter how deeply we understand the brain and the cosmos that it creates."[49] Over the ages mystics, poets, artists, religious from all stripes of observance, and those with none have sensed what Simone Weil expressed in her spiritual autobiography *Waiting for God*. Namely, that there is an Ultimate Reality that transcends our ordinary human lives; an Ultimate Reality whose Spirit hovers over our lives and engages with us providentially if we are open to such engagement.

---

48. Lehrer, *Proust was a Neuroscientist*, 197.
49. Ramachandran, *The Tell-Tale Brain*, 239.

In his *My Bright Abyss,* the contemporary poet Christian Wiman talks about the necessity of being open to God's impingement in our everyday lives. He says "if you do not 'think' of God, in whatever way you find to do that, if God has no relation to your experience, if God is not *in* your experience, then experience is always an end in itself, and always, I think, a dead end." In the writing of poetry, Wiman notes some "mysterious resonance" between the thing imaged and language, between mind and matter, which is a kind of revelation of reality beyond what we can see, or touch, or measure.

This is a book about our human lives and their potential to flourish to the very end. This is a book about aging well, if you will; this is a book about living well until our last breath; this is a book about telling a good life story, giving it a coherent wholeness with value and positive meaning. Our marvelous brain gives us the rich potential to achieve all of that. To this purpose, I am going to draw from all these human sources of truth—science (as I certainly have in this chapter, laying the biological foundation for embodied wholeness), and art in the form of song, dance, and story, and theology—that quest for Truth beyond words and worlds. Ultimately this book is about faith in life, yours and mine. Faith in the "ongoingness of it, the indestructibility, some atom-by-atom intelligence that is and isn't us, some day-by-day and death-by-death persistence insisting on a more-than-human hope, some tender and terrible energy that is, for those with the eyes to see it, love."[50]

With that, let's continue our journey together.

---

50. Wiman, *My Bright Abyss,* 58; 51; 36.

SECTION I

Wired for Friendship, Knowledge, and Joy

Building the Story

2

"If I Had a Hammer"
The Protest Generation and Idealism Writ Large

> On April 30 [1970], President Nixon announced the movement of American and South Vietnamese troops into Cambodia. On May 4, four students were killed and nine wounded at Kent State. On May 14, two more were killed and twelve wounded at Jackson State. Campuses across the country were swept by a prairie fire of protest. In all, 448 campuses were either on strike or were completely closed down. Columbia President McGill called it "the most disastrous May in the history of American higher education" and, in a Gallup poll, the American public called campus unrest the nation's most important problem. Momentarily, at least, the baby boom had burst out of control.[1]

****

THE SCENE BACK THEN: THE AGE OF "AQUARIUS"

Spring, 1970, the campus of Indiana University, Bloomington. I was in my senior year at IU—a psychology major. We were in our last week

---

1. Jones, *Great Expectations*, 115–16.

of classes, and I remember being sorry that my seminar that afternoon had been canceled. In fact, about all classes had been canceled because the students had gone on strike. And most of the professors—especially the younger ones—supported the shutdown. Instead of classes that afternoon, students had been "invited" to meet with the university president to discuss their grievances and to be reassured, I suppose, that all was under control.

Thus, I, along with hundreds—maybe by then thousands—of students marched across campus to the large auditorium in the middle of campus. There we pushed and threaded our way into the cavernous building, filled to overflowing at that point with students who came in general protest of all things establishment, or who came out of curiosity—after all, this was where it was happening. No classes and you wanted to be where the action was, to see what was going down.

By the time I had pushed my way into the auditorium, there were no seats left. So I was pushed and shoved by those behind me to the top of the last balcony, and I sat with others on the stairs leading up. About that point, the president of the student body appeared down on stage and a hush settled over the mass of students gathered. I remember about then feeling quite uneasy as he reminded us of a recent stampede of spectators at some South American soccer game where hundreds had been trampled to death. He delivered this warning to us in order to urge us to remain orderly, or the same thing could happen to us that very afternoon in that very place! Not very comforting, but he sure got our attention with that sobering thought.

Next, the university's president sauntered out onto the stage. I do not remember what he said, but I—along with most others—realized after a few minutes that he was not quite speaking coherently. Apparently, at least according to rumor, he had been drinking that afternoon before the gathering took place. So his message was somewhat incoherent. Anyway, nothing came of that meeting that I recall, other than a show of force by the students who had closed down the campus for the day and other than the fact that no one got trampled in the process.

Now the campus at Bloomington, comparatively speaking, was tame that spring, as well as in the years of unrest that preceded it—nothing like Kent State or Jackson State or Columbia or Berkeley. But still, we had our moments. Around that time my future husband, Leon Levy—a full professor in the psychology department and director of the clinical psychology program, along with his fellow faculty—got phone calls at about 5 AM from someone in the administration, asking them to get onto the campus as fast as they could. Students had surrounded the administration building, and the faculty were being asked to surround the students, forming a protective barrier between them and the Bloomington police. It's possible that this episode followed Kent State and obviously there would have been great anxiety that a similar outcome could occur if the police were provoked by shouts of "Pig!" and the like. But other than drama, no such calamity occurred.

I find it interesting that when I look back on my past, these are the years that I first recall. My memories extend much further back, and we'll explore some of those in the pages ahead—as well as early memories of other Boomers whose biographical sketches appear in these chapters. But the late '60s and early '70s were the years of tremendous personal growth; these were the years when my—and our—identity was shaped into who we became and who we have now carried into middle age and beyond.

Of course Boomers were not then and are not now a uniform cohort. We differed vastly in terms of educational attainment and economic prosperity. But it was the educated elite, the pampered radicals of the Me generation, who set the tone for others of our cohort to follow—in dress, in music, in style and individual strivings, in at least initial optimism that life held great promise and offered multiple options.

On my campus as well as others, there was a sort of tribal sense of communal bonding. Within our tribe, you could sense a certain smugness, a self-righteousness that lay beneath the protests. There was a militancy—even at IU, as tame as it was—to our sense of entitlement. In my graduate student days there (which followed immediately after graduation in the spring of 1970), teaching assistants threatened to go on strike with the cry, "Students are niggers!" reflecting our sense of general injustice meted out to our (privileged) lot. We demanded "relevant" courses—psychology, sociology, political science, religious studies—and not dead subjects like Greek or history. During the four years I was a graduate student at IU, qualifying exams for a PhD became "individualized"—tailor-made to a student's own tastes—and the traditional requirement for proficiency in a foreign language was dropped in favor of the election of a "tool skill." I elected for my "tool" speech pathology—practical and relevant to my budding clinical interests.

These were also my "existential days," and I became quite taken with Merleau-Ponty's *Phenomenology of Perception*, Victor Frankel's *From Death Camp to Existentialism*, and Heidegger's *Being and Time*. My "tailor-made" qualifying exam included a concentration on Freud and the theories of existential and humanistic psychologists like Rollo May and Eugene Gendlin. We read Saul Alinsky's *Reveille for Radicals*, and in my Religious Studies 101 class—for which I wound up as a teaching assistant during my first year in graduate school—we read Mark Twain's *The War Prayer* and Martin Buber's *I and Thou*. Even if you may not be familiar with these works, there were common threads that bound them together: themes reflecting a deep respect for human beings as such, and a protest against the military/industrial and technological (that is, dehumanizing) *status quo*.

And thus I shaped myself. I fashioned my frame of mind and colored my perception of the world that I and my generation assumed we would perfect in time. And others of my cohort did the same.

As to our music—as Daniel Levitin observes in his *The World in Six Songs*—"the rock stars were our poets; we felt that they had hard-won life lessons to pass on to the rest of us."[2] Our countercultural idealism was expressed so well we thought by such songs as "War (What Is It Good For?)," and Arlo Guthrie's "Alice's Restaurant," where just fifty folks banding together became a "movement." We lived out our brave new world coming just over the horizon as we experienced the rock opera *Hair*. We thrilled as the last "innocent" scene of the actors appeared pure and self-righteous on stage in their "coats" of nudity. They strode onto the stage singing "Let the sun shine . . . let the sunshine in . . . the sunnnnnn . . . shine in,"[3] as they proudly faced down the Establishment in all its hate-filled militarism and racism . . . striding forth in all their (and our vicarious) righteousness to confront the evil society surrounding us.

There was indeed a religious revival feeling to our "movement," a community of visionaries who were going to change the world. You just felt it—and it was so! There was a *zeitgeist*, a spiritual feeling to the time, with students not only flocking to religious studies classes, but embracing Eastern religions, moving into ashrams, appearing on the streets in long garb with flowers in their hair. There was ecstasy brought on by music, as well as hallucinogenic drugs.

Now I have to confess that I didn't do drugs. I think maybe once I took a puff of a marijuana "roach" being passed around at a party. But I didn't even smoke cigarettes and the drug scene never really took for me. And I didn't go to Woodstock, either—although in our imaginations, we all did. By August of 1968, my first husband joined the faculty at IU (hence, what brought us to Bloomington, but more about that later). We had two small sons—aged two and four—and I was working hard to juggle it all and finish my undergraduate studies. So I didn't go to Woodstock along with the other 400,000 students, hippies, and other members of my protest cohort who poured into the little town of Bethel, New York, that summer. About this be-in, Jones has the following to say:

> Their prolonged adolescence seemed to have conditioned them with a craving for group support. The music at the concerts was

---

2. Levitin, *The World in Six Songs*, 30.
3. MacDermot et al., *Hair—Vocal Selections*.

no more important than the ritual; the cheering and waving of lighted matches had all the emotional richness of a religious revival. Before many rock concerts, hundreds of students would wait in the line overnight, huddling in sleeping bags and passing joints from hand to hand.

At Woodstock, they could meet and see more people than anyone could ever imagine. "The roar after a song!" remembered Country Joe McDonald. "It was scary, God, I had never seen so many people." Kids who returned from Woodstock spoke less about how Jimi played, or what Joe Cocker had said, than they did about sloshing together—together!—in the rain and the mud.[4]

In 2012, an entire issue of the journal *The Gerontologist* was devoted to research reports on Boomers who are now entering mid-life or senior status. And on the cover of that issue, an older couple is shown, grinning and holding a snapshot taken of them at Woodstock. There they were, huddled in the rain, with not much on but blankets to protect them from the weather. Apparently they eventually married and were still together in 2012—which as we shall see, was frequently not the case with those married during the early Boom years. This couple's identity and the identity of their cohort were shaped by the Woodstock mentality of that day.

Of course as we saw in chapter 1, this group bonding, this felt ecstasy in response to moving in rhythm, has both evolutionary and biological roots. Thus, it is not a phenomenon arising solely with this Boomer generation. William McNeill, in his often-cited and now classic book, *Keeping Together in Time*, began his writing with memories of marching in drill formation during World War II. He remembered marching around the military post during training, and recalled having a sense of "enlargement; a sort of swelling out, becoming bigger than life, thanks to participation in collective ritual."[5] As we saw in chapter 1, he says:

> Words and ideals matter and are always invoked; but keeping together in time arouses warm emotions of collective solidarity and erases personal frustrations as words, by themselves, cannot do. Large and complex human societies, in all probability, cannot long maintain themselves without such kinesthetic undergirding. Ideas and ideals are not enough. Feelings matter too,

---

4. Jones, *Great Expectations*, 133.
5. McNeill, *Keeping Together in Time*, 2.

and feelings are inseparable from their gestural and muscular expression.[6]

Ritual movement—dance, marching, protest chants, and yes, rolling in the mud at Woodstock—helped us form group solidarity, the sense of being part of a tribe with its own language and dress, ideals and purposes in life that would one day change the world for the better. We knew where we were going and it felt good!

Of course, not everyone went to college. Not everyone was part of the educated, entitled elite. If you ever saw the wonderful coming-of-age film *Breaking Away* (filmed in Bloomington, by the way, and all about what life was like growing up in that university town), then you saw the tension that did—and still does—exist between those who were privileged and those who were not. As that film told the story, blue-collar laborers of the Boom generation remained alienated from their more privileged cohort mates who were led by the Jerry Rubins of the day.

In that movie, the "town versus gown" tension was wonderfully portrayed. This mutual wariness and dislike of the Other played out between the protagonist—a townie, referred to as a "stonee" or stone-cutter—and the boys who lived in the large fraternity houses dotting the campus. Bloomington was the heart of limestone country, and most of the buildings on campus were covered in limestone cut by the town laborers—the GI fathers of the town kids. The crisis gets played out when the stonee who pretends to be French invades the college territory—the college boys' chief sources of recreation: sorority girls and bicycle racing.

It's a lovely tale well told. The movie painted a picture of life in small towns dominated by universities that hired the local staff, created the cultural climate, kept separate behind gates and stately walls, and whose faculty and students—if not openly or consciously—nevertheless looked down upon the locals. We stayed within our "ivory towers" and the locals perceived us as viewing their own lives as ignorant and unenlightened.

Along these lines, Landon Jones points out that "those who went to college formed their values and attitudes in a completely different world from those who did not. Baby boomers who did not go to college were not part of Youth. They were forgotten. In fact, the point of view of college youth became so pervasive in the sixties and seventies that it was the mass of working-class youth, once the backbone of the American system, who showed the most evident signs of alienation."[7] Jones goes on to point out that the liberal styles of the college student elite typically percolated down

---

6. Ibid., 152.
7. Jones, *Great Expectations*, 100.

to their blue-collar peers in about five years' time. As an example, he points out that in the '60s, long hair was *de rigueur* on campus; by the late seventies, those who were still wearing their hair long were actually wearing a sign that they had *not* gone to college.

For us the sense of elitism was real, absorbed from the culture around us. I remember visiting my parents in California during my undergraduate years when I was on summer break. For some reason I viewed with disdain the older diners at the next table who seemed to me to be ignorant. I dismissed them with a passion as I overheard what I thought was their inane conversation—even though they were complete strangers and I had absolutely no grounds to view them as I did. Except that they were not from my generation and so by definition, were not "with it" as far as I was concerned. I did consider my parents, however, as an exception. Except that they were totally wrong about politics and their social values! But I loved them anyway and so forgave them their benighted ideas.

From my parents' point of view, in many ways this cohort of Boomers was not only self-righteous and smug, but at times aggressively hostile to differences—principally marked off by educational attainment—in the culture around them. "This generation did not seem to have its quota of alienated 'hoods'—the Fonzies of the fifties—because they all looked and sounded alienated."[8] And thus, the "generation gap" was born. What *was* new with my generation was that this special sense of Self didn't disappear with the coming of age.

In fact, both early and late Boomers, as well as elite and blue-collar Boomers, have more in common than not. We are all sometimes strident individualists in one form or another, striving for relevance in mid and later life, and idealistically driven—whether our politics are far right, far left, or independent, depending on the persuasiveness of the current rock star candidate and our own personal social tastes. Even though Frank Sinatra was from my parents' generation, his song "I Did It My Way" resonated in our lives and still does.

If you think about the lyrics to that song of Sinatra's, and as I look back across those years in my life—at least until now, when I think I've become a better version of myself (as Tom Hanks recently said in a television interview)—there was a core selfishness to this Me generation that came out in multiple ways. One of the ways it came out was in what happened to the institution of marriage during those early years. "The women of the baby boom . . . were the first generation to escape what was previously the primary economic basis for marriage—the security provided by a working

---

8. Ibid., 101.

husband. If a marriage came under pressure, they no longer had to accept it."[9]

In citing Erik Erikson's description of early adult development and the need for individuals as they journeyed through their twenties to develop the capacity for intimacy and the ability to abide by such commitments for the long haul, Jones sees the Boomer cohort as wanting in this regard. Oh, we were able to make political and social commitments as a self-defined group, but when it came to individual commitments, we remained infantile in our development. "Why should one limit one's prospects when the choices still ahead were so thrilling?"[10]

The lyrics to our songs perfectly mirrored our attitudes toward the changeable scene of relationship commitment—or non-commitment, as the case so often was. Carole King's refrain in "It's Too Late"—"and it's too late, baby, now it's too late, though we really did try to make it. Something inside has died and I can't hide and I just can't fake it"[11]—is a perfect reflection of this time-to-move-on-to-something-better attitude of many of us in the '60s and '70s. Gordon Lightfoot's "If You Could Read My Mind" echoes this me-first sentiment.

Thus, the popularity of "no-fault" divorce rose in the late '60s and early '70s, and folks walked away from marriages and even children, but could still "remain friends." "It's just that this isn't working anymore." In my case, I fit right in. But let me back up a few years to our Waltham, Massachusetts days and even a bit before.

Half of my undergraduate days were spent at St. Mary's College in Notre Dame, Indiana. I had finished my sophomore year there and was engaged to, of course, a Notre Dame boy. Sam (not his real name) was a year ahead of me in that grand school across the road, and as we entered my junior year and his senior year there, I got it into my head that we should get married. I was tired of school and really, I couldn't think of anything else I wanted to do with my life at that point.

I also decided right then and there that I was tired of being in school and so why not get married. I also decided that "Hey! I don't want to take the fall semester finals either." I was warned by the good Holy Cross sisters that if I "signed out" for Christmas break with an unexcused absence before I took my final exams (those were the days when we had to sign in and sign out in the dean's office), I would forfeit an entire semester's worth of

---

9. Ibid, 215.

10. Ibid, 217.

11. Written and performed by Carole King. Copyright 1971 by Colgems EMI music Inc/Sony/ATV Music Publishing LLC. 8 Music Square West, Nashville, TN 37203.

credits—thus wasting my parents' money; furthermore, I would get a "W-F" for all courses, that is, failure due to unauthorized withdrawal. But despite the warning and in my last days there—with my parents' support, by the way—I continued to take the bus into South Bend in order to buy my wedding gown and outfits. As I packed the last of my things and headed for the bus home, a way overweight nun who was stationed that day as hall monitor in my dorm exclaimed to me as I headed to the elevator, "You're going to regret this day!" I never actually did.

Sam and I were married at the end of January in Our Lady's Chapel in the large, gothic church at the center of the Notre Dame campus. After honeymooning in Chicago at the old Edgewater Beach Hotel, we set up house in a two-room apartment in Niles, Michigan, with just a short drive south to the Notre Dame campus where Sam finished his undergraduate degree. By the time he graduated, I was pregnant with our first son, Brian—born ten months after we were married (Sam's parents counted carefully on their fingers for that one!).

We moved to Boston after a summer job for him in Washington, DC, and rented the upper floor of a duplex in Waltham to be near Brandeis University where Sam worked on his PhD in physics. I turned twenty-one that fall, and Brian was born that November of 1964. A short nineteen months later, our second son, Kevin, was born in 1966. As I remember it, before our first son was born, I thought I wanted five children. After Brian, I thought maybe four. After Kevin was born, I decided three—no maybe two was a good number.

If you were a Catholic in those days—especially an educated one—you began to question the Church's stand against birth control. We read the *National Catholic Reporter*; we belonged to the Newman Club on campus and became close friends with the University's Catholic chaplain. We decided to shift from the "rhythm method" to the diaphragm in quick order. Of course, once you start thinking for yourself, your own reason becomes a major guide for such decisions. One night, the chaplain came to our apartment for a drink, and we laid out for him the arguments in favor of birth control. And he was way ahead of us. Without officially giving us his blessing, he didn't say no. Thus the decision was made—and paved the way for many "did it my way" decisions that followed.

In actuality, we were children playing grown-up. Two children playing grown-up in those Brandeis days, having two small babies and fashioning a family life as we imagined one might be—making our way into an adult world, growing up in the process. Or beginning to grow up in those years of study. When Kevin was six months old, I went back to school, taking night classes at Boston College. I quickly decided that not only did I want to get my undergraduate degree in psychology, but I wanted to get a PhD in clinical psychology. And that became my goal, come hell or high water.

After Sam finished his PhD, he got a position on the faculty at Indiana University. Hence, our move to Bloomington. I did finish my undergraduate days there, getting a bachelor's degree in psychology with a minor in religious studies. The year was 1970. And I immediately entered graduate school, getting my PhD in 1974, with a residency spent at the Indiana University School of Medicine in Indianapolis the following year.

To make a long story short (as they say), during this time of campus unrest and student power, I grew up—at least I became an academic professional with an identity and with the political and social values of my Boomer tribe. During those years, because there were lots of graduate student wives in Bloomington, especially the foreign students' wives who couldn't find work, there were many hands available to help us take care of Brian and Kevin while I devoted a great deal of my time to study. Sam's schedule was also flexible, so life was made easy for me in terms of child care. The boys were also enrolled in half-day nursery and preschool from the age of three onward, so I was free to pursue my goals.

Unfortunately, at least for the boys as well as Sam, I developed into a different person than Sam had married. To put it mildly, we grew apart. There was little holding us together except our mutual love for our sons. And apparently that was not enough to keep me in the marriage. We arranged a "no-fault" divorce, even using the same lawyer at the time to work out joint custody for the boys and to divide our assets such as they were—Sam got the Volkswagen and I got the equity out of our house (which had been bought through my inheritance from my grandmother). So eleven years after the Our Lady's Chapel wedding at Notre Dame we walked out of the courthouse in Bloomington with Sam inviting me to go with him for a cup of coffee. I didn't. But he was—and is—a very sweet man.

But unfortunately for him at the time, I knew what I wanted. I wanted a new life. And that included a marriage that suited me more than our growing-up one did. I had a view of options and possibilities that my parents' generation would not have even considered. Although my grandmother was divorced in a day when a woman did not do such things, she had a good reason and little choice. My grandfather—whom I never knew—was, as she said, "a philanderer." He walked out on her when my dad was an adolescent, and she really had no choice in the matter. But I did. And I took it.

> Previous generations were taught that life is hard, times must be borne. But the baby boomers were not willing to make the risky and often painful compromises their parents did. Just as

they had great expectations for themselves, they had great expectations for their marriages. Life was too short to live with an unhappy marriage. If they could switch to another TV channel, why not switch husbands or wives? In fact, their satisfaction and sense of self-obligation practically demanded it.[12]

And so that is what I did. I switched husbands and married Leon Levy in 1975. As I mentioned earlier, Leon was on the faculty at Indiana University, although I prided myself that I never took a course from him (well, maybe one summer course in personality theory, but let's not count that). This insistence that I was not his student was in order to avoid fitting too patly into the usual stereotype of an older faculty member (he was eighteen years my senior) and a young (or in my case, a youngish twenty-nine-year-old) graduate student pairing up.

But we did just that. Thus, at age 49, Leon assumed responsibility for helping to raise Kevin and Brian—then seven and nine—a fact that some of his fellow faculty members found amazing. We bought a large house in Bloomington suburbia. Sam moved east to join the faculty at George Washington University; and shortly after that remarried—to someone much better suited to him than I had been. The boys stayed in school in Bloomington and spent summers with their dad and his new family in the east. This remained our pattern for their growing-up years.

After three years in Bloomington, Leon and I moved east to Baltimore, where he became chair of the psychology department at the University of Maryland Baltimore County, and I wound up at the National Cancer Institute in Bethesda. We lived in Columbia, Maryland, and that is where the boys finished high school at Mt. St. Joseph's College—a Catholic college prep school in Baltimore. Again, the boys spent summers with their dad and his wife and, by then, a son of their own.

"The idea that the normal destiny of a man or a woman is to live within one family has been broken. These baby boomers have first families and second families and stepchildren and a whole new raft of relations . . . . Ex-brother-in-law? Ex-stepsister . . . ."[13] And thus, the era of "blended families" came to be. Brian and Kevin grew up with a half-brother; I had with Leon (now the boy's stepfather) three stepchildren who are now my "former stepchildren by marriage," as I remarried again after Leon died after thirty-five years of our marriage.

I go into all this because my own life course in this regard is typical of the divorce/remarriage cycle that we Boomers created in our strivings

12. Ibid., 219.
13. Ibid., 219–20.

(in hindsight in many ways quite selfish). We sought existentially meaningful lives in all regards, taking care of Number One first and picking up the pieces of the wreckage in the wake of our lifeboats as we sailed off into our envisioned futures.

So I married too young and then remarried again to better suit my lifestyle and personal values—including my full embrace at that point of the academic life and research enterprise. For all of my middle years Leon became my partner, my colleague, my best friend, my firm supporter (and I his, by the way). What drew us together and kept us that way was both a deep love, attraction, and friendship—and also a shared vocation that created a base for our life together.

I have spent the past number of pages attempting to capture the Boomer scene as we came into our own in the '60s and '70s. But we didn't just spring up and blossom that way in our late adolescent and early adult years. No, we were shaped and we shaped ourselves from the crib onward. We were rooted in both our biology—our evolutionary gene pool and the structures of our malleable brain wiring—and in our own personal development within a cultural setting that nurtured and shaped us, and that we shaped in turn.

For our purposes in this work, I covered our biological roots in the last chapter. So I will not repeat myself here other than to say a bit about our evolutionary source of selves as creators of the world and the neurochemical base of communal experience. I will spend most of this next section focusing on our personal development and ourselves as authors of our own life story. But first a visit to the land of memory and the beginning of my story as a developing self.

The Source of the Scene Back Then

In the fall of 1960 I was sixteen and had entered my senior year in high school. My dad had taught me to drive when I was fifteen and a half. I practiced in the high school parking lot on Saturday mornings in the 1959 avocado green Chevy he had bought me—a straight shift, no less, with fish tails and all. Although I was the only girl in my class with her own car, most if not all the guys had cars. Landon Jones notes that nationally one out of every five high-school senior Boomers drove his or her own car, so my classmates and I were not unique in this regard. But Bremen, Indiana was a farming community. And although I lived in town, many of my classmates lived outside the town limits and thus, the need for wheels to get about.

Once I got my learner's permit, off I went to the surrounding countryside, which meant the little towns circling our little town in northeast Indiana. One Saturday morning, I found myself in the next town over called Napanee, where I had taken my driving test as soon as I hit that magic age of sixteen. For some reason I don't remember now, I found what I was looking for—a Roman Catholic Church named St. Isidore's. No one was around as I entered the sanctuary, but I remember the smell of incense in the air, soaked into the very walls of that silent space. Standing in the back of the church, I looked over the various pamphlets displayed in a rack there, and slipped a number of them into my handbag. They all had to do with what it meant to be a Catholic, what the Church meant, what the rituals were about, what the symbols stood for, what the statues represented, what the large crucifix hanging above the altar signified.

I think I decided in that moment that I was going to become a Roman Catholic, despite the fact that no one in my family was one—except for three cousins living out of state who I very rarely ever saw. Okay, I was dating a Roman Catholic boy at the time, but he had no idea what was on my mind in terms of conversion. By the time I told him, it was a done deal. I had already approached the Catholic priest in town, who agreed to give me instructions in the faith (and who later left the priesthood to marry an ex-nun—as many of his kind did in the mid to late sixties).

Now not to belabor this, but as my dad was one of the business leaders of the community and employed a fair share of its populace, the leading citizens in this little farming town of 3,500 were aghast at my bold move. My parents, needless to say, were also horrified that I was bringing a "foreign" way into the household.

And boy did I bring a foreign way into the household. My bedroom wound up looking like a shrine. I drove to South Bend to a Catholic religious goods store (owned by two elderly sisters), and brought home a very large statue of the Virgin Mary that I placed by my bed, and a very, very large crucifix that I placed on the wall above my desk—and that I have in my bedroom to this day. I stopped eating meat on Fridays, attended daily mass at the little church named St. Dominic's, and faithfully fingered the rosary given to me by Fr. Larson's housekeeper when I was confirmed as a Catholic.

I tell this story for three reasons. First, I was attracted to the rituals and rich symbols of the Roman Catholic liturgy as I still am to this day in my "high church" Episcopal version of Anglicanism. Second, even at the age of sixteen I was hell-bent (perhaps not the most fitting term here!) on creating my life on my terms and on doing it my way—no matter the opinion of others. I decided firmly that I was going to become a Catholic, and as much as

I loved my parents, and as close as I felt to my father in particular, nothing and no one was going to get in my way.

Third and most to the point I want to make here, I was at that adolescent period of my development as a person—that point when we begin to pull together a coherent life story. As we shall see in some more detail in the pages ahead, this story that the "I" weaves about the emerging "me" with a past and future is usually based on some broad philosophy of life that pulls our actions, our values and motives, and our overarching story together into a coherent whole. From adolescence to old age we tell and retell our story, shaping our story as it shapes our self in the process. My story that I created began on that Saturday morning in St. Isidore's Catholic Church in the little town of Napanee, Indiana—that story I'm still writing and living out to this day, with several twists and turns, several setbacks, several decision points along the way.

****

The Evolutionary Source of the Scene Back Then: "Good Morning Starshine"

Reaching back a few millennia before our own crib experience, recalling our earlier discussion of our evolutionary roots, our ancestors—being social creatures—emerged from the cave to live in larger groups where the advantages outweighed the risks. We could hunt farther, defend ourselves better, have a wider selection of mates to pair with, raising the possibility of happy and favorable mutations along the way. Larger groups required intragroup cooperation and shared purpose, and as language developed, communication allowed more creative problem solving, as well as the advent of storytelling as we sat around the fire at night.

Before we told stories for entertainment, we sang songs to our offspring perhaps to soothe away fears. As we saw earlier, art in a variety of forms arose before language emerged, and our ancestors sang and danced as their brains developed and allowed rhythmic movement over time. With Levitin, picture some clever tribe member hitting on the idea of beating some drum-like instrument in rhythm to scare the enemy away or warn fellow tribe members of an imminent attack. The development of such rhythmic art—in this case, drumming—had survival value and thus was passed on to future generations as adaptive. Now picture a group of kids at Woodstock sharing drumbeats and dance and in the process, creating bonds of group solidarity and tribal cooperation—same brain base, same adaptive function as our singing and dancing Neanderthal cousins.

Had you been around our earliest ancestors back then and asked one of them why he or she was dancing to the rhythm of the drum beat, they may not have been able to deliver a very coherent answer. But scratching stick symbols on the wall of their cave or clapping and moving in dance around the fire likely did convey a sense of playful creativity, a sense of self as creator of new meaning beyond the concrete and rote movements of habit. In reviewing the evolutionary base of narrative, Brian Boyd affirms that art in all its forms generates this sense that we can transform the world of our experience and fill it with new meaning—for our Neanderthal and *homo sapiens* ancestors and for us both in our youth and now.

And we did see ourselves as creating a new world coming as we sang "Aquarius" and "Good Morning Starshine" as we swayed to the music of the rock opera *Hair*. And as we sang, we bonded with each other as the neurochemical oxytocin bathed our brain cells, raising our trust level—trust extended to at least those under thirty. "Humans around the world report not just strong emotional bonding from synchronized, coordinated movement together, but feelings of a spiritual nature—a sense of there being a collective consciousness, the presence of a superior being, or an unseen world that is larger than what we immediately experience."[14]

We were also the Me generation raised on Bill Haley's "One, Two, Three O'Clock, Four O'Clock Rock," Presley's "Heartbreak Hotel," and the invasion of the Beatles, sensing ecstasy as Jerry Lee Lewis pounded out "Whole Lotta Shakin' Goin' On."

> "It began with the Music," Jeff Greenfield has written perceptively. "Nothing we see in the counter-culture—not the clothes, the hair, the sexuality, the drugs, the rejection of reason, the resort to symbols and magic—none of it is separable from the coming to power in the 1950s of rock and roll music." The Woodstock Nation was originally the Rock Nation. Kids all over the East Coast were sneaking upstairs, closing the door, and listening to the disc jockey Alan Freed playing "Stagger Lee" on New York's radio station WINS, juiced up to 50,000 watts.[15]

From the war protests to the free speech movement to women's lib to anti-racism, the songs created a sense of cohort solidarity. We were "all bound up into one big cause, into 'us against them'. The songs seemed to hold

---

14. Levitin, *The World in Six Songs*, 56.
15. Jones, *Great Expectations*, 72.

wisdom, encouragement, and motivation.... Just *knowing* that there were other people like you throughout the country, hundreds of thousands or millions of protesters, singing the same songs, chanting the same slogans"[16] where just fifty people, banding together, became Arlo Guthrie's movement. The songs opened up our hearts and planted seeds of change.

Thus, we sang our stories and created our worlds, then and now. So let's shift our gaze from our evolutionary roots of song and story as they provided the base for what shaped us as a generation, to our specific human capacity to create and articulate the story of our lives over the time we've been given.

The Creation of the Life Story that Began Back Then

In his seminal 2013 article,[17] Dan McAdams—one of the leading lights in the research area of narrative psychology—speaks of our developing sense of selves as actor, agent, and author of our lives. Although I want to focus on ourselves as authors of our life stories, briefly let me summarize those two other aspects of personality development.

If we think of our subjective sense of a self, the "I" who peers out of the crib and who gazes into its mother's face as she nurses and cares for it, at around the age of about two years this "I" develops a sense of itself as a separate "me" inhabiting the world. Remember the "terrible twos" that maybe your own children went through? The cries of "Me, me!" "Me wants that!" "Mine!" "No!" facing off the sibling rival and omniscient parent as the Other against my willful Me-space of wants and needs. Between one and two years after birth, we experience ourselves as separate creatures, as actors apart from others who inhabit our home space. And our earliest memories harken back to this period. For me, I have a hazy memory of taking an afternoon nap in my bed (crib?) on the sun porch of my grandmother's apartment.... and a bit later on, of lying in bed, safely tucked in with blankets over me, sick with some germ confining me to that place, and Daddy bringing me toys from his appliance store on Bardstown Road in Louisville, Kentucky. I felt safe and secure and loved.

So emerges a sense of myself as actor in my surrounding world, as a separate Me already expressing genetically given traits such as shyness or bold extroversion—as a behaving subject—in my case, as a Me who gets spanked when caught having pulled up my grandmother's flowers in the

---

16. Levitin, *The World in Six Songs*, 60.
17. McAdams, "The Psychological Self as Actor, Agent, and Author."

back yard of her house, discovered under the back porch, a guilty actor caught in the act.

Around the age of six or so, our "I" self begins to see itself as an agent, as a goal-directed "Me" who aims purposely for what is of value to that Me. Before that, of course, even in the crib we reached for the mobile hanging just above it, reaching out to grab the desirable flicker of color and light above our heads. But not even by age four or so could we have understood ourselves as goal-directed, not having the self-reflective capacity to transcend our concrete actions and claim a sense of overall purpose to our activities.

But by the age of six or seven, we self-consciously adopt goals, for example good grades, gold stars for perfect attendance at school, or new toys bought with an allowance that gets saved over the months. We purposely strive for things we value, and compare our achievements with those of our peers. Our "I" feels self-esteem or failure depending on whether our "Me" reaches the goals the "I" has set. The "I" comes to feel pride or shame as we compare ourselves to others as the "Me" makes its way in the larger world of school and playing field. By the age of seven or so we have also come to understand ourselves in trait terms—as shy, or bold, or cheerful, or cautious, and so on—as well as in terms of the roles we play in the family and school, having begun to embrace purpose and goals as our own. McAdams puts it this way:

> By the time children are 8 or 9 years of age, then, they are defining and evaluating themselves through experiences in the family, among peers, on the playground, and in school in terms of culturally valued goals and their progress, or lack thereof, in accomplishing valued goals.... In the ever expanding Me, specific goals to be accomplished in the future ("I want to be a good baseball player"; "I plan to get Jennifer to like me") join with attributions about traits ("I am an outgoing person") and social roles ("I am a good sister"). In other words, features of the motivated agent now sit side by side in the Me with features of the social actor.[18]

As we'll see when we turn our attention to the Now of our current lives, how we see and characterize ourselves in terms of our traits does not change much over the course of our adult lives. For example, I've always been a bit of an introvert, although again, I've learned to harness that inner tendency when the need arises and to work a room—at a cost—with the best of the rest. But our goals, projects, and plans shift and change over our entire adult

18. Ibid., 277.

lives, even into old age—"I choose my goals; I have my traits." Dropping some goals, shifting plans, serve adaptive purposes as we age, as we shall see in due course. But in general, "individualistic societies like the United States typically place a strong premium on goals that enhance the autonomous, achievement, and power of the individual person, over and against the group."[19]

It is in our adolescence that the author, the "I," begins to pull together a coherent life story, one that ties together significant remembered episodes from the past (for example, my visit to St. Isidore's), colored by meaning created by songs and stories, by conversations with significant others, by ritual and tradition of community life, by society's and family values—in short, by meanings given by the surrounding culture—and projected into an expected future life. "We are the plagiaristic authors of our own identities . . . . The autobiographical author borrows and appropriates a culture's prevailing narrative forms, images, metaphors, and plots and fits his or her personal experience to them—taking great literary license, for sure, but always within culture's narrative constraints."[20]

Based on memory and expectation, the "I" creates a sense of self with a history and a future, a sense of cohesion, as a comprehensive life story incorporating, but not replacing, my earlier self as actor and agent. It is in adolescence that all three layers of the self cohere into a single story that gives overall meaning to my life. "The I becomes an autobiographical author; the Me becomes the story it tells."[21]

> Developmental research shows that autobiographical reasoning skills begin to emerge in late childhood and continue to grow through the adolescent years. Older adolescents and young adults show more facility than their younger counterparts in (a) deriving organizing themes in their lives; (b) sequencing personal episodes into causal chains in order to explain their development; (c) illustrating personal growth over time; (d) identifying clear beginnings and endings in their life narrative accounts; and (e) incorporating foreshadowing, retrospective reflection, and other markers of mature self-authorship . . . .[22]

Thus, we begin to pull our life stories together in our early teenage years and continue to tell and retell our story—more or less into old age.

---

19. Ibid., 287.
20. Ibid.
21. Ibid., 279.
22. Ibid., 280.

Interestingly, research has shown that the audience for our stories shifts as we develop through our teen years. In her 2005 report, Kate McLean describes findings from her study looking at the telling of the smallest unit of the life story, our autobiographical or episodic memories. The latter are specific memories we carry around for particular, concrete events that happen in our lives—for example, my St. Isidore's episode—that finally get pieced together in our story as we develop. But the audience for these discrete autobiographical memories change as does the purpose in the telling. McLean's findings suggest that adolescents tell their memories first to their parents (or I suppose parent surrogates such as a priest or a trusted teacher) in order to work out the meaning of the events, to regulate emotional response to a memory. Later on, the same event can be remembered and relayed to peers in order, this time, to entertain and to form social bonds with others their age.[23]

Now of course this is all in the abstract. There are individual differences between us, aren't there, even if we're born into a cohort or generation shaped by its times. At the level of actor, we are each born with a different set of genes, with a different temperament, with a different style of navigating our way in the world. As I said earlier, I am basically an introvert, comfortable in my own skin, preferring a few close friends over dinner, or even dining alone, to a room full of smiling faces chatting away over cocktails.

And certainly at the level of agent we are even more varied, with different life goals, different values, different purposes played out in the choices we make. And for both actor and agent, the culture in which the self is a part has a major impact on the shape of our personality. How our traits are expressed, for example, or how we act in our social world is shaped by what is permissible and desirable in our immediate culture. We might define

---

23. I actually don't think this is age-related; I think the same differential function occurs across our lives. For example, an excruciatingly embarrassing event occurred when my husband, Leon, and I were being interviewed for faculty positions at the New School for Social Research in New York City. We had been taken for lunch at a little bistro near the New School. It was a rainy day and I had an umbrella that I laid on the floor beside my chair—which happened to have only three legs, a sort-of stool. As we finished lunch, I leaned over to retrieve the umbrella and the whole chair tipped over and I went sprawling on the floor in front of the four senior faculty members who had taken us to lunch. I really wanted to die, I wanted the floor to open up and swallow me. I was humiliated.

However, years later, I told and retold this episode seared into my memory like it was yesterday—in this case, for purely entertainment purposes, but also for social bonding purposes. I was saying "See, I'm fallible, I'm human, really embarrassing things have also happened to me in my life, just like to everybody else."

Thus, our purpose for telling—whether in adolescence or in later years—shifts as a function of the audience we select to hear the tale told.

ourselves, our "Me," as basically shy or introverted, but over time our "I" can learn to inhibit the expression of our traits, can rise to the occasion if you will, can overcome trait tendencies to a certain extent and at a certain cost. As I said earlier, I have learned to overcome my introverted tendencies and speak and preach publicly with ease, but it drains more energy from me than others, and I then need downtime to recover. As for the goals I choose, I select from a menu of possibilities afforded by my social world that gives me the opportunities arrayed before me. If I grow up in a poor ghetto and choose to become president of the country, the odds are against me. (But then there's a Nelson Mandela, yes?) In my case, my values and my choices—as first academic and then clergy—were offered by my culture and happily were within my reach, so I grabbed them as goals to be won.

But we are most unalike, or perhaps I should say we are most unique with respect to the story of our lives, that story that we began to put together in our teens. "Cultural effects may be ubiquitous, but the most pronounced and dramatic cultural effects are to be expected for the self as autobiographical author."[24] And for me, the cultural menu I chose from was colored by religious symbols and stories. Going back to my experience at St. Isidore's, I began to pull together my life story with the Church, with God, with a religious vocation at its center.

Of course as I've already pointed out, some come to tell better stories than others; some create life stories that despite setbacks have some sense of redemption at their core, while others remain stuck in a story grown rigid, cynical, and hardened by dead ends. Even in adolescence, research has shown that those youths who reported successfully dealing with some major turning point in their lives while in high school, incorporating reverses into their emerging life stories, by grade twelve had a stronger sense of psychological well-being than those who were unable to create some positive meaning out of such losses (for example, interpersonal conflicts, geographical moves, accidents, sickness, death in the family, academic difficulties).[25] Research has also shown that the same findings hold true for adults' meaning-making across the life course. All lives have turning points, both very good and very bad, turning points that challenge us to make meaning and incorporate these episodes into some coherent whole in order for us to flourish.

---

24. McAdams, "The Psychological Self as Actor, Agent, and Author," 286.
25. Tavernier and Willoughby, "Adolescent Turning Points."

Interlude I: Meet Paul

Let me introduce you to Paul, a sixty-year-old lawyer, a public defender of the poor and the unfortunate. Paul and I have known each other for nearly four decades and at times in our history, have been at loggerheads over big issues ranging from God (especially) to lifestyle—me fairly conventional and Paul at times outrageous, at least in my eyes. Paul has always known how to push my buttons, as they say, and I used to take it personally. However, as we both get older I have come to understand him as a gadfly, as someone who pokes at convention in general, and not just me in particular. We have also come to deeply appreciate and love one another over the years, to embrace our differences and see beneath them to the person within.

Paul is also a quintessential Boomer. I think his life reflects many of the aspects of our generation that I've described here, drawing from research and social commentary. So allow me to let him speak for himself.

> ... my work as a criminal defense attorney has dominated my adult life, and before my current stint as a bureaucrat, for the past three decades I served thousands of poor clients, many of whom were locked behind bars. These people, each of whom I sought to know well and treat with dignity and respect, often had lives of incredible suffering and, on occasion, inflicted the same on others. This was not easy work, and the conditions of employment—relatively low pay, constant conflict, little appreciation—were difficult. Thus, the need to party often and well! And, more generally, to enjoy life and remember that luck plays a large roll in what side of the jail door I stood by at the end of the day.

> ... [When I was in law school] I got to know, and then be very close with, classmates who went to law school to become, or continue being, activists for political and social change. In time, we coalesced into a chapter of the National Lawyers Guild, a politically progressive lawyer organization, hosting our own regional conferences with inspirational radical lawyers, and attending similar programs elsewhere in the Midwest. Naturally, of course, drugs, sex, and rock and roll played a good part in all of this, in addition to a fervent commitment to the cause.

I include here this excerpt from a longer autobiographical sketch Paul provided for this chapter because it nicely shows a life narrative shot through with idealism. And although he probably didn't actually go to Woodstock, nevertheless he captures that "tribal" sense of collective bonding as his guild met and seemingly partied with abandon at their gatherings over the years.

We'll return to Paul in the next section of this chapter as he describes his current life as he has entered his sixties. But the story he tells here—the origin of his thirty-year vocation—began early and reflects a coherent narrative of his life as a whole, despite the setbacks that have bedeviled him as they have bedeviled us all across our days.

Circling back to the overall theme of this book, our brains are wired for story, in all its forms—the stories we make of our lives as Paul just told of his—the stories we've been discussing here, the stories we sing, the stories we dream, good or bad, coherent or fragmented, hope-filled or filled with despair. As McAdams repeatedly points out, self as author becomes layered over self as motivated agent, and both levels of personality development become layered over the self as actor on our stage of life. As we'll see later on, each of these aspects of the self offers challenges across the life course. As we turn our attention to the Now of our present lives as we've come this far—in this chapter and in the ones that lie ahead—we'll have an opportunity to address those challenges as we consider the stories of our lives as they are unfolding before us.

THE NOW OF OUR LIVES: ON PARADISE DRIVE

So here we are. In our late fifties or deep into our sixties and approaching (or just having approached) that very strange year that Simon and Garfunkel sang about so long ago. Landon Jones's *Great Expectations*—all about that Baby Boom generation that was changing the world—appeared in print in 1980, when the Boomers were approaching middle age. Howe and Strauss's *Generations*—which includes an in-depth look at the Boomer generation termed by them "Idealist"—was published in 1991 when we were all a decade older. The latter authors also interestingly hazarded a prophetic description of that cohort as they (we) age, reaching "Post-Elderhood" by 2026.

Howe and Strauss predicted some social crisis occurring in the mid-2010s—primarily economically driven—where Boomers' expectations of entitlement clash with the spiraling cost of health care and with an underfunded federal pension system. "A straight-line extrapolation of recent productivity, fertility, and longevity trends indicates that by the year 2025, younger workers would have to hand over 30 to 40 percent of their payroll to provide old Boomers with G.I.-style public support."[26] Some of these authors' predictions are indeed prescient—eerily apt as we look around at the

---

26. Howe and Strauss, *Generations*, 402.

current economic debates regarding the future of Social Security and the fate of the Affordable Care Act in the months and years ahead.

Tracing out the lives of the Boomer generation to the year 2030, Howe and Strauss conclude their description of this cohort thus: A person born in the 1940s

> ... will recall growing up indulged, coming of age at an exciting if hazardous time to leave home, and passing through rising adulthood in an era that prized consumption and careerism. Among Boomers lucky enough to last eight decades ... the second forty years will be just as memorable. Boomers will have spent mid-life in an era well suited to the sober realizations of mature parents and community leaders, entered old age just as elder wisdom was newly venerated, and reached their collective deathbeds knowing the necessary deeds had been done, allowing heirs to live happily ever after (or so it may seem at the time). If this all comes to pass, this generation may be eulogized as Franklin Roosevelt was by Churchill, for having died "an enviable death."[27]

To reiterate, we are born with traits that can be socially shaped and molded in their expression. But it is in our goals and especially in our stories that our culture and our historical place in time have the greatest impact and make us both unique as a generation and unique as individuals within our cohort's span of time.

We have focused until now on the Me generation—idealistic according to Howe and Strauss, individualistic, at times selfish in our sense of entitlement, pursuing personal goals with the aim of achieving a meaningful life for the self above all. But that cohort characteristic is also embedded in a broad-based cultural story that spans generations across our American history.

In his delightful work *On Paradise Drive*, David Brooks takes a hard look at what he calls our "Paradise spell," a myth of exceptionalism, a sense of being called by our Creator to serve as a beacon upon the hill, to shine brighter than other stars on the distant horizon, "roaring into battle with visions of virtue on our side and evil on the other."

> Born in abundance, inspired by opportunity, nurtured in imagination ... this Paradise spell is the controlling ideology of American life. Just out of reach, just beyond the next ridge, just with the next home or entrepreneurial scheme or diet plan; just with the next political hero, the next credit-card purchase,

---

27. Ibid, 408.

or the next true love; just with the right all-terrain vehicle, the right summer home, the right meditation technique, or the right motivational seminar... just with the right beer and a good set of buddies; just with the next technology or after the next shopping spree, there is this spot you can get to where all tensions will melt, all time pressures are relieved, and all contentment can be realized. Prosperity will be joined with virtue, materialism with idealism, achievement with equality, success with love ... thereby producing a new Eden.[28]

Of course, this is an oversimplification of the American ideal, and Brooks does go on to talk about our hope as a "trickster," where we've sacrificed security for opportunity, where there's an underlying, uneasy sense that even if you win the rat race, you're still a rat—with hope running up against disillusionment and cynicism rising as the perfect life still alludes us.

And yet. Philip Caputo has recently written a fascinating account of renting a trailer and traveling overland, with his wife, from Key West to the Arctic Ocean. In *The Longest Road*, the author made every attempt to stay off interstate highways, and travel instead through small-town America, chatting with folks along the way. As he carried on these conversations in bars and restaurants and other various stops in their travels, Caputo always finally got around to asking the question, "What holds this country—as diverse as it is—what holds it together?" And his conclusion at the end of their journey was the overriding importance of hope, asserting that optimism is our "quintessential American trait." As we shall see in the pages ahead, McAdams and his fellow researchers have studied what they refer to as the "Redemptive Self," the self-story of redemption experienced by those who have weathered loss and suffering, and yet have been able to triumph in the end—authoring a life story consistent with the American myth.

So perhaps we can say that our generation's Boomers, with our own cultural history and shaped by our times, draws from and interacts with a national predisposition to mythically triumph as individuals, transcending the worst that life can throw at us—and like Horatio Alger, rising to the occasion: experiencing the self as still good, still entitled, still strong despite the road blocks encountered as we traversed our mid-life and older years.

---

28. Brooks, *On Paradise Drive*, 268–69.

The Scene in Mid-Life and Beyond: The Me Generation Grows Up . . . Still Doing It Our Way

In 1997 I came to Richmond, Virginia, to assume the rectorship of St. Mark's Episcopal Church in a trendy, museum-dotted area of the city. In 2004, tired of vestry meetings and budgets and personnel issues and program development—and wanting to spend more of my time writing— I resigned from St. Mark's and left active ministry for the writing life. I had just come back from a sabbatical summer in Cambridge, England, where I had a grant from the Lilly Foundation to begin work on my book, *Imagination and the Journey of Faith*. I thought when I returned I could continue work on the project but found that pastoral demands had to take priority. So after some months of deliberation, I walked away from the parish that I and a team of wonderful clergy and lay volunteers had rebuilt from years of decline. But that's another story for some other time.

Leaving St. Mark's because I felt called to return to a life of scholarship (I thought in those terms), and I made up my mind to follow my passion in that regard. But looking back, I see that this was the pattern of my entire adult life, from my first academic job at Indiana State University in Terre Haute, Indiana—I'm sorry, not the earth's most charming spot—then heading east with my husband, Leon, searching for greener pastures. After a brief landing as psychologist in the Division of Disability Studies in the Social Security Administration (so brief that it's not even on my CV), I grabbed the opportunity to become a research administrator at the National Cancer Institute, part of the National Institutes of Health. There I was also able to carry out my own research project on psychological, as well as biological, factors as predictors of breast cancer survival. That initial project subsequently led to a meteoric career studying biological mediators of behavior and cancer outcome.

If you've ever worked for the government, you know that you can arrive one morning and find your office erased from the organizational chart (or as my dad would have colorfully put it, discover that you had the only desk chair that flushed!). Thus, although I had headed the Behavioral Medicine Branch in the Division of Prevention and Cancer Control at the NCI, I got caught in a web of animosity from on high, and was unceremoniously summoned to an administrator's office (may he rest in peace—the fellow died from a brain tumor some short years later) and informed by him with some glee that my branch was no more. However, I landed well on my feet, heading to the University of Pittsburgh in 1984, where I became Associate Professor of Psychiatry and Medicine, and later, Associate Director of the Pittsburgh Cancer Institute. I stayed there until 1991, surprising everyone—including my shocked and dismayed staff—when I resigned to head off to seminary.

Before leaving my academic post, I had begun to read again for pleasure. For example, I read Gail Godwin's *Father Melancholy's Daughter* as I was getting ready to leave Pittsburgh and enter the seminary in Alexandria, Virginia. It is the story of an Episcopal priest and his daughter, who herself becomes a priest in the end. I was inspired by Godwin's description of "Father Melancholy" as "neither a self-transcendent guru nor one of these fund-raising manager types who have become so sought after lately by our Holy Church. He's just himself—himself offered daily . . . . He's lonely and bedeviled like the rest of us, but he has time for it all and tries to do it right. He lives by the grace of daily obligation."[29]

That last line about living by the grace of daily obligation stuck in my brain as I went off to seminary and as I made my way into the life of the parishes I have served. It's a wonderful ideal appealing to my own sense of trait-self as conscientious, reflecting my purpose and goal in leaving the university and heading off for a life of service, becoming part of my story as I rewrote it in the years ahead.

After seminary, I was called to Lexington, Virginia as Assistant and then Associate Rector of R. E. Lee Memorial Church (no kidding—he had been on the vestry there after the Civil War). I then abruptly left there after three years when I was offered the rector's position in Richmond.

I recite all this because I want to make a point that I think is well illustrated with my professional life course. When I informed the rector at R. E. Lee that I was beginning to search for a rectorship of my own, he was a bit unhappy—to say the least—because he had long planned a sabbatical in England, a trip that he hoped to take with his son who was approaching college age. He had also hoped (and planned) that I would run the parish in his absence, gaining good parish administrative experience in the process. But I had decided to move onward and upward, and was very soon called as rector of St. Mark's in Richmond.

I had an excuse—that my husband, Leon, had some physical problems at the time and that a move to the city of Richmond, with its health care resources, was a reasonable and prudent thing to do. I also wanted to have my own church. Just before I left Lexington, a retired priest by the name of Monty Pierce visited me one day at home. And as we sat in the breakfast alcove, he gave me some feedback. He said that he saw me as someone "with blinders on," one who was hell-bent on a goal, and single-mindedly pursued it, letting the chips (or in this case, people) fall where they may. I was

---

29. Godwin, *Father Melancholy's Daughter*, 199.

surprised at this picture he drew of me, startled really, never having seen my life choices in that light. But his characterization had a ring of truth to it. It didn't cause me to magnanimously forego the move to Richmond, but that picture of my drivenness haunted me from that time forth. And as we shall see, it prompted some soul searching in the years ahead.

Now I have gone over all this to illustrate Howe and Strauss's description of the career choices made by many in my generation. "A growing flood of late-starting boomers began to spread ('free agency') traits throughout the economy. They insisted on having 'meaningful' (read: un-[parent]-like) careers."[30] More educated than previous generations, we had drilled into us from early on our "extraordinary promise year after year . . . while growing up. [We] had been richly educated and planned to use it."[31] And we became the teachers, preachers, and writers of our generation.

We also became self-perfectionists. Not only did we work on ourselves striving for meaningful perfection in the workplace, we worked on ourselves then and now in order to stay fit by jogging, by eating low-fat foods, and going organic. In mid-life and beyond, we reach for the Greek yogurt, the gluten-free chip, the fair trade, decaffeinated coffee—smug in our rightness, judgmental as we approach our old age. In summing up the best and the worst personality characteristics in our late mid-life and aging cohort, Strauss and Howe see us positively as principled, resolute, and creative—again, many of us becoming writers, publishers, teachers, preachers, lawyers (as you'll see ahead), and radical in one way or another (think Newt Gingrich or Hillary and Bill). These authors also view us negatively as capable of ruthlessness, selfishness, and arrogance. And looking back at my life as I have lived it, certainly most of their characterization does ring true for me. At least, up to a point and up to the ground we have covered in these pages so far.

Interlude II: Paul Again

We met Paul some pages back as he recalled some of his law school days and early career as a public defender. Creeping toward sixty years of age, he is now nearing the end of that career, still drawn by the humanistic idealism that lured him into public service law that he has practiced for over thirty years. He also volunteers his time as a board member of an organization—the Circus Project—that helps at-risk youth build healthier lives. And he is

---

30. Howe and Strauss, *Generations*, 311.
31. Jones, *Great Expectations*, 198.

still a countercultural free spirit, a sometimes maverick who playfully pokes fun at staid convention on occasion.

> As I approach my sixtieth birthday next year I continue to wonder, as I'm sure you and others do as well, at what age I will finally grow up. I know I'm aging, of course, since I look at my hands in a certain light and see old man skin. And I'm slower in nearly every way, from my thinking and talking to swimming my laps and riding my bike and running on trails with my old man shuffle. But I'm still having the darndest time being serious about myself or those around me. I hide it well, usually. I don't very often say inappropriate things, at least not when it might offend or get me in serious trouble. At work it's a challenge, since being a lawyer, especially in state government, presents all sorts of opportunities for hilarity, usually when people are trying their hardest to be serious. But, really, what can I do when stakeholders gather to identify core competencies in order to assign action items and deliverables for going forward? Hardly a day passes without wondering if I'm on the wrong planet . . . .
>
> [Now maybe all this] may be a slight misstatement of my current circumstances, at least objectively observed. That's because in my real present life I have just spent a week being pretty serious. I have been home exactly one night of the last five as I lectured at and attended conferences and meetings in different parts of the state having to do with representing clients in family abuse and neglect cases, handling death penalty cases, and managing public defender services. And now, finally home on Saturday night, I prepare to leave for three more nights in Arizona for a "leadership summit" on defending juvenile delinquency cases. I describe all this in order not to brag or complain but to provide evidence of my present life.
>
> The picture can actually be drawn in finer detail if I also share that at the beginning of last week, during a nice luncheon at the Eugene Hilton, a good friend had me bang on the glassware so he could share with everyone the news that a man we've all known and adored for decades had died unexpectedly. This kind of news is arriving with increasing frequency (my own doctor, a paradigm of fitness and health, also dropped dead recently), leaving me to daydream . . . about the day they make the announcement about me . . . . As "the end" slowly becomes more real, though, my overwhelming thought is that I better work even harder at having fun, since most of the things I want most

to do—mostly having to do with outdoor adventure—need to happen before my body parts wear out....

I think I have a good life. I have a loving relationship with my wife Judy, a good dog, and an extended family of good and supportive people, including you, of course. Judy and I regularly engage in what might be called self-betterment activities, like the classes, workshops and gatherings we enjoy to play the guitar (me) and the mandolin (her). She's always taking yoga and related workshops, and teaches yoga as well in a women's prison and to a group of physically disabled adults. I took a class recently on making kim chee. And of course, I've now been involved with the Circus Project for quite a few years, first with my own aerial classes and now as a board member for a group that provides circus training and performances for at-risk youth. We have a good group of friends, too, whom we often talk about as family.

Before we leave Paul, let me share one more bit of the interview with you because his words so beautifully reflect that rebellious, occasionally outrageous behavior that absolutely challenges the bourgeois and conventional status quo so typically of our protest generation.

Paul happened to mention, almost as an aside, that last spring he had visited the Portland Art Museum "completely naked except for sandals"—in conjunction with an annual naked bike ride around Portland participated in by about 7,000 riders and escorted by police. I think this museum episode shows nicely not only the countercultural values that still drive his life (even though in general he sees his professional life as conventional because he has held the same job as a public defender for thirty-some years). But it also shows how the sense of euphoria and even ecstasy—in this case, in an aging Boomer—can develop within a kind of group ritual. He says:

To say you had to be there probably isn't a good answer, although it's the best one. Picture yourself, first, in Portland, which cherishes and nurtures its wacky ways. Then understand that every year, for at least the last five or so, there has been an annual naked bike ride, at least one of which went past our house, that draws thousands of participants and which, thanks to a court case here a few years ago, is now totally legal and so big that the police close off streets to cars and escort the ride. And then add in that this year the said staid art museum, which was featuring an exhibit of vintage bicycles at the time, offered admission to naked ride participants, charging only a dollar for each item of clothing worn (which had to include, at a minimum, shoes or sandals). All this intrigued Judy and me. So we rode our bikes downtown on a beautiful spring evening, with enough clothing to visit a little restaurant for dinner before arriving at the museum with hundreds of others in an extremely festive mood. The museum, of course, could not accommodate the thousands who would eventually show up for the ride that evening, which happened to coincide with the annual Grand Floral Parade of our venerable Rose Festival, which brings hordes of tourists to downtown Portland (and who would later line the beginning of our mass bike ride across town). But Judy and I were fortunate to get into the museum, entering with enough clothing still on to cover our modesty, as they say. Once inside, however, the urge to shed clothing became stronger, and eventually was overwhelming. I have photos and video of the event, which would show you just how ordinary it all really was. Certainly, there was absolutely nothing sexual or exhibitionist about it. People of all sorts, and all body types, were simply carrying on like normal museum goers, but without any clothing (except shoes, of course). Some people did have a rationale for being naked—to protest this or that, or expose our vulnerability to this or that, or whatever—but for most I think the idea was just to do something a little different for a change and to have fun. Ultimately, that's why Judy and I were there. And, indeed, it was great fun!

****

"Those were the days, my friend, we thought they'd never end."[32] But they did. And here we are, sixty and beyond, keeping fit, still idealistic and egocentric—embracing careers in public defense law or church leadership, while many of us spend to the hilt at fitness centers with personal trainers, on exotic vacations, on houses in trendy neighborhoods that reflect our values and tastes. Some of us (like Paul and Judy) elected not to have children, or to have only one or two at best. Recalling the crisis that Howe and Strauss predict in the coming years, the economic implications of our "baby bust" are now playing out here and will get worse in the years ahead.

Not all of my generational cohort followed the marriage/remarriage cycle. Many elected not to marry, or to divorce and not remarry—opting for the solo life instead. I mention this now because as you will see later in this chapter, those decisions—the numbers of Boomers moving into retirement who are living alone for one reason or another, and/or who have no children

32. Hopkin, "Those Were the Days."

as they now age—matter a great deal in terms of the retirement years and the possibility of a son's or daughter's help as physical decline sets in.

Using national survey data, the researchers I-Fen Lin and Susan Brown reported that "the proportion of midlife Americans . . . that are unmarried has increased by more than 50 percent since 1980. Today, one in three Baby Boomers is unmarried. The vast majority of these unmarried Boomers are either divorced or never-married; just 10 percent are widowed. As Boomers move into older adulthood, the unmarried share will grow as married Boomers continue to experience divorce and widowhood."[33] These researchers draw the conclusion that obviously this rise in unmarried Boomers by mid-life will leave these aging Boomers vulnerable as they move into their frailer senior years—especially the unmarried in general, and men who never married in particular.

We are now the new consumers, buying the newest iPhone, or Viagra-alternative pills or underarm sprays boosting testosterone levels for the male side of our cohort, checking our investments for retirement savings, beginning to think about downsizing to just the right kind of place—a condo with a Jacuzzi in the bathroom. The nostalgic music we still listen to glorifying our past when we came of age, and the books that we now read that continue to shape us (for an example that's on my bedside table at the moment, Anna Quindlen's *Lots of Cake, Plenty of Candles*) reflect the ideals of meaning-striving and ego satisfaction that we still value in our lives—reinforcing the ideals that drove our choices over the years.

As in all things human, of course, there is a downside to our generational picture of Now. In an op-ed piece in *The New York Times* titled "All the Lonely People," Ross Douthat observes that one in three Americans over the age of forty-five identifies themselves as chronically lonely. Douthat quotes Judith Shulevitz: "With baby boomers reaching retirement age at a rate of 10,000 a day . . . the number of lonely Americans will surely spike."[34] He points out that neither Facebook, nor a life coach, nor an institutional bureaucracy can replace the role of family or religious community.

Reflecting back on Howe and Strauss's prophetic warning of an emerging economic crisis sometime in the mid-2010 decade, a crisis due to the large crop of Boomers entering their "golden" years with a shrinking workforce to support their entitlements (a shrinking workforce in part a result of two-professional Boomer marrieds preferring no or few children in their upwardly mobile households), a recent policy study by Robert Hudson and

---

33. Lin and Brown, "Unmarried Boomers Confront Old Age," 163.
34. Quoted in Douthat, "All the Lonely People."

Judith Gonyea[35] sees our cohort as increasingly fractionated in the years ahead. The relatively affluent aging Boomers will resist the identity label as "old" and will also resist any encroachment on their social safety net that they—like Reagan's microphone of yesteryear—paid for and also richly deserve. In contrast, the less affluent—less educated, less powerful, less elite members with a lifetime of blue-collar occupations at best—will be more likely to identify themselves as old and in need of those same benefits in a shrinking pot. "For the first group, maintenance of benefits will continue to require a muscular political presence; for the latter group, their needs will continue to be acknowledged by others. The logic of this divide... is that the more affluent will remain as Contenders, whereas the more vulnerable will return to their original categorization as Dependents, relying on the goodwill and charity of the larger public to assure a modicum of well-being."[36]

This economic divide for our generation is only one source of fractionation as we age. In a fascinating study reported in that same issue of *The Gerontologist*, Erin Roth, Lynn Keimig, and their colleagues describe what happened to the social environment of a retirement community when Boomers started joining that facility. Because the Boomers preferred to see themselves as special members of a culturally shaped cohort, they did not integrate easily into the social life of the community. In fact, on the whole the Boomers refused to see themselves as like those Others who were perceived as older and not "with it" in terms of shared music and interests.

Interestingly, these researchers also reported that both the older, original residents and the somewhat younger Boomers, all shared an "ageism," a distancing from those of their peers who were beginning to slip mentally or physically. They characterize a "third age" identity as still active, "youthful," fit, and mentally sharp. In fact, there was such a rejection of even the notion of becoming frail, that the staff couldn't get many of the residents to support increasing the available resources to allow "aging in place." As far as most were concerned, they believed they would not need such extended services "any time soon—or perhaps ever."

Even though both newcomers and older residents alike clung to the image of the still vital "third-ager," the incoming Boomers refused to identify with the older residents—defining themselves by chronological age as an exclusive, closed club. They developed their own LISTSERV, met together as a closed group, and listened to "their" songs of the '60s and '70s, refusing to mingle with those they perceived as older and Other.

---

35. Hudson and Gonyea, "Baby Boomers and the Shifting Political Construction of Old Age."

36. Ibid., 281.

The "fourth age," in contrast, was an identity defined as showing illness, decline, and approaching death. Even the impaired themselves knew that they were perceived as "Other," avoiding community events knowing that others might be "averting eyes when the ragged tooth marks of time begin to appear around the edges of a neighbor's mind or body."[37]

Well, of course we all won't wind up in an adult retirement community . . . at least by election. I for one will remain in my own home, on my own terms, in my own space as long as I can possibly hold out. Frankly, I can't imagine wanting to move to a retirement community and would have to be well into my "fourth age" to do so. Still, as the writer Carolyn Heilbrun said, "the human irony is that those of us who have reached seventy . . . since we did not wish to die, surely we must have wished to grow old?"[38]

I suppose if we put it in those terms, aging is a good alternative, giving us a chance to be better selves—better versions of the self we have been—with our collection of genes and the shaping of their expression by culture, by the choices we have made and continue to make, as we write and rewrite, as we finish our stories—developing, if we're lucky, some wisdom along the way.

We do face challenges to this life project across the areas of personality that Dan McAdams so nicely summarized as actor, agent, and author—challenges to those of us who grew up in a culture of protest and fierce individualism. As we've already seen, self as author is actually layered over, but does not replace, self as actor and agent. That is, the comprehensive, mature self in adulthood is comprised of all three functions or aspects, but it is the self as author that is the most fully comprehensive of the three.

****

"Listen. To live is to be marked. To live is to change, to acquire the words of a story, and that is the only celebration we mortals know."[39]

When I started my research career over three decades ago, I interviewed seventy or so recent retirees from Indiana University and Indiana State University (where I was then on the faculty). I sat in their homes or borrowed offices and asked them a series of questions: how would you describe your

---

37. Roth et al., "Baby Boomers in an Active Adult Retirement Community."
38. Heilbrun, *The Last Gift of Time*, 6.
39. Barbara Kingsolver quoted in King and Hicks, "Whatever Happened to 'What Might Have Been'?," 634.

current life, your current situation? And after they had done that, I asked them to describe their past lives . . . wherever they wanted to begin the narration. Finally, I asked them to imagine their future, what they expected life to hold for them as they peered down the next years.

The experiences I had with those aging faculty and staff from the two institutions were fascinating and powerful—powerful in the sense that as they pulled together a picture of their whole life, their stories unfolded before us as we sat facing each other by fireside or at the kitchen table. According to McAdams, the ability to create a sense of autobiographical continuity—a sense of a Me continuous with my past memories and future hopes—depends on both an intact memory for specific episodes in my past life (episodic memory), and a semantic memory (made up of general facts and attributions of the self, for example, "I'm usually timid and shy," "I'm an extravert," "I'm somewhat careless about details, that is, not very conscientious about things").

But there's a challenge in rewriting and retelling my story as I move through time and as I age. And the challenge is this: to create a sense that despite all that I have been through, all the changes and chances of my life that have befallen me, that I am the same, continuous "Me" over time. And this sense of coherence, of continuity, depends first on what researchers refer to as *phenomenological continuity*, that moment-by-moment feeling that I'm the same person this morning who went to bed in my bedroom last night, that I'm the same person who steps out of my car in the grocery store parking lot as the one who got in my car to drive to the store fifteen minutes ago. This is the minute-by-minute sense of continuity that can get scrambled in a psychotic break, or bizarre dream sequence, or ecstatic occurrence in daily life.

In addition, a sense of self-coherence over a lifetime despite choices and losses along the way also depends on *narrative continuity*. As McAdams puts it, such continuity "refers to a constructed sense of the self as a character in the many different scenes that comprise a story, extending back to the past and forward to the future."[40] And it is this sense of personal continuity that emerged powerfully in the early interviews that I carried out at the two midwestern universities, and that presents a challenge to our aging selves as our roles and goals change, as our physical health and energy wane, as we enter the last decades of our lives.

There has been solid research in recent years on the nature of life stories that people tell, especially on evaluating how those folks deal with

---

40. McAdams, "The Psychological Self as Actor, Agent, and Author," 284.

trauma and loss in their life.[41] Much of this work has been descriptive and correlational, examining life turning points (or antecedents) and life satisfaction, mood, maturity, continuity (consequences) of "good" and "bad" stories. Because this book is concerned with stories that shape us and stories that we create out of our imaginative brains, I will return to some of this research as we traverse the chapters ahead.

So my questions: as members of a special generation reflected in our music and myths of righteousness and purposeful mission, where do we go from here? And where is God amid all the complexity of our lives then and now? To begin to answer these questions and with this basic look at self-creation over the life course, we'll turn now and look at our idealistic cohort as moral and ethical selves, as righteous warriors who marched for justice . . . on our terms and in our own judgment.

---

41. Pals, "Constructing the 'Springboard Effect.'"

3

"Which Side Are You on, Boy?"
Education of the Moral Sense

THE SCENE BACK THEN: "BLOWIN' IN THE WIND"

Boston. Fenway Park. It was the presidential race of 1968 and there we were—Sam and I—to hear Eugene McCarthy give his stump speech. But before he came onto the field, Pete Seeger warmed up the crowd by strumming his banjo and singing his heart out for the cause. I don't remember a thing about McCarthy's message, but I do remember Seeger loping out onto the infield, and we were thrilled to hear the great man in person.

Shortly after that night, Sam and I drove—with our baby sons, Brian and Kevin—to visit my parents who at that time were living in Thomasville, Georgia. Now if you know anything about Thomasville, it's in the Deep South—just north of the Florida line. It was (and maybe still is) antebellum South. Visiting the place then was like stepping back into the last century in terms of conservative lifestyle, social values, and political persuasion.

So to drive from Waltham, Massachusetts to Thomasville, Georgia, with a "McCarthy for President" bumper sticker plastered on the back of our car was a deliberate, in-your-face move on our part. We made the trek without incident other than some frowns of disapproval from bystanders, including from my parents who were staunch Republicans and members of the John Birch Society for at least a while.

If I haven't made it clear before now, I was raised in a very conservative household. My dad was—as they say—a "self-made man." He had pulled himself up by his own socks—in fact, a favorite expression of his was "pull your socks up!" meaning pick yourself up and just do it without whining. He had overcome great odds to finally make it financially, owning a plant that manufactured automotive needle bearings in the little town where I grew up. I remember him later referring to Kennedy as "Old Narrow Eyes," and Jimmy Carter as "Mr. Liver Lips." (He was not kind to those with whom he disagreed!)

My dad's dad (my Grandpa Louis whom I never met) abandoned Dad and Grandma when my dad was a teenager and Dad had to work part-time while in high school to help make ends meet. He didn't attend his high school graduation because he couldn't afford to buy a suit to wear to the occasion, and he never forgot what it was like to be hungry. When he and my mom got married, their honeymoon dinner was at a local White Castle hamburger joint. Together they built an appliance shop in the back of their apartment where my dad taught himself how to repair just about anything folks cared to bring in for him to fix.

Dad kept track of every penny that came in, and kept a careful record of all expenses and credits in a little green notebook that my brother and I found in the back of his desk when he died at age eighty-nine a few years back. Having fought in World War II and Korea, he retained a suspicion of all things foreign, and a particularly virulent hatred for the Japanese. So needless to say, he was politically incorrect and conservative to the bone. A McCarthy bumper sticker on the back of our car told him that something indeed had happened to me along the way.

And of course what happened to me along the way was that I had gone off to college. Despite dropping out of St. Mary's in my junior year to get married, my life had veered off into an entirely different (and to my parents, foreign and baffling) world from the one in which I was raised. They considered Indiana University in Bloomington a hot bed of "pinko" communism, and that hot bed is precisely the place—during undergraduate and graduate school—where I developed into my own person during my twenties.

While in Bloomington, I joined the Catholic underground church in defiance of the "above-ground" institution, and we generally adopted all things liberal—antiwar, anti-military, anti-gun, antiracist causes—celebrated especially in the songs that shaped us. The title of this chapter, "Which Side Are You on, Boy?" was popularized during the civil rights struggle by Pete Seeger. And the story behind it captures the sense of the righteous quest for justice and freedom that drove our social unrest.

As the story goes, the scene was Selma. A young black youth approached a clerk in a hardware store, and the clerk asked him, "Which side are you on, boy?" Reportedly the youth answered "I'm on the side of freedom." At that, the clerk drew out an axe handle and proceeded to beat the kid with it.

I first heard this song on an audiotape of Seeger's folk hits, and I can still hear him singing the lyrics in my head.

> Which side are you on, boy, which side are you on? Everybody.
> Which side are you on, boy, which side are you on? [Refrain]
> Don't "tom" to Mr. Charlie, don't listen to his lies
> Us black folks, we ain't got a chance unless we organize. Oh. [Refrain]
> My daddy was a freedom fighter, and I'm his freedom son
> I'll stick to this freedom fight, until every battle's won. Oh. [Refrain][1]

Such songs shaped us Boomers fundamentally, and will be a focus in this chapter. But books—particularly autobiographies—were also important in their brain-shaping effects. For me, Victor Frankl's *From Death Camp to Existentialism* and *Man's Search for Meaning* gave powerful witness to the human forging of meaning in the face of profound evil. Memorably, Frankl wrote that even in the circumstance of a Nazi concentration camp, one can give witness to what it means to be human—in the deepest and finest sense. One who gave such a witness was Dietrich Bonhoeffer—political martyr *par excellence*.

Bonhoeffer was a German theologian and ordained minister who had a temporary appointment at Union Seminary in New York during the rise of Hitler's power and reach. Later in World War II he elected to go back to his country to help organize a movement opposing Nazism. He was finally arrested, imprisoned, and hanged at Flossenberg shortly before the camp was liberated by the Allies. Especially his *The Cost of Discipleship* and *Letters and Papers from Prison* (which I believe was a model for Martin Luther King's *Letters from a Birmingham Jail*) elevated and inspired us who read these works.

Notice that the examples I give here, the songs and autobiographies that were important to us at the time, were all sung or written by

---

1. Written originally by Florence Reece, "Whose Side Are You On?" as a labor organizing song. Copyright 1931 by Bicycle Music Company and administered by Hal Leonard Company. Interestingly, Seeger adapted this song to other causes. I first heard a recording of his singing it in support of unions—exhorting the listeners to join the union effort with the refrain, "Which side are you on? . . . which side are you on?," omitting the word "boy" from the lyrics. But both causes were served because the lyrics challenge the protesters in both the civil rights and labor movements to buck the *status quo* and stand up for justice.

pre-Boomers—Pete Seeger and Bonhoeffer as mere examples of leaders who influenced later Boomer activists, espousing causes that others had also fought for before them. In fact, human history is littered with protest movements and tribal conflicts across the millennia. It's in our DNA. In their book, *Generation Ageless*, J. Walker Smith and Ann Clurman put it this way:

> Much of what shaped Boomers as they grew up became important and influential not because they created it, but because they adopted what others had conceived. Maybe these things would have emerged anyway without the commitment of millions of Boomers, but there's no way of knowing since they signed on in droves.[2]

Smith and Clurman note that for the three great passions of the 60s and '70s—sex, drugs, and rock 'n' roll—Boomers became mere followers of the previous generation of rebels. Alex Comfort of *The Joy of Sex* fame, Betty Friedan, author of *The Feminine Mystique*, Timothy Leary, LSD guru, Jerry Rubin and Abbie Hoffman, defendants in the Chicago Seven trial—were all born either in the 1920s or 1930s. But all were also powerful icons of social change for Boomers who followed them.

So we did not invent protest in the service of the various righteous causes that we espoused. But we took our turn. There were so many of us. And we were affluent enough to massively consume recordings that played over the airwaves. Thus we rode the wave created in the wake of earlier social protests.

The Source of the Scene Back Then: The Music and Culture of the '60s

The overarching theme of this chapter is that songs and stories that convey important life lessons—resonating and reflecting our best moral intuitions—are cultural forms ideally suited to our human brain. If we learn the positive lessons well, they will keep us from going too far astray. As I have underscored in these pages, we author our stories and they create us in turn.

In the first section of this chapter, I plan to focus mainly on the music that played such a large part in shaping our ideology back then and thus, shaped our brains at the most basic level of experience. In the introduction to this work and in the first chapter, I wrote about Daniel Levitin's idea that music, especially songs with lyrics, can be sorted into six basic categories.

2. Smith and Clurman, *Generation Ageless*.

And one of those categories he referred to as "knowledge"—conveying important life lessons for those who hear it.

Levitin, along with others, makes the point that knowledge has an emotional base. We pay attention, recall, remember what's important to us, what we're motivated to care about. And as we discussed earlier, we can trace an evolutionary base to this cognitive process. Likely our early ancestors conveyed important information about tribal boundaries, about foods that were safe to ingest, about heroic deeds performed in the past by exemplary leaders who played a role in successful hunts that insured tribal survival through harsh times.

The Bible is replete with psalms and hymns that teach and celebrate what its listeners and readers need to pay attention to and remember about the past. And to make the point today, children learn their ABCs and memorize which months have how many days by songs and poems. In fact, the only way I can remember how many days a month has is by reciting the old "Thirty days has September, April, June and November . . ." and so on. Let me offer this somewhat lengthy quotation from Levitin, because I think it's important as a whole.

> Of the millions . . . of possible facts about the world we memorize, document, and pass on to others, we *select* those that we think are important, and this is an emotional judgment. We are motivated to care about some and not others, and . . . emotion and motivation are two sides of the same neurochemical coin. It is true that the mere fact that 2 + 2 = 4 . . . is without emotional content. But the fact that we *know* these things, have gone to the trouble to learn them, reflects interests, priorities, motivation—in short, reflects emotion. Scientists are motivated by intense curiosity and a desire to interpret and represent reality in terms of higher truths . . . of course artists do the same thing, taking their observations and trying to formulate *them* into a coherent whole that we call the painting, the symphony, the song, the sculpture, the ballet, and so on. *Knowledge songs are perhaps the crowning triumph of art, science, culture, and mind, encoding important life lessons in an artistic form that is ideally adapted to the structure and function of the human brain. We need to know. And we need to sing about it* [emphasis added].[3]

But beyond conveying emotionally laden and important information and passing it on to others, especially the young, music—as we have discussed in earlier chapters—releases neurochemicals such as oxytocin. When folks sing and dance together, such music binds participants into a communal

---

3. Levitin, *The World in Six Songs*, 186.

whole. And this whole dynamic process is bi-directional. That is, emotions (stirred by musically conveyed meaning) motivate action (for example, marching or dancing or throwing rocks); and such action, in turn, builds emotional response (for example, joy, ecstasy, or rage), which may, in turn, motivate further action.

In this sense, the protest songs of the '60s and '70s were educational in the way Levitin means. Songs such as Arlo Guthrie's "Alice's Restaurant" (where Guthrie sings about being arrested for littering but then being found highly acceptable by the local draft board in order to "kill, kill"), Joan Baez's rendition of "We Shall Overcome," and Peter, Paul and Mary's "Blowin' in the Wind"—all convey pointed protest aimed at war and racism. (You can fill in memories of your own favorite songs here, these are just some of mine.) Political movements fueled by such songs are a form of social bonding, stimulating and motivating the participants to action.

In his book *The Republic of Rock*, Michael Kramer argues that the protest movements of the 1960s—antiwar, pro-drugs, anti-establishment in general—raised basic social questions about the meaning of citizenship and work, but in the end they didn't provide any answers. As cultural critics of the Boomer generation have repeatedly pointed out, we grew up in the age of post-World War II prosperity. We were children of affluence—protesting in velvet jump suits behind ivy-covered walls—paradoxically seeming to oppose the establishment that allowed us the luxury of such opposition. And the music of the times was the vehicle that carried us in the cause.[4]

The questions Kramer sees as being raised by the '60s protests, roiling a decade of social unrest, seem to boil down to these two: what does it mean to be a free citizen within a community that has to set limits on each one's freedom for the sake of an equitable and peaceful social order? And what does it mean to embrace work that has authentic meaning for me, and yet still contributes to the overall good of society?

In Kramer's fascinating work, to examine the first question, he describes the scene played out in the streets, dance halls, and city parks of

---

4. In an earlier chapter, I noted that not all Boomers went to college, not all were affluent, protesting in velvet, not all marched in the streets against the Vietnam misadventure or popped acid. But in fundamental ways, we were more alike than not: Individualistic, self-expressive, and self-absorbed—seeking some deeper meaning in our work and relationships. However it was the elite who made the noise and shaped a signature culture, and it was those affluent elite who modeled a lifestyle in dress and manner that was adopted by our blue collar peers over time. My point here is this: I think it is important to keep in mind that there were—and are—class differences that also separate us within my generation—politically, religiously, and morally—differences that should also be kept in mind. We'll revisit those differences from time to time in these pages.

San Francisco—the Haight-Ashbury scene of flower children and drug-induced ecstasy. To examine the second question regarding the existential meaning of work and the demand for individual rights within the work environment, Kramer focuses on the San Francisco-based rock music radio station KMPX FM. He describes it as an experimental new form of "hip capitalism," "embedding psychedelic rock in a wide-ranging, disc jockey-controlled programming format."[5] Still capitalistic because it bowed to the necessity of advertisements for income purposes; but hip, nevertheless, at least in conception, supporting "artistic freedom" by allowing disc jockeys a free hand in programming.

Kramer traces the rise and fall of both protest efforts. The drug scene had petered out by the end of the '60s as civil society imposed legal constraints on drug consumption, due largely to outrageous excesses spilling out from the fringe and causing social backlash. The radio station lost its innocence by selling out to commercial interests. In fact, both strands of protest, fired by the basic questions raised about citizenship, freedom, and individual rights in the work and wider social environment—carried by the day's rock music—became co-opted by commercial interests and either died or became institutionalized in turn.

But, under it all, and carried beyond our shores to eastern Europe and the troops in Vietnam, lay a quest for *communitas*, for some utopian ideal of authentic community where free individuals would bond into a brother- and sister-hood of human family, where peace and love would reign for all. "Attending a free concert in the Golden Gate Park Panhandle or listening to a psychedelic rock record ... seemed like a gateway to a new utopia—all you had to do was join in; if everyone did, then global social transformation would surely follow.... This was a powerful quality of rock [but] the music also became a means of critically confronting the present."[6]

In his *The Lyre of Orpheus*, Christopher Partridge views protest from the fringes of society as exposing the sacred beneath the everyday normative tolerance of social wrongs. Seeger's refrain, "Which side are you on, boy?" and the whole of that folk song's lyrics are "transgressive" (to use Partridge's term) in the sense that they transgress normative (white society's) tolerance for racism. They go against the grain of the assumed order of social arrangements. Such protest songs uncover and reveal the sacred bonds of our common humanity, with dignity and worth deserved by every human being.

Just so, folk songs like "The Big Muddy," also made popular by Pete Seeger, "War, What's It Good For? Absolutely Nothin'!," "Where Have All

---

5. Kramer, *The Republic of Rock*, 69.
6. Ibid., 21.

the Flowers Gone?" and "Blowin' in The Wind" expose the horror and injustice of war, assumed and tolerated by the larger society. For Partridge, such songs also reveal the sacred truth concerning the sanctity of all life submerged beneath that norm. In short, when the everyday world comes to tolerate injustice in the form of war, white lynchings, the death penalty, mistreatment of migrant workers, and absence of a living wage, then protest arises from the minority fringe in the form of songs and the actions they motivate.

I've made the point in these pages that both music and story in other forms—ritual, dance, fiction, biographies, and visual art—all participate in shaping us, as we in turn create and shape these cultural products. But I'm focusing on the music of the '60s and '70s here because it was a particularly potent force in pulling in those who heard it, sweeping us up in an emotional response, communicating and shaping important lessons and values. "Through the construction of [emotional] space it [music] contributes to the development of identity, by which we mean, broadly speaking, our sense of self and who we are in relation to others and to what we collectively experience as 'the sacred.'"[7] The bond forged between the artist and audience sets up a conduit where the singer can "pour his soul directly into theirs," shaping emotional meaning and memory in the process.

Partridge's understanding of transgressive protest songs as uncovering the sacred beneath the taken-for-granted wrongs of everyday, normative society, takes on a somewhat nuanced shading in his discussion of the boundary between the sacred and profane in the social world of human endeavor. Where exactly does the boundary lie that needs to be crossed over in order to reveal the sacred truth beneath the mundane norm? It turns out that that boundary is not fixed, but movable, depending on the cultural context that changes over time.

Let me give an example here, one Partridge himself uses to make his point. He argues that some forms of music, for example, Gregorian chant, carry with them what he refers to as "affordance." That is, chant "affords" or carries with it an emotional meaning that conveys a sense, a space for the holy or a sense of transcendence. If chant is then introduced into a metal rock song with a beat and lyrics that seem to celebrate sexuality, the dissonance created by the juxtaposition of the chant's affordance of sacredness and the rock beat which calls for exuberant dance and sensual bodily expression is jarring and, it turns out, an extremely potent experience. Does the musical experience suggest perhaps the sacredness of the body and sexual expression? Or not?

---

7. Partridge, *The Lyre of Orpheus*, 58.

The answer to that question a generation or two ago would have been "No." The juxtaposition of chant and sensuality suggesting raw sexuality would have been viewed as a perversion and a profanity. But now? In today's culture, with its celebration of embodiment and a holistic understanding of being human, we might indeed hear and experience the music as a daring exposure of sacred incarnation within the sense of holiness itself. Partridge quotes here from my friend, John De Gruchy—South African philosopher and theologian—who notes that "Christianity—the religion of the incarnation—has too often been guilty of denying the body, the sense and human creativity."[8]

Partridge's thesis concerning popular music's role in shedding light on social evils, uncovering transcendent truths beneath profane social arrangements, is an important one. Listeners caught up in the music's experience not only are moved to dance in the streets, but can become deeply transformed and motivated to act in the cause of sacred values.[9]

In summing up the best of the '60s protest efforts, Kramer has the following to say, which I find very persuasive:

> The counterculture was never just the naive blossoming of a simplistic ideology of peace and love, nor only the torrid pursuit of ecstasy in a hothouse of sex, drugs, and rock 'n' roll . . . . It was all these things, but it was also something more: the music fostered an efflorescence of civic engagement that continues to matter because the need remains to invent modes of citizenship suitable for the difficult conditions of more recent times. Rock, the counterculture, and the whole sixties mythos are important

---

8. Ibid., 46. In the area of the visual arts, another example comes to mind. The well-known photograph by Andres Serrano, which depicts a crucifix half submerged in urine, has offended many a viewer. On the other hand, this breaching of the boundary by such art was meant to open up the possibility that nothing of the body is necessarily profane—that all can be made holy. In that sense, even the urine reflected the sacred truth of God's creation.

9. We'll return to some of Partridge's thinking in the chapters ahead when we discuss the shaping of meaning by music related to religious experience and human love. But let me say here that when I first took up Partridge's work, I was left with the impression of a totally non-critical acceptance of protest from the extreme fringes in order to push the boundary line in search of the sacred beneath all forms of expression. This is especially true in his treatment of contemporary "Dionysian" music and performative female sexual expression (*a la* the Russian group Pussy Riot). He says "this then is the intriguingly ambiguous nature of the sacred—the pure can contaminate [that is, cease to reflect the sacred by veering off course] and the impure can sanctify. That the impure can communicate the sacred is enormously interesting and socially significant. Again, it is this insight that opens up the Dionysian world of popular music to the study of the sacred" (Ibid., 69).

not because they come from some lost magical era, some garden to which we must get back, some time when "you had to be there, man," but rather because they offer a history of how struggles over citizenship often take place in surprising ways: within dominant systems as well as against them; simultaneously at levels of deep philosophical and intellectual questioning and through intensely sensorial bodily experiences; both in immediate contexts and across vast distances; and most of all through commodified forms of leisure, pleasure and culture that intersected with the conventional sphere of politics.[10]

Taken together, these two works by Kramer and Partridge—both written in today's cultural context but Kramer's reflecting specifically back on the protest movements of the '60s—embody the way humans experience their culture, and how cultures are then shaped from without and from within. And of course this process of human community and its transformation has a deeply rooted evolutionary base, much of which we've already discussed in earlier chapters. I'm now going to draw from that earlier discussion, as well as take a look at some recent psychological research that sheds light on the origin of intuition and virtue in our lives that we express in community.

Going Deeper Into the Sources: Evolution, the Brain, and God

After I get ready for bed at night, I like to read for a half hour or so before I turn out the lights. A couple of weeks ago, as I was reading, I heard what sounded like a muffled boom, followed by . . . a strange sensation . . . a slight movement beneath me. I remember my eyebrows shooting up, likely my eyes widening a bit, and wondering "What the hell . . . ?" Then after a few seconds, I recalled that there had been a forecast of storms in our area, and I then told myself—assured myself, really—that the muffled boom must have been a very strong clap of thunder somewhere in the distance that shook the ground even under my house.

That explanation satisfied me enough that I could go to sleep soon after the shake-up. Still there was a nagging sense, an intuition if you will, that the sensation of slight movement beneath me was odd. Oh well. Probably just a very strong clap of thunder in the distance. But still . . .

The next morning I read in the paper that not far from my neighborhood—in the western part of the county—a mild 2.4 earthquake had occurred, rattling windows and generating the strange sensation I had felt the

---

10. Kramer, *The Republic of Rock*, 22.

night before. No damage done, but there could be more aftershocks to follow. In fact, about three years ago, a rather strong earthquake had occurred near here, so more were definitely possible—possible enough to cause me to contact my home insurance folks and initiate the adding of a rider to my policy to protect from earthquake damage.

But what is the point here in my telling you this little story? The point is that my brain perceived *via* my senses something odd, an unusual sensation that put me automatically on the alert for possible danger. The sensation got my immediate attention and I then groped around with my reason for an explanation of the experience. And I came up with the clap of thunder reason (explaining the muffled boom) and the shaking the ground aftermath—which turned out to be quite wrong, but nevertheless calmed my fears of the moment.

Now I believe that all of this has something important to do with what we've been discussing so far in this chapter. We've been focusing on story, primarily sung in lyrics that uncover and convey meaning and teach powerful lessons to those who hear them—shaping our meaning-giving brains in the process. In previous chapters, we've also considered the evolutionary origin of language and here, the primacy of song in passing on important information to others, especially to the young—cementing communal or tribal bonds in the process.

But what about our brain that has evolved allowing us to sing and find meaning in the stories and songs we listen to, as well as create? What about that interconnected network of neurons, the brain centers that each of us has inherited from our early ancestors? What bearing does current brain science have in informing our discussion of moral development within social groupings? Let's look.

Music moves us. Songs trigger memory centers in our brains that affect emotional experience. As I have said here, drawing from Levitin's and others' work, songs are potent stimuli for motivating us to action, from dance to hand clapping to marching and manning the barriers to protest and maybe challenging socially unjust acts. Music stirs powerful feelings of love, altruism, or outrage.

In the 1990s, Daniel Goleman—psychologist and popular journalist—wrote a very accessible and ground-breaking book titled *Emotional Intelligence*. The emotions we inherit as part of our human equipment—fear, anger, joy, surprise, love, disgust, and sadness—motivate us to act in response to the emotional experience. As he says, they prime us to act. But these emotions, located in centers deep within the brain, the amygdala (site of our emotional impulses) and hippocampus (housing our emotional memories), have to be controlled, have to be tamed in order for us to live in peaceful society with others. And the work of taming and controlling our emotions so that they don't run amok is done by centers in our forebrain, in the neocortex which allows us to reason, delay gratification, reflect and understand the feelings of others or empathize with others' plight. This executive controller of motivated action directs us to the appropriate response based on sizing up the situation as a whole.

There are two neural pathways that incoming stimuli can take in our overall assessment of what's coming at us at the moment. The first signal alerting us to danger or surprise—catching our immediate attention—enters through our sensory apparatus (for example, kinesthetic, aural, or visual), then travels via neural pathways through the thalamus to the amygdala; the second, slower signal travels from the thalamus to the neocortex, where again our frontal brain centers get to work sorting out the meaning of the stimulation.

If you think back to my experience of the recent earthquake, my ear picked up the muffled boom and my kinesthetic sense picked up the strange movement beneath me—both catching my immediate attention. The second signal reached my forebrain and after a minute or so I had sorted out the meaning of the experience (wrongly it turns out), dampening my emotional response and calming my fear.

Usually, unless some pathology prevails, the first and second signals, or more generally, the midbrain and forebrain centers, work in tandem. In order to make realistic and accurate sense of my world around me, feelings are essential. But feelings have to be tamed and controlled, or our fear, rage, sadness, etc. are not constrained and we run into great trouble living with others in community. And for all of us, life is a rather continuous battle between our impulses fueled by emotion and restraint exercised by reason and empathy.

For example, when some guy cuts me off in traffic, my immediate response is that I'd like to punch him out or at least give him "a piece of my mind." I've never done the finger thing, because that's too crude. But I do gesticulate by raising my hand up high and shaking it at the windshield, my palm facing me, as if to say "you idiot, what are you doing?" I'm sure the guy looks in his rearview mirror and feels my road rage and that is satisfying in itself. But then, my forebrain kicks in and I tell myself, "Maybe his wife's in the car about to deliver a baby," and I calm down. More likely, of course, he's just being a jerk. But now I feel calmer about the road insult anyway.

Nor can we develop much of a sense of ethical altruism without the ability to feel with, empathize with the plight of unfortunate others—or in the case of social protest to sing and act from the margin and uncover the sacred buried beneath an unjust *status quo*. Which brings me back to why

I think this discussion is relevant for our topic here. For Goleman, the opposite of empathy is indifference.

If you know the story of Lazarus and the rich man in the Bible, the sin of the rich man is that he didn't even see Lazarus who sat at this doorstep, begging for food every day. He was totally indifferent to Lazarus's desperate condition displayed right before his eyes. In Goleman's terms, there was no emotional response whatsoever informing his rational sizing up of the begging display; hence, he was completely unmotivated to have pity because the scene had no emotionally informed meaning for him. The rich man's forebrain and midbrain centers did not work in tandem in this case, and hence, he had no empathy for Lazarus's condition. Of course, if you know the story, it did not go well for the rich man in the end. But that's another issue.

I think more recent work than Goleman's (and certainly more recent than the writings of those who authored our sacred Scriptures)—work by Jonathan Haidt and his colleague, Craig Joseph—can add to our understanding of the origin of ethical, and indeed, virtuous behavior within the community setting.

In their work they distinguish between intuitions and virtues. Intuitions are the "judgments, solutions, and ideas that pop into consciousness without our being aware of the mental processes that led to them." For these scientists, these intuitions are innate and inherited from our evolutionary past. "Moral intuitions are a subclass of intuitions, in which feelings of approval or disapproval pop into awareness as we see or hear about something someone did, or as we consider choices for ourselves."[11]

In this significant line of research, these psychologists refer to the same two neural processing tracks in the brain that I referred to earlier when describing Goleman's work: social cognition operates like other cognitive processes in response to incoming stimuli. Most of our perceptive meaning-making occurs at the automatic level, that first fast track where our brain registers and makes sense out of what's out there in milliseconds. "Most social cognition occurs rapidly, automatically, and effortlessly—in a word, intuitively—as our minds appraise the people we encounter on such features as attractiveness, threat, gender, and status." The second, slower neural path from midbrain to forebrain then allows us to reason and evaluate our social decisions and review our snap judgments about others. The master control center in the neocortex helps us sort through occasional moral dilemmas when confronted with intuitive gut feelings that run counter to our moral understandings. Yet Haidt and Joseph caution:

---

11. Haidt and Joseph, "Intuitive Ethics," 56.

Research in social psychology suggests that the responses to such dilemmas mostly emerge from the intuitive system: people have quick gut feelings that come into consciousness as soon as a situation is presented to them.

... As with the visual system, we can't know how we came to see something; we can only know that we see it. If you focus on the reasons people give for their judgments, you are studying the rational tail that got wagged by the emotional dog.

They—and we—are interested in the relationship between the culturally shaped, rational tail controlling ethical reasoning, and the moral, embodied intuitions uncovered in protest songs and stories. Thus, I'm going to spend a bit of time here looking at Haidt and Joseph's work before returning more explicitly to the chapter's discussion of Boomer protest and the basic social questions addressed in the 60s scene.

Based on earlier studies, Haidt and Joseph assume at least four hard-wired, evolutionary-based moral intuitions: Suffering, Hierarchy, Reciprocity, and Purity. Displayed in a table in their 2004 article, they show the original, evolutionary-based "triggers" that elicited the development of these four intuitions; contemporary triggers that call forth these hard-wired moral responses; the typical emotions associated with these moral impulses; and the culturally learned virtues or virtuous behaviors expressed in response to such emotional reactions.

As an example, they show the following. Suffering originally evolved in response to our ancestors seeing vulnerability and suffering in their offspring (i.e., the development of this moral sense had survival value for our species). Examples of contemporary triggers to this intuitive, hard-wired moral response are photos of baby seals being clubbed to death or pictures of malnourished and starving children in Bangladesh. A typical emotional response to such suffering is compassion, and the relevant virtue is charitable giving, joining the Peace Corps, or working in a soup kitchen.

Haidt and Joseph follow the same line of reasoning for each of the other moral intuitions. The moral sense of hierarchy evolved in our ancestors confronting physical size, domination, and protection; modern triggers of our intuitive sense of hierarchy include responses to "bosses" and to God; emotional resentment or awe follows, calling forth the virtue of obedience and loyalty. Similarly for reciprocity, the intuition became hardwired in our brains as a function of group cooperation and food sharing; current triggers include marital fidelity or vending machines that work or not; emotional responses include guilt or gratitude, and the culturally shaped virtue associated with this moral intuition is fairness and trustworthiness. Finally, our sense of moral purity originally arose in response to tribal members displaying parasites or disease, or the sight of animal waste products that could contaminate; modern triggers include taboo subjects such as incest or cannibalism. A typical emotional response to impurity is disgust; and the associated, culturally learned virtue is cleanliness or chastity.

Interestingly, these moral intuitions that we have inherited from our earliest ancestors, and that come unconsciously bidden when triggered by events, both major and minor, can also be elicited by what these researchers refer to as "third party" displays. That is, our moral outrage or compassion, our anger or our disgust can also be aroused in response to novels and memoirs, to films, to song lyrics. We are moved by the stories told that trigger our deep-seated intuitions about a moral universe. Clearly this line of research is consistent with Partridge's vision of protest songs uncovering (at their best) sacred universals beneath the assumed everydayness of sometimes unjust social arrangement.

Developmentally, the virtue that becomes embedded in one's character is shaped primarily by culturally given models found in childhood stories, novels, films, worship practices, parental displays, and biographies of virtuous lives. Relevant to this, Haidt and Joseph describe what they refer to as the "warping" or distortion of a universal moral intuition by cultural forces. Children can be taught to be cruel bullies or racists. Do you remember the Broadway hit and later film, *South Pacific* and the song, "You Have to Be Carefully Taught?" The point being that we are not born hating skin color different from our own; you have to be taught the targets of your hatred, the Other to be feared.

When President Obama was running first time for the White House, the fellow who cuts my hair mentioned that one of his other clients made the remark about Obama, "Can you imagine them sleeping on the White House sheets?"—said with a sneer. You have to be carefully taught. True, there is an evolutionary base to fear of the Other—the one not of our tribe, a potential enemy, one who may take our food or our mate. But the target, the trigger of that hard-wired disposition is shaped by cultural prejudice. It can also be deflected away from any difference marked by skin color by careful parental modeling of "color blindness." But you do have to be carefully taught.

In fact, let me end my discussion of Haidt and Joseph's work for now with this strong observation they make about the learning of virtue.

> One of the crucial tenets of virtue theory is that the virtues are acquired inductively, that is, through the acquisition, mostly in childhood but also throughout the life course, of many examples of a virtue in practice. Often these examples come from

the child's everyday experience of construing, responding, and getting feedback, but they also come from the stories that permeate the culture. Each of these examples contains information about a number of aspects of the situation, including the protagonists' motivations, the protagonists' state of being (suffering, disabled, hostile, rich, etc.), the categorization of the situation, and the evaluation of the outcome offered by more experienced others.[12]

Our emotional brain is what scientists refer to as an "open-loop system." A closed-loop system, like our circulatory system, is self-regulating if working properly. Andrew Root, in a piece written for *The Christian Century* in 2013, points out that our emotional system, centered in the midbrain, but with extensive neural connections widely dispersed throughout the higher cortical regions, depends in part at least on external, social sources to manage itself. "We rely on connections with other people for our own emotional stability."[13] Mirror neurons, allowing us to experience what we observe others experiencing, and more generally our emotional intelligence— allowing us to grasp and "read" other minds as we develop from the crib into old age—close the distance across the "social synapse."[14]

As Haidt and Joseph observe, "the mind like the brain itself, is a network that gets tuned up gradually by experience."[15] Again reflecting back on the 60s and the heady protests of that period, with the social unrest and the emotional highs generated by our songs of love, justice, and freedom, we bonded across that social synapse into a self-righteous force. The songs that knit us together were, as Levitin puts it, "knowledge songs," arising from our moral, intuitive depths. We did sense a sacred reality beneath the assumed civil arrangements that were impure in our eyes. Songs like "If I Had a Hammer," ringing out freedom . . . and "We Shall Overcome" and "Which Side Are You on, Boy?" emerged out of a visceral, moral intuition that reflected some universal truth, "encoding important life lessons in an artistic form that is ideally adapted to the structure and function of the human brain . . . . [Such] music connects us to something larger than our own existence, to other people, or to God."[16]

Speaking of God, let me raise here the question of God's role in all of this. Recalling my earlier discussion of where I am—at the theological

---

12. Ibid., 62.
13. Root, "Wired Together," 33.
14. Ibid., 34.
15. Haidt and Joseph, "Intuitive Ethics," 62.
16. Levitin, *The World in Six Songs*, 186; 243.

level—my own theology is informed by the concept of theistic evolution. God created the world *de novo* "in the beginning," and made use of evolution and the unfolding of creation from its inception to this day.

But here's a question: does God tell stories? If you grew up in one of the monotheistic traditions—Christian, Judaism, or Islam—you were likely taught that God created the world and all things in it. So God is creative. You may also have been taught that the Holy Scriptures are the story of God's dealing with God's creatures over time. But in asking whether God is still actively telling stories, whether we are part of God's ongoing narrative as God creates it over time, I think this casts the creative question in a new light.

I'm going to return to this question of God's ongoing storytelling, "imaginative" vision for all creation, including human history and where you and I might fit into God's story, in a later chapter. But just as we can consider human beings from multiple levels—socially, behaviorally, psychologically, and neurally—we might consider here in our discussion of neuroscience and brain function, God's activity at the level of synapse. My suggestion is that God as Creator is still actively, dynamically engaged with all creation, and at the level of our human brains, could perhaps also be considered as "God of the synapse." Let me explain.

In his *Synaptic Self: How Our Brains Become Who We Are*, Joseph Le Doux, a well-known neuroscientist, argues primarily from a reductionistic vantage. The self is nothing but . . . nothing but a well-integrated brain (if we're developmentally lucky), comprised of "plastic" or malleable neural pathways connecting brain centers at multiple levels of integration. The building blocks of such plasticity or molding potential are the synapses between neurons, bathed in chemical neurotransmitters such as dopamine and norepinephrine—released by incoming sensory input, exerting an inhibitory or excitatory role in cell firings. As many have noted, cells that fire together, wire together. Thus, sensory, emotional, and motor experiences become encoded in midbrain memory centers. Such experience-based learning can shape our brain synapses (inhibiting or fostering cell firing) and hence our perceptual awareness and self-consciousness over time.

Each of us is unique because we are not only born with different genetic material inherited from both parents; but each of us also has different experiences that help mold our brains as we move through life. At the very end of his book, Le Doux observes that "the self is synaptic [and this] can be a curse—it doesn't take much to break it apart. But it is also a blessing, as there are always new connections waiting to be made. You are your synapses. They are who you are."[17]

Sounds pretty reductionistic to me. I don't see much room for God there. But I don't want to be unfair to Le Doux. He does seem to leave the door open for mystery. Early in the book, he has this to say:

> As we begin to understand ourselves in synaptic terms, we don't have to sacrifice other ways of understanding existence. The idea that the self is created and maintained by arrangements of synaptic connections, in other words, doesn't diminish who we are. It instead provides a simple and plausible explanation for how the enormously complex psycho-spiritual-socio-cultural package of protoplasm we call our self is possible.[18]

In chapter 1 of this book, I echoed what many other scientists have asserted: that ultimately science can never reduce our sense of self, our subjective sense of actor in our world, to the level of our brains. "No map of matter (synaptic or otherwise) will ever explain the immateriality of our consciousness.... Like a work of art, we exceed our materials."[19] In the last analysis, the purposeful self, engaged with its world of meaning, is a mystery that we try to understand at multiple levels.

In terms of theistic evolution, the final and transcendent Mystery is God. John de Gruchy, South African philosopher and theologian, says "this mystery to which we bear testimony is not within the domain of scientific exploration, nor is it to be discovered in the gaps of human knowledge, or reduced to a controllable formula; it is the core of reality, the ultimate Mystery we name God.... We do not discover or unpack this mystery; it discloses itself in ways that take us by surprise, changing lives, restoring dignity and transforming the world."[20]

What I am suggesting here is that God engages humankind at multiple levels—from the synapse to the final story we write of our lives—perhaps even as part of God's larger, ongoing narrative. At base, our moral intuition, our virtues that develop and are shaped through our practices, may very well be God's mysterious call, God's action in our lives—drawing us on toward God's Mystery and purpose.

---

17. Le Doux, *Synaptic Self*, 324.
18. Ibid., 12.
19. Lehrer, *Proust was a Neuroscientist*, x.
20. de Gruchy, "Convocation Address," para. 9.

****

Well, we've come a long way from McCarthy at Fenway to God of the synapse. But I think it all fits together here. The music that bound us affected our emotional centers, perhaps uncovering the Sacred, or in Haidt's terms, stimulating our evolutionary-based, moral intuitions about justice. It also motivated us to act and so we marched and otherwise protested. We shaped our story and our brains were sculpted in the process. And at the center of it all from cell to culture—then and now—is Mystery.

Let's turn now and meet a middle-aged Boomer who I believe exemplifies the best we had to offer on the social scene of the '60s and '70s. Just as we met Paul in chapter 2, I want to introduce you now to Beth in this next interlude.

Interlude I: Meet Beth[21]

Beth grew up in a midwestern university town—a popular girl with friends and an outgoing openness to life. After graduating from high school, she attended a private, midwestern college, and while there, "discovered"—or finally confirmed—that she was a lesbian. She wrote her family, and—unlike many who "came out" in those days (and since)—Beth was supported and embraced by her parents and siblings.

Beth dropped out of college at some point, and moved to Indianapolis, where she initially organized kitchen workers at a midwestern university nearby. She became a serious labor organizer, acting as chief negotiator for the university service and maintenance workers, dealing with fair wage and benefits issues with the university administration. At some point, Beth was hired by the American Federation of Federal, State, and Municipal Employees union (AFFSME) and for some time was their only full-time paid staff member in the area where she worked. She continued with AFFSME until she uncovered some corruption among the union leaders, threatened to expose the corruption, and became a target of harassment from the union hierarchy herself.

Somewhat disillusioned, Beth quit the union job and began to search for some other outlet for her labor organizing efforts. At the time her dad (himself a professor) urged her to think about finishing undergraduate

---

21. Because of the sensitive nature of "Beth's" current position, I have taken the liberty of changing her and her partner's identity and some of the particulars of her story in order to protect her identity. But the contours of her life are true despite intended anonymity. In this section and in the next, she is an excellent example of a life lived in pursuit of moral integrity.

classes and applying for law school. After all, if she really wanted to change labor conditions and work for justice at an effective level, it would be far better to function from a credentialed base than as freelancer with little power or leverage.

And that is just what Beth did. She finished her undergraduate education and then applied to a midwestern university's law school—one of the best in the country—all the while being quite open about her personal life and, by that time, her living with a committed partner in a stable relationship. And she was also quite open about her labor values and her history of organizing university employees for better wages and benefits. She was accepted into law school there, and turned out to be an exceptional, talented law student.

Beth also had a family by then. Her long-term partner, Mary (who holds a master's in education) is African American, and they decided early on that they wanted biracial children. Because Mary had been treated for breast cancer, she was advised not to try to become pregnant. So in the middle of law school Beth decided to conceive a child by artificial insemination—to her father's consternation, since he feared this would jeopardize her progress in law school.

To make a long story short, not only did Beth give birth to a little girl (who is now a talented student at Yale University), but shortly after that (having just completed law school) she also gave birth to twin girls—from the same donor so that the three children would be biological siblings. The twins are now college age, and have both been accepted into first-rate schools. The amazing point I want to make here is that Beth did it all. She succeeded in creating a family with her partner and she succeeded brilliantly in one of the toughest law schools in the country.

As a mark of her success, when she graduated from law school, Beth applied to clerk for a federal judge in the area. She was one of maybe 200 or so applicants, and she was the one he selected. During the years Beth clerked for that judge, they became good friends, and in fact, he became like a grandfather to her and Mary's three children. We'll revisit Beth in the next section as we look at her life as a middle-aged Boomer.

I think Beth's story is remarkable. She fought the good fight—true to her own sense of personal integrity—faced down corruption when she saw it, fighting for workers' rights and enduring some personal peril in the process—staying the righteous course as she saw it, from college dropout to a talented law career dedicated to making a difference in civil rights for minorities often caught in an unfair system.

Beth has been driven her whole life to represent and fight for those on the fringe of society—herself having experienced prejudice as a lesbian woman who faced closed doors and at times lost opportunities simply because of who she was. She has marched to her own drum and spectacularly won the war she began nearly forty years ago. Beth is a prime example of all we have discussed so far in this chapter. Her moral intuition regarding universal justice for all has been expressed in virtuous practice as she has built a life for herself and for her family. Again, we'll return to her current, meteoric story in the pages ahead.

THE SCENE NOW: POLITICS AND PURPOSE OR "WE SHALL [STILL] OVERCOME"

> The green van speeded down the dirt road toward us. It looked a little like an ice cream truck such as you might see in your neighborhood. There were about sixty of us in the adjacent field, and we crowded up against the fence that kept us from the roadway. As the "ice cream" truck advanced, I saw that it was trailed by two police cruisers, racing along as escort sentries.
>
> We watched them pass us, the silent ones among us holding candles and standing vigil by the fence. We watched their tail lights disappear into the blackness of the rural night. Another green "ice cream" truck, carrying the body of a man killed only moments before by the state of Virginia in my name.[22]

In an earlier chapter, I mentioned that I had never really been much of an activist in my Boomer youth. Having dropped out of college and married early, I was much taken up with caring for two infant sons. After I did go back to undergraduate and then graduate school, I had to balance family life with studies, with not a lot of time left over for protest marches and such. And besides, I had been raised in a socially conservative home, and was still developing into my own person as an adult. Certainly, the times shaped me and my ideas swung leftward—to my family's dismay. But still, other than my memory of the student lock-out at Indiana University and my liberal-tainted arguments with my parents, I never had been inclined to take to the streets over social causes.

That is, until sometime shortly before I wrote about the state-sponsored execution described in the above quote. I became radicalized over the death penalty issue after reading Sister Helen Prejean's *Dead Man Walking*—a powerful narrative of murder by both the defendant and the

---

22. Levy, "Primitive Symbolic Consciousness and the Death Penalty in American Culture," 717.

state that ended his life. There are those who claim that reading stories—both fictional and biographical—can affect our emotional state but rarely motivate our actions. But my reading of Prejean's book and the aftermath prove a strong counter example to that argument. I was emotionally moved by reading Prejean's words against state-supported killing. She wrote: "An execution is ugly because the premeditated killing of a human being is ugly. Torture is ugly—gassing, hanging, shooting, electrocuting, or lethally injecting a person whose hands and feet are tied is ugly. And hiding the ugliness from view and rationalizing it numbs our minds to the horror of what we are doing. This is what truly 'coarsens' us."[23]

Not only was I moved by those words, but I also acted on that experience by contacting an anti-death penalty group in Richmond and became an active member of that committee. I began to take to the streets and march, carrying anti-death penalty signs, standing vigil when the state executed another death row inmate, and preaching against the death penalty from the pulpit. (The only time I had a parishioner walk out on a sermon I was in the middle of giving was in response to one of those messages.) I even have a photo of me in clergy collar standing on top of a soap box—literally—with a megaphone held to my lips while I led the group of protesters, gathered before the state house, in prayer.

I go into this for two reasons. First, as I said above, I am a living example of someone radicalized by what I read to become actively engaged in a social cause rooted in what I believed it meant to be human in the deepest moral sense of that word—holding all life as sacred. In living out that cause in what I believed as righteous action, I was also reflecting a key characteristic of my Boomer generation in middle age and beyond.

But second, in thinking about what shaped our social consciousness in our youth and what shapes that consciousness now, I was struck by the fact that music played such a major role as we grew up and achieved adulthood in the '60s and '70s, but in our middle age and later years, it is not the music that shapes our ideology as much as it is the books we read—as Oscar Wilde said—when we don't have to. Not that books played no role in our youthful shaping. Of course they did, from childhood on. As an example in my life, the writings of Thomas Merton had an enormous influence on my world view as it took shape through my twenties and beyond.

However the music of the '60s and '70s—the songs of Seeger, Baez, Carole King, Don McLean, and others—burrowed deeply into our emotional brain memory centers . . . and remains there to this day. I think there are no more songs that affect us so deeply in our middle years. As we discussed

---

23. Prejean, *Dead Man Walking*, 216.

earlier, in adolescence and early adulthood, our brain is particularly malleable. Emotionally laden memories become fixed in the memory centers of our midbrains. While other music of course moves us as we age, it is the music of our youth that remains ours—reawakening our past and affecting us still.

No, now more likely it's the books—as well as stories in whatever electronic form in our Internet age—that shape "the way we perceive and interpret reality, determining what we hope for and hold dear—making us ... who we are,"[24] as Oscar Wilde observed.

The Source of the Scene Now

In their book, *Generations*, Howe and Strauss characterize Boomers—both early and late ones—as primarily "Idealists," still self-absorbed in middle age and beyond, smugly arrogant, embracing what they refer to as "neo-puritanism." "From Jonathan Schell to Jeremy Rifkin . . . Boomers are still doing what they have done for decades: giving America its leading visionaries and 'wise men'—or just its preachy didactics— . . . boomers today stand midgame in a many-pronged reworking of American society. The righteous fires of People's Park are still smoldering."[25]

In a chapter titled "Having a Purpose," Smith and Clurman see Boomers now as still embracing their generational focus on the self—myself as independent, myself as expressive, myself striving for meaning even if that requires going up against the system I view as corrupt. Determined to matter, even as we slip toward elderly status, work and politics remain foci of committed concern for many of us.

When I decided to leave full-time ministry in order to assume the life of a writer, I completely rejected the word "retired" as applied to me. In fact, when the diocesan newspaper listed clergy who had recently retired from their parishes and I found my name on the list, I requested a written retraction in the next edition. The idea that I would "retire" was abhorrent to me. I intended to matter, to be productive, to contribute to society as a writer and scholar, until I dropped in my tracks. The lesson I learned when I was young became glaringly obvious in my life: "Pursue your life's passion through your work and make no compromises in following your own path."[26]

Of course we Boomers are passionate about many things beyond our work lives. We are also passionate—and in many cases, stridently so—in

24. Douglas, "Saved by Fiction," 27.
25. Howe and Strauss, *Generations*, 316.
26. Smith and Clurman, *Generation Ageless*, 59.

our political beliefs. In viewing the political landscape of today, Smith and Clurman do note our highly polarized terrain. Although our country was founded on political strife and political ideologies have always generated civil turmoil and upheavals across human history, the authors see that today's "uncompromising political style" has emerged with the rise of Boomers on the political scene. All we have to do is look at the dysfunction of today's Congress and the demonizing by both the left-leaning Democrats and the Tea Party conservatives to witness the breakdown of the governing machinery of state.

Even the neighborhoods we live in comprise what the authors refer to as *de facto* segregation by politics and ideology. As a local example, most of my suburban neighbors are conservative if I can judge by the get-out-the-vote signs planted on lawns during election times. In contrast, there is a neighborhood in the city called the Fan or the Museum District (where St. Mark's is located, by the way) that is and has been for many years openly liberal and inclusive of alternative lifestyles.

Dan McAdams and his colleagues have done some very interesting research into the psychological roots of political ideology. In interviews with political conservatives and liberals, these researchers found that conservatives emphasized moral intuitions regarding respect for social hierarchy, allegiance to one's in-group, and purity or sanctity of the self; liberals tended to emphasize moral intuitions regarding reciprocity/fairness and human suffering/harm issues.

Recalling our earlier discussion of Jonathan Haidt's research on evolutionary, universal moral intuitions that generate gut feelings of right or wrong, good or bad, and the cultural shaping of virtuous behavior based on such intuitions, this work of McAdams and colleagues builds on that earlier work. But further, it also helps explain the polarized political convictions that are tearing at our nation's fabric.

Importantly, these investigators also suggest a way to approach those who disagree with us by understanding that they are not just being intransigent, but are drawing on deeply embedded moral intuitions which inform their own political stance. "Social scientists have long suspected that political beliefs and behaviors are less a function of rational calculation and more a matter of deep personal significance."[27]

In short, conservatives and liberals are emphasizing different moral intuitions based on harm, fairness, loyalty, authority, or purity. Increased understanding and good will might follow from seeing our opponents' political stance as based on deeply held moral beliefs—opening up a space for

---

27. McAdams et al., "Family Metaphors and Moral Intuitions," 988.

a different level of conversation, as well as affording the possibility for joint action when moral values overlap.

Let me circle back now and consider—in the light of this discussion of moral intuitions— some of the reading that shaped me in this Now of my life. I described the profound impact that *Dead Man Walking* had in galvanizing my anti-death penalty action as both a private citizen and as leader of a church community. But there were other books that played a shaping role. A prime examples is Kent Haruf's *Plainsong*—the beautiful story of what it means to be family in the most unconventional sense.

In Howard Mosher's endorsement of *Plainsong*, he says that it's the "marvelous story of how seven extraordinary members of a tiny prairie community—two dedicated teachers, two young boys wise beyond their years, a pair of wonderfully idiosyncratic rancher brothers and a pregnant high school girl—come together, in the face of great difficulties, to form the most appealing extended family in contemporary fiction." At the time I read *Plainsong*, I was rector of St. Mark's, that inclusive community of urban believers of all stripes and lifestyles—"inclusive" was the code word for welcoming gays and lesbians before it had become less of an issue, as in today's culture. The book spoke to me in a deeply moving way, as I was growing into a broader and deeper understanding of family in my church and in my own family.

In the light of Haidt and colleagues', as well as McAdams and co-investigators' moral intuition research, my response to both of these books and likely others I could name was rooted in my intuitions regarding fairness/justice and personal harm/vulnerability. The books' themes were consistent with those prominent intuitions deeply embedded within me and expressed in "virtuous" behavior shaped by my liberal cultural context—including the Episcopal Church and my friendships then and now.

Stories that engage us—fiction and nonfiction alike—can affect us deeply, as research on the effects of reading has repeatedly shown. Fiction and nonfiction that pull us into the reading—where the reader's mind meets the mind of the author in the co-creation of meaning—"helps us pattern in newly nuanced ways our emotions and perceptions; it bestows new knowledge or increased understanding; and gives the chance for a sharpened ethical sense, and it creates new forms of meaning for our everyday existence."[28] At least part of the reason for this cognitive/emotional impact is that good stories that engage us also touch us at the level of our evolved, inherited

---

28. Zunshine, *Why We Read Fiction*, 164.

moral intuitions—motivating at times our ethical or culturally learned "virtuous" behavior.[29]

Well, as Jonathan Gottschall puts it, "if you want a message to burrow into a human mind, work it into a story."[30] Every good preacher knows this, and I think we have our own experience as well as abundant research evidence to suggest this is true. And now we have some sense, I think, of one reason why this is so. Because a good story touches our deepest moral intuitions about what is good and what is bad; what disgusts us and what delights us and fills us with hope. Circling back to the overall theme of this book: Our brains are wired for story. From early adolescence to the end of our lives, we tell and retell our story as author of our own lives.

In his 2013 review article describing his narrative psychology research, Dan McAdams describes what he refers to as "redemptive life stories" typically told by "highly generative" or high-functioning, productive Americans—deeply characteristic of the Boomer generation, but extending beyond and across generations representing an American, culturally shaped prototype.

> The story-teller or author of his or her own life typically (a) enjoys a special advantage or blessing early in life, (b) expresses sensitivity to the suffering of others or societal injustice as a child, (c) establishes a clear and strong value system in adolescence that remains a source of unwavering conviction through the adult years, (d) repeatedly overcomes adversity, (e) tries to integrate experiences of power and love, and (f) looks to achieve goals to benefit society in the future.
> . . . [He or she is] a gifted hero who, equipped with clear moral values, journeys forth into a dangerous world, confronts and experiences suffering of various kinds (e.g., loss, failure, pain), and eventually gives back to society, while emerging better or wiser for the pain and suffering endured.[31]

McAdams goes on to note that this American prototype, built on inherited moral intuitions but shaped by our culture—evolving from the Puritans to Oprah—has "morphed into many storied forms . . . as Americans have

---

29. See also Gerrig, *Experiencing Narrative Worlds*, for his discussion of "participatory responses" on the part of the reader or viewer to not only fiction and nonfiction, but in response to TV, newspaper articles, and movies, where we actively supplement the "text" with our own creative work. Also see Mar et al., "Exploring the Link between Reading Fiction and Empathy," and Kidd and Castano, "Reading Literary Fiction Improves Theory of Mind."

30. Gottschall, *The Storytelling Animal*, 118.

31. McAdams, "The Psychological Self as Actor, Agent, and Author," 288.

sought to narrate their own lives as tales of atonement, emancipation, recovery, self-fulfillment, and upward social mobility."

McAdams and his colleagues have always distinguished between good stories and not so good stories. The good or redemptive life story as described above is told in one form or another by adolescents and adults who are able to pull together their past, emotionally laden, episodic memories, linked with future hopes, all integrated into a cohesive life story filled with forgiveness, hope, and positive meaning. As we have seen, such redemptive stories following life's losses can be contrasted with some self stories that remain rigid, closed, and filled with cynicism and regret. Not all Boomers are idealistic and righteously purposive into middle and older age. But all do have the potential to tell a good story in the end.

One middle-aged Boomer who fulfills that American prototype is Beth—now a highly placed federal government official—to whose biographical sketch we return to now as we round out this chapter concerned with story and ethical action in our lives, both then and now.

Interlude II: Beth Again

In the fall of 2013, Beth was nominated to become a high-ranking federal government official. This past March she was sworn into that office. As she appeared with other federal nominees before a congressional subcommittee, her partner Mary and two of their children stood behind her as she was welcomed by the committee before the hearing began. Not an eye batted as she introduced her partner to the gathering. After more than an hour of questioning, her nomination was unanimously approved; when it finally went forward to the whole Senate, her nomination was also strongly supported.

In the years that stretched between law school and clerking for that federal judge and her ascendance to high federal office, Beth spent her entire working life fighting for the rights of minorities, true to the moral intuitions that have motivated her entire life work. On a personal note, Beth and her long-time partner Mary were legally wed in Washington, DC in 2013. At a small gathering of friends and colleagues after an informal ceremony welcoming her to her new position, Beth said "I came out as a lesbian in 1977—before some of you were born—and when I opened that closet door, other doors closed. But our country is changing, and the fact that this door has opened for me means that it is open for many others."

A remarkable story of a remarkable Boomer at mid-life. Moving from the fringe of society to the center of civil power, she has fought the good fight fought by others before her. Beth is a person of integrity, true to her gut sense of right and wrong, shaped by moral intuition regarding justice and fairness. She will make a very fine government official, indeed.

CONCLUDING THOUGHTS

In 1994, Pete Seeger said "the key to the future of the world is finding the optimistic stories and letting them be known." And in 2009, he also said that "his task was 'to show folks there's a lot of good music in this world, and if used right it may help to save the planet.'"[32] He apparently disliked loud rock music, because the beat of the noise would drown out the lyrics that would teach valuable life lessons.

Seeger embraced the notion that one has to be carefully taught those life lessons—starting in childhood. Thus, he recorded these lessons for children to sing along with him, singing songs of justice and freedom, shaping the stories in their heads, creating and strengthening emotional meaning and motivation centers in their brains in the process.

We are peoples of story—from beginning to end. Our identities, yours and mine, Beth's sense of who she is from where she has come from, Paul's lifelong work for justice as a public defender—all these unique identities are constructed and reconstructed from remembering our past, anticipating our future (including imagining its setting, its scenes we carry in our head, its likely plots, its major life themes), all tied together by our evolving life stories.

One of my favorite writers, Thomas Lynch, makes the following observation:

> How we come to be the ones we are seems a useful study and lifelong query. Knowing how we got to where we are provides some clues to the perpetual wonder over what it is we are doing here—a question that comes to most of us on a regular basis. Indeed, a curiosity about one's place and purpose keeps one, speaking now from my own experience, from going too far astray.[33]

Our understanding of what it is that we are doing here is a function of the stories we tell ourselves, the stories we make of our lives. As McAdams and

---

32. Quoted in Nader, "Pete Seeger-Character, Personality, Intuition and Focus," para 12.

33. Lynch, "How We Come to Be the Ones We Are," 8.

others have shown, our very identity is a life story that is always evolving.[34] And the theme of this chapter is that songs and stories that convey important life lessons, resonating with our best moral intuitions, are cultural forms ideally suited to the structure and function of our human brains. If we learn the positive lessons well, they will keep us from going too far astray. We author our stories and they create us in turn, as Mystery hovers in the synapses within and between us.

"We need to know. And we need to sing about it."[35]

---

34. McAdams, *The Redemptive Self*; McAdams, Josselson, and Lieblich, eds., *Identity and Story*.

35. Levitin, *The World in Six Songs*, 186.

4

"I'm on Fire"
The Celebration of Life

The envelope had a return address of the journal—*The International Journal of Aging and Human Development*. I had submitted a research manuscript to them a couple of months before, and my hands now held my future—or at least the likelihood of whether I would someday get tenure at Indiana State University . . . or not. I tore the envelope open and there my future read: "We are pleased to inform you that your manuscript . . . has been accepted for publication, subject to a few minor revisions which we have indicated in the enclosed comments by one of the reviewers." I didn't read much further than that when I literally—not figuratively, but literally—leaped for joy in my living room that day. I must have also whooped it up, pumping my fist in the air, high-fiving myself along with the jump off the ground and a quick dance around my living room as I absorbed the news that I believed the letter held about my whole future as a research psychologist.

Now I go into all this because, first off, you may have guessed by now that I am not a very demonstrative person. No, actually I'm a rather restrained and, as I have already said, introverted self who is much more comfortable alone with my thoughts or with a close friend or two than with a crowd of others. And I do not normally jump for joy or otherwise behave in an unseemly fashion in either public or private. So at about age twenty-nine or so, I surprised myself that morning in my living room. Somewhere in me arose a motor response motivated by absolute elation at that turn of events. Obviously all these years later, the memory of that leap remains marked as an episode of some significance in my developing life story. I can still see where I stood, the dining room table in front of me in our L-shaped room, the glass doors to our patio just beyond the dining area.

Yes, I am normally restrained in my motor movements, my emotional displays . . . unless I'm dancing to music with a beat—as I recalled in that Fort Myers swimming pool incident a few years back. True then, true now. In fact, as far back as I can remember—through high school and before—at the end of the day, I turned on the records and danced, mesmerized by the music and its beat—whether Porgy and Bess's goin' to the picnic scene . . . Carmen's wild dance by the fire in that mountain camp scene, to the '60s "Here Comes The Sun," . . . or "Ain't No Mountain High Enough" . . . Sonny and Cher's "And The Beat Goes On" . . . and the song "Happy Together"—up to last night—but more about our present lives in the pages ahead.

Of course there's nothing unique about my generation's response to music that moves us, triggering feel-good chemical hormones in our brains and provoking rhythmic motor responses in sync with the beat we hear. My mom could dance a mean Charleston step in her day. As you should anticipate by now, this is all part of our evolutionary, biological givens that we are born with, each of us to some extent or another. But in our slice of history, "our" music carried with it culturally derived meaning that became wired together deep within our Boomer midbrains and continues to play an important role in our daily lives as we age.

On a blog titled "Baby Boomer Bliss," Julie Georges writes:

> From infancy, we are fascinated by the rhythms and melodies we hear and feel, in our older years, we are instantly transported to youth and vitality just by hearing an old tune. With music, we can connect with others, even someone we've just met, even if they speak another language. When I listen to music, I can go from tired to energized, from a feeling of sadness to one of absolute joy. When I play music, I can truly express myself at those times when mere words would not suffice. When I play music with other musicians who share that same joy, I feel a wonderful connection that could not be achieved in any other way. Music can transport any one from a state of mediocrity to state of bliss.[1]

Reflecting back to the beginning of these pages, Daniel Levitin lists six universal categories of existential concerns, categories that we humans take up in our stories and in our songs. As we shall see below, songs and stories reflecting human exuberance beyond mere endurance are our heritage, giving

---

1. Georges, "Music and Happiness," para. 8.

as well as reflecting zest for life—celebrating the lives we have been given and carrying us through even the darkest of times. Let's spend a bit of time examining the root sources of joy as part of our human condition.

SOURCES OF THE SCENE BACK THEN: "AIN'T NO MOUNTAIN HIGH ENOUGH"

Maybe we've already said enough about my generation's growing up on rock 'n' roll, the swelling tide of media that dominated our days—from AM rock stations to the rise of FM music from the margin to the center of our waking lives. Enough said about rolling in the mud of Woodstock and bringing in a new day with the drop-out revolution of the drugged '60s. Many of the lyrics of our music were dark and rebellious, but there was a craving for group support in facing our brave, new world order. And what could cement that social connection more completely than the music that bonded us together. Landon Jones traces the roots of this group craving to what he refers to as our "prolonged adolescence." He says 'the music at the concerts was no more important than the ritual; the cheering and waving of lighted matches had all the emotional richness of a religious revival.'"[2]

As we've already seen in earlier chapters, these classic works analyzing the Boomer phenomenon then and now—Jones's writing, but also others such as Neil Howe and William Strauss's *Generations*—insist that the times that shaped our generation made an indelible print on our character. Our idealism, individualism, and yet our craving for community and tribal bonding have held over the decades. Jones puts it this way: "The twinkle-toed, bell-bottomed look is gone, but many of the attitudes nurtured at Woodstock lasted through the seventies and are part of the baby boom today."[3] Our music may have shifted from the "light rock" of the '60s through the rebellious "hard rock" of the '80s, but the underlying message is the same: Our mission is one of sanctification—of society and of our spiritual selves in the process. "Boomers flocked from drugs to religion, to 'Jesus' movements, to evangelicalism, New Age utopianism, and millennialist visions of all sorts."[4]

And at the heart of our social lives was our music that we created and which shaped us in turn. As I and many others have argued, universally there is such a thing as human nature. Our genetic givenness has richly endowed us with the capacity to create art in all its forms and in the process, to sculpt and shape our brains individually, as well as to develop our emotional

2. Jones, *Great Expectations*, 133.
3. Ibid., 135.
4. Howe and Strauss, *Generations*, 303.

intelligence—the existential meaning of our collective cohort to this day. In fact, each generation is marked as a kind in a particular way. That is, there is something unique—a stamp if you will, a signature marker for each generation as it comes along. And we do have ours.

In the pages ahead we will explore the evolutionary base of joyful exuberance. But to anticipate, a few years back Barbara Ehrenreich wrote a delightful book titled *Dancing in the Streets: A History of Collective Joy*. In that work, tracing the history of joy-filled, participatory gatherings such as festivals and carnivals, Ehrenreich's main thesis is that humans have an inherent need to express freedom of movement in the form of parades, ritual processions, maypole circling, even frenzied rhythmic group dancing—all provide outlets for our excess energy and need for release in bodily movement. She traces such embodied expression from its preliterate evolutionary roots through biblical descriptions of songs and festivals (including King David dancing naked and ecstatic before God's tabernacle and disgusting his wife, Michal), and early Christian ecstatic strands of enthusiasm marked by such practices as Spirit-filled speaking in tongues or glossolalia.

As the church became more hierarchically controlled and organizationally protective, such free expression of spirit-filled freedom of movement became threatening and such things as dancing in the churches became frowned upon by church leaders—which only drove festivities into the streets, providing an outlet for the people's energy and also providing a certain leveling across classes as many were drawn into the swirling gatherings. These festivities also often gave vent to mockery of those attempting to control them.

The church tried to harness the people's excess energies by declaring Saints' days and holding processions to satisfy the masses' need for pageantry. Still, dance manias would occasionally break out, infecting whole towns with frenzied excess. As Ehrenreich notes, by the thirteenth and fourteenth centuries the frequency of festivals—both church sponsored and not—made for "one long outdoor party."[5] Finally, the Reformation and the rise of the Protestant work ethic, along with the requirements of mass discipline in order to shoot well and wage war, brought a slow end to public expression of such joy-filled, exuberant spirit. Ehrenreich includes a succinct quote from Peter Stallybrass and Allon White's analysis of what they refer to as transgressive movements in history:

> In the long-term history from the 17th to the 20th century . . . there were literally thousands of acts of legislation introduced which attempted to eliminate carnival and popular festivity

5. Ehrenreich, *Dancing in the Streets*, 92.

from European life.... Everywhere, against the periodic revival of local festivity and occasional reversals, a fundamental ritual order to western culture came under attack—its feasting, violence, processions, fairs, wakes, rowdy spectacle and outrageous clamour were subject to surveillance and repressive control.[6]

Ehrenreich concludes both early in her book, and again at the end of her analysis, that this "loss, to ordinary people, of so many recreations and festivities is incalculable; and we, who live in a culture almost devoid of opportunities either to 'lose ourselves' in communal festivities or to distinguish ourselves in any arena outside of work"[7] are the losers in this dearth of joy-filled expression.

But then there was the "rock rebellion" of living memory for those of us who lived through it, and the potential—as we shall see—for ecstatic joy is still embedded deep within us. As Ehrenreich notes, we rebelled against being spectators only, and not as players muscularly moving within the rock scene. As the author points out, rock had its origins in an African-rooted musical tradition with its intimate ties to dance movement. She says "rock and roll is part of a family of music that it is almost impossible not to respond to with dance or some other form of rhythmic involvement."[8] Jerry Lee Lewis ("Goodness, Gracious, Great Balls of Fire!"), Elvis ("Jailhouse Rock"), and later, Jim Morrison and the Doors ("Light My Fire"), along with Jefferson Airplane and the Rolling Stones—all are heirs to ecstatic religious music sources, whether acknowledged or not. Ehrehreich concludes her discussion of those early Boomer years by admitting that "*something* happened in the rock rebellion, traces of which persist not only in today's club scene but in the most banal settings for rock ... like supermarkets. Rock and roll reopened the possibility of ecstasy, or at least a joy beyond anything else the consumer culture could offer.... [T]he news is out, and has been at least since the 1960s: We are capable of so much more."[9] And so we are.

Let's take a little deeper tour now, again through our wonderful brain structure—this time our brains on joy since this is the topic at immediate hand.

---

6. Quoted in ibid., 99.
7. Ibid.
8. Ibid., 216.
9. Ibid., 224.

Going Deeper Yet: This is Your Brain on Joy: "Here Comes the Sun"

"By being able to celebrate our good feelings, sense of well-being, and positive emotions, we were better equipped to share our emotional states with others, a key ingredient in being able to form societies and cooperative groups."[10] In essence, this statement captures the rationale for including joyful music in all its forms—expressed in songs, dance, rhythmic movements of all kinds—as an evolutionary adaptation that became embedded in our genetic inheritance from our proto-human ancestors. Because of the positive survival benefits to group bonding, the brain developed in such a way that neurochemicals that were themselves rewarding came to reinforce musical displays in tribal members. Those who sang and danced best, drawing others into trusting social bonds, tended to pass their genes on to their heirs. But why *joy* songs? Why uplifting rhythms with a "happy" beat? Levitin gives the following answer:

> Fundamentally, we have joy songs because moving around, dancing, exercising our bodies and minds is something that was adaptive in evolutionary history. Stretching, jumping, and using sound to communicate felt good because our brains—through natural selection—developed rewards for those behaviors. *Joy songs today give us a jolt of good brain chemistry as a biological echo of the importance they held over thousands of years of evolution* (emphasis added).[11]

In Levitin's chapter on joy songs, he reports a conversation he had with a musician friend of his. His friend, who apparently has done a great deal of thinking about the matter, speculates that maybe the first song arose in our earliest ancestors when one caveman started fooling around, playing with rhythm and some sort of singing sound or humming, moving to some beat he heard only in his head. Others sitting around the fire joined in, and all discovered that this felt good! It felt very good indeed! And so they kept doing it, and thus shaped and grew a proto-human brain that afforded music a place in our evolutionary history.

Recent brain studies have shown—in response to musical upbeat rhythm—an increase in "feel-good" neurochemicals such as dopamine and serotonin that sooth the brain and calm the emotions, again suggesting an ancient, evolved advantage to playing music in our earliest ancestors. Researchers have speculated that such neuromodulators may have diffused

---

10. Levitin, *The World in Six Songs*, 109.
11. Ibid.

hostility within tribal groupings, raising levels of trust and social bonding, dampening aggression and even murder within primitive gatherings. (Skipping down some millennia, the Hebrew Bible records the story of David, playing music for crazy King Saul, calming his distress at least temporarily—until Saul tossed a spear at David, but that's another episode in the story!)

Levitin and others point out that in terms of neurochemical "feel-good" release of synaptic agents such as dopamine and serotonin, there appears to be no single "pleasure center" within the brain, but rather diffuse neuronal centers across the brain layers that respond to musical input—pathways directly connecting incoming aural sensation to midbrain areas stimulating emotions and memories, triggering movement in motor neurons, and then extending to the forebrain where the imagination provides layers of significance based on both memory and meaning now.

Like Levitin's mother, my mother—she who danced a mean Charleston—lived to a very old age, in my mom's case almost 101. And also like his own mother, my mom retained a sense of rhythm to nearly the end of her life. She would sit in her wheelchair, or recline in her comfort chair—hugging her stuffed dog in her lap and tapping her fingers to the music of her own memory, a CD of Glenn Miller tunes. And like Levitin's musing about his mother, I also wonder whether her retention of rhythm until the end was a mere marker of her programmed longevity or if somehow the health benefits of music responsiveness played some role in her longevity—in a causal sense. Again, anecdotally, music therapists report amazing benefits from playing music for those sick and elderly confined to nursing homes and hospital beds.

Of note, there is—beyond anecdote—some evidence that music might play some role in promoting health benefits. For example, Levitin reports that several recent studies have shown an increase in one important antibody that fights infection, serum immunoglobulin A, following music as one form of treatment. Other studies have shown an increase in melatonin—a hormone important in regulating our sleep and waking cycles—as a result of musical input.

This is all a long way from proving longevity benefits or major health outcomes as independent effects of music therapy. But where there are anecdotes, science often follows. And the logic of looking for such a potential relationship is reasonable given the known brain effects of response to music. Which brings me to the whole question of individual differences in music response.

As I and others have said all along, we are pro-social beings—inherently communal in nature, from our earliest evolutionary roots. Reaching back into my own former academic work and knowing the field pretty well, there is evidence from animal studies, as well as human clinical and epidemiological research, evidence that clearly demonstrates a strong association between social engagement and support and positive outcomes, including survival itself. But the question arises here whether music responsiveness might play some role in this association.

Very few studies that I have reviewed have carefully examined the trait of music reactivity in multiple samples of individuals, along with the role such reactivity might play in social engagement. But a very recent series of studies by Chris Loersch and Nathan Arbuckle has done just that. And in short, these researchers have found that first, musical reactivity and general emotional reactivity are distinct from one another, and that the former was an independent predictor of social motivation. Specifically, they found that musical reactivity was a significant predictor of what they refer to as "belonging motivation." That is, those subjects who responded positively to a questionnaire with items such as "When I listen to music, I can feel it in my body" and "When I hear music, my foot starts tapping along with the beat," had a stronger desire for personal social attachment to others than those who reported less reactivity.

So the question that I raise here, before moving on to recent related work on joy, "mindfulness," and brain reactivity, is whether musical reactivity as an inborn trait characteristic might be an important causal factor related to health status—with social engagement as a mediator between music responsiveness and both mental and physical health outcomes. Again, where anecdote and speculation arise, science follows in their wake. But the possibility is tantalizing. And also hopeful, because although passed on as trait, music appreciation can be learned. Traits can be shaped, and even introverts can learn to modify and mold their behavior and brains in the process.

Joy, the Practice of "Mindfulness," and the Brain

Now here's a puzzle. Given the fact that as part of our evolutionary heritage, we each have within us the capacity to experience and express joy in all its manifestations, why then do you and I not live more joyful lives? Why do we walk around preoccupied with worries—real and imagined? Why are we depressed and fearful much of our waking lives?

One answer—returning again to our evolutionary roots—is that we are born to be vigilant, to scan the horizon for all possible threats to our well-being. This is a basic biological imperative and of overriding importance to our very survival. And even if we are no longer threatened by now-extinct giant tigers and enemies from other tribes (well actually, I guess we still are, as we witness the desire of the shoe bomber and the like to kill us all in a very personal way), still there are other, learned threats to our well-being—loss of job, loss of prestige and status, as well as loss of health or loss of loved ones—with serious survival consequences.

But beyond these obvious threats to our lives and well-being, we tend to pile up worries with negative preoccupations on a daily basis—many with little or no foundation in reality. We ruminate thoughts like "Maybe my boss doesn't really like me because she had a tone in her voice this morning that seemed kind of sharp to me. Maybe she's getting ready to fire me and that's an early signal of what's to come later this week," when in reality she had a bad night and thinks she's coming down with the flu, and so on. Worry over nothing!

This kind of piling up of negative thinking is part of a pattern of waking consciousness referred to as "negativity bias," a tendency to think the worst, to catastrophize the worst outcomes on an ongoing basis. In response to this habitual negative thinking pattern that tends to destroy any hope of joy-filled experience in our daily lives, a whole industry has developed around the practice of what's referred to as "mindfulness" training. I recently came back from the annual meeting of the American Academy of Religion, and I attended one of the sessions on mindfulness and the practice's effects on our brains. The opening presenter announced at the beginning of the conference session, "Mindfulness is everywhere!" And so it is. Countless books have been written describing this practice and its benefits. Books such as Earl Henslin's *This is Your Brain on Joy* and Rick Hanson's *Buddha's Brain* are examples of this genre. Let me try to summarize the basic message that these works and others hold, before offering my own critique—both positive and negative—of this current practice.

I came across a rather succinct summary of the rationale for mindfulness practice recently. A blog site called *PsychCentral* posted an interview with Rick Hanson, the author of *Buddha's Brain*. Hanson says:

> If you routinely dwell on your resentments and regrets, the neurons involved in that particular mental activity will fire busily together, and automatically start wiring together as well. Which will add one more bit of neural structure to feeling discontented, mistreated, angry, or sorrowful. On the other hand, if you regularly focus on the good facts around you and inside you—like your own good qualities, such as patience, determination, or kindness—then the neurons involved will wire together, stitching more resilience, hopefulness, confidence, and happiness into

the fabric of your brain and your self.... The mind takes the shape of what it rests upon. Modern neuropsychology is starting to shed light on how, exactly, this happens—how the fleeting flow of thoughts and feelings, hopes and dreams, sorrow and suffering, gradually, inexorably sculpt the brain[12]

Hanson's "takeaway point" from the interview is that we should be careful about the quality of the mental activities we indulge in. Drawing from modern brain science as well as ancient and contemporary contemplative practices, you can use the mind to change your brain and thus your mind for the better—experiencing more peace and joy on a daily basis, and enhancing the lives of those you touch in your daily life across the board—at home, at work, and in the marketplace as well.

Given the fact that we can't avoid suffering and, at times, unsettling changes in our lives, in Hanson's book, *Buddha's Brain*, he insists that while "pain is inevitable... suffering is optional." While this author does recognize the rightful place of occasional negative passion in our lives—for example, in response to observed injustice or evil aggression—he says "most of the time we're just overheated—caught up with some carrot or struggling with some stick. Then we feel driven, rattled, stressed, irritated, anxious, or blue. Definitely not happy."[13]

Given these losses that occur to every one of us over the course of our days, Earl Henslin's book, *This is Your Brain on Joy*, gives a very practical and detailed discussion of concrete ways you and I can enhance the experience of peace and joy in our everyday life. For some years, Henslin has collaborated with a neuroscientist and psychiatrist, Daniel Amen. Amen has used single photon emission computerized tomography (SPECT) for diagnosing various mood disorders such as crippling depression and anxiety. Working with the basic premise that we can shape our brains and hence, our emotional experience and expression though mind control, the book offers very practical advice aimed at achieving a fine balance between the executive control exerted by our rational forebrains and our emotion and memory centers generating response to inner and outer stimuli, shaping what we value and coloring our world view.

Drawing from an extensive SPECT database, the author describes five brain centers that "light up" when associated mood disorders are present, followed by prescriptions to counter such disturbances that involve in each case enriching the environmental context (for example, listening to music, watching a humorous show, reading something pleasant or comic, and so

---

12. Quoted in Goldstein, "The Neuroscience of Happiness," para. 5.
13. Hanson, *Buddha's Brain*, 79.

on), enriching the "inner world" (for example, practicing prayer and meditation, practicing the relaxation response, taking naps, learning something new), and enriching the body/mind chemistry through good nutrition and exercise.

Section two of Henslin's work summarizes the SPECT findings for the five mood disorders of concern in his work: Attention Deficit Disorder (if you know the Winnie the Pooh story, they refer to this as the "Tigger" effect, with poor "executive control" over the manic flow of thoughts and feelings as they arise in the mind), obsessive/compulsive worry, anxiety disorder, clinical depression, and disordered anger expression. Without my going into all the brain details at this point, the overheated brain centers range from a poorly integrated prefrontal cortex to excessive neural firing in areas of the deep limbic system of the midbrain.

Interestingly, the practical advice pretty much remains the same across the brain areas, tailored a bit to the mood disorder at hand. For example, those showing an overactive deep limbic system with symptomatic expression of depressed mood are prescribed "happy songs" to listen to, as well as reading hope-filled Scripture passages, watching amusing films, and so on. Those with anger management issues are advised—beyond certain prescribed medication—to practice "self-soothing" techniques such as deep breathing, playing soothing music, practicing progressive muscle relaxation, praying, self-talking with quotes such as "anger is a bad counselor," exercising, and so on.

Section three of Henslin's very practical and practice-focused work is titled "Joy Everlasting." The advice is simple and straightforward but I think worth sharing here. Henslin opens this section by saying "I do not need a perfect world [which none of us will get anyway!]; I need perfect peace." And so, I think, do we all. As an ideal to be striven for, if not completely, finally attainable in all times and places where we find ourselves dwelling. The author then lists what he terms six "secrets" to attaining joy, which do contain some wisdom worth sharing.

First, he says "reframe your chains." That is, you can say "If only _____ would happen, then I would be happy." Whatever you fill the blank in with, he says, that's your "chain." So as someone has said, be careful of what you wish for, because nothing—or at least very few things—turn out to be the panacea you hoped they would be. Interestingly, Henslin cites the words of Victor Frankl—a Jew and author who survived the evils of a Nazi concentration camp. Frankl talked about some prisoners who—even amid such horror—were able to comfort and give hope to others, giving witness to the fact that all can be taken from you but one thing: "the freedom to choose one's attitude in any given set of circumstances, to choose one's own way." Such prisoners' acts of self-giving bore witness to what it means to be a noble human being.

The other "secrets" to experiencing joy in one's life include "shrinking irritants" such as letting go of anger at specific others in your life through forgiveness; practicing gratitude to counter anxiety or depression; and stocking your mind with rich food for thought—filling your life with times spent in your favorite cozy chair, sipping a nice Merlot before the fire, savoring smells that make you happy, living your life generously with "deep-spirited friends." After all, someone has said that "sorrow is halved and joy doubled when shared." In fact, Henslin concludes his writing by emphasizing the importance of giving and receiving love from others ". . . to love others, to be deep-spirited friends, to put aside our own needs long enough to lend a helping hand . . . who would have thought that the path to real joy is to happily, sacrificially, kindly, and deliriously . . . give your life away in the service of Love?"[14]

Before leaving the topic of mindfulness, a word of caution. There are many positive things that can be said about attempting to quiet down our "gerbil minds," and relinquish as many negative habitual thought patterns as we can possibly shed. Life is tough enough in reality without adding additional burdens to our emotional lives.

Having said that, I do not believe that "disinterestedness" is finally a desirable state to strive for. Even though Hanson, in *Buddha's Brain*, insists that the ideal of mindful equanimity is neither apathy nor indifference, he says the "primary point of equanimity is not to reduce or channel [emotional] activation, but simply not to respond to it. This is very unusual behavior for the brain, which is designed by evolution to respond to limbic signals, particularly to pulses of pleasant and unpleasant feeling tones."[15] Hanson recommends instead making every effort to attend only to what he calls "neutral stimuli," no longer reacting to emotional signals but staying comfortably focused on neither threats nor rewards, neither on past meaning nor future expectation that supply emotional meaning in our lives, so that eventually the "neutral tone can become . . . a *"doorway to the eventless" of the neutral now"* [emphasis added].

As I read the above words, I couldn't help but hear in my own mind Simon and Garfunkel's lyrics from their song "I Am A Rock, I Am An Island" . . . where nothing and no one can finally reach me or disturb my peace as I smile and bob along like a cork amid the swirling stream of life. What I am basically questioning even the possibility of "living in the present moment."

---

14. Henslin, *This Is Your Brain on Joy*, 216.
15. Hanson, *Buddha's Brain*, 112.

There is much philosophical and psychological literature—from Edmund Husserl and the existential phenomenologists to the early phenomenological psychology of William James to the vast literature in the area of narrative psychology drawn from here, as well as the neuroscientists who I have also cited in this writing that altogether suggest that to be human is to shape our phenomenal world as temporal beings—that both points back to a history and expects a future. The shape of human consciousness—how our brains are wired whether awake or asleep—is inherently a narrative shape, with retentions of the past memories and what is technically referred to as protentions of our future lives both coloring and giving meaning to our present reality.

So let me leave it there. I have discussed the recent mindfulness literature because I believe it has something important to say about how we live our daily lives. Someone has said that "how you live today is how you live your life." A sobering thought indeed. I think we all want more joy and peace and happiness in our lives, and the concrete practices suggested in this literature—finding refuge places for calming our distress, exercising, praying, listening to happy music, and such are all good practices to try to incorporate into our daily lives.

But in the end, I believe that the ideal of an atemporal, nonreactive life is not finally humanly attainable, or frankly, even desirable. Thus, in my view (and I hope I'm not being totally unfair here) some of the ideal end states described in the mindfulness literature—unless you're a monk living in Tibet—are not based on a sound understanding of human consciousness, but on an idea imported from Eastern cultures and the meditative practices of those who devote their lives to reaching Nirvana.

Excessive Joy or Too Much of a Good Thing?: Springsteen's "Dancing in the Dark"

Daniel Levitin notes that uninhibited joy is usually associated with a positive outlook on life. And music that is joyful pumps us up, makes us feel better all the way around. As I get ready for bed at night, I turn my iPhone to my Pandora app and tune in to the Simon and Garfunkel or Fleetwood Mac station. And no matter how lousy my day was, I usually go to bed happy, humming along, dancing a little on my way to bed. And as Levitin says, there probably was an evolutionary advantage to being optimistic, emerging as the leader of the pack who can attract tribal followers and strike out into new territory.

But also as part of our evolutionary-based antennae that scan for and pick up trouble, we tend to be suspicious of folks who are way too optimistic—the nuts, the fanatics, the over-the-top salesmen who promise the moon and lead others astray in the process—like the seller of trombones in the musical *The Music Man*.

Yes, there seems to be a fine balance between having a positive outlook, which usually accompanies a joyful disposition, and being overly optimistic, setting oneself up for a lifetime of disappointment when hopes become pinned on visions that disappear in the crush of reality. As Levitin says (quoting Barack Obama by the way), "hope is not blind optimism." He says "an overoptimistic person is going to experience a large number of failures and find he has expended considerable energy for no rewards . . . . The best adaptive strategy . . . has been shown to be the adoption of an attitude that is slightly over the halfway mark, on the optimistic (joyful) side of realistic."[16]

But how much is too much joy? A few years back, Kay Redfield Jamison—at this writing a psychologist on the faculty at John Hopkins University in Baltimore—wrote a delightful little book titled *Exuberance: The Passion for Life*. In it, she covers much of the ground that we've already covered in this chapter, describing exuberant manifestations of zestful living in biographical portraits of historical figures (such as Theodore Roosevelt) and fictional characters, like the irrepressible Toad in the children's book *Wind in the Willows* and Snoopy in the *Peanuts* cartoon series. Having spent her professional scientific life studying mood disorders such as depression and mania, Jamison discusses the evolutionary roots of diverse temperaments, but focuses in this work on manifestations of the extrovert's "ebullient brain" (to echo her use of Coleridge's term).

Jamison cites brain research that has located the left frontal region of the forebrain as one area associated with joyful emotion, with neurons in the right frontal region playing a role in dampening joyful exuberance. In this and other works Jamison argues for a clear association between extroverted exuberance—even mild forms of mania—and the creative mind. In fact, she sees a bi-directional association between a joyful exuberance and creativity, as creative achievements feed back into a high mood, positively reinforcing the creative process.[17]

16. Levitin, *The World in Six Songs*, 102.

17. Some time back, I read Susan Cain's book *Quiet*. I was very persuaded by her writing—in part, because she was talking about me. That is, what she said fits me to a tee.

In short, Cain makes a strong case for quiet introversion as a significant contributor to creativity. She notes that about 40 percent of us are born introverts—more or less.

In a chapter titled "Throwing up Rockets," Jamison reminds the reader that emotions are contagious. As I have repeatedly emphasized, we humans are social creatures and as such, live within an open loop and are responsive to others around us. Dark mood and anxiety bring us down while ebullience "answers despair with hope."[18] Consistent with the central theme of this present writing, Jamison emphasizes the importance of joyful music which calls forth in us a like response. Emotion motivates action pathways deep within the brain, and she insists that it is in our actions that our moods are most fully expressed. "For it is in action, in dance and in music, in the kinetic thrusting upward of arms and legs and the throwing up and back of the head, that great joy finds its highest expression."[19]

Toward the end of her book, Jamison raises the troubling issue of manic disorder. That is, she opens up the question of joy-filled overload, of inadequate brain control over exuberant optimism. She says, "exuberance can veer off sharply into disturbing territory." And she should know, because Jamison herself has suffered from bouts of manic-depressive psychosis—where mania at its best is zestful and enlivening, and at its worse, reflects "fanaticism, poor judgment, and at its extremes, evil."

Jamison does raise the question that I asked a page or so back: Where does exuberance end and mania begin? It's interesting that for a scientist who has spent her life studying mood disorders, and who herself has suffered from one very serious one, she answers that we do not know. The "edge" of mania, called hypomania, can be, as she says, exhilarating, attractive to others, creative in expression. She also points out that many who appear especially exuberant personalities have darker, frequently unrecognized mood disturbances—a depressive undertone to their hypomanic

---

introverts are folks like Cain and me who are very comfortable being alone with our rich inner world and who often prefer our own company. Folks like us are in fact overrepresented in such occupations as writers, poets, preachers, scientists—in short, those who are creative contributors to our culture. Most of us learn to rise to the occasion and exert ourselves socially when community expectations require it. But such "extrovert" behavior tends to exhaust us. Thus, we need to withdraw, and have some alone time in order to replenish energy that such social engagement depletes.

I go into this because when it comes to personal creativity, it seems to me that the situation may be more complex than either Cain or Jamison makes it. When it comes to creativity at least they strike me as arguing from opposite points of view—in part, but importantly based on their own life experience. And since my own experience synchronizes best with Cain's, I feel compelled to insert this note in my discussion of exuberance and its role in creative contributions—especially here in response to Jamison's argument in favor of hypomania as an inherited trait causally contributing to creativity in her and others' lives.

18. Jamison, *Exuberance*, 138.
19. Ibid, 135.

actions and antics (think Robin Williams.) Many have argued that the most successful comedians also have a core of deep depression that they mask through humor. Joy and grief "inhabit close and traversable lands."

But then for us all there are unavoidable life losses. Jamison concludes that in fact in addition to the controlling function of our forebrain and rational thought, melancholy arising from more ancient midbrain emotional centers does also dampen and control an exuberant mood. "Sorrow adds ballast," she says. Thus, such "ballast" supplied by a well-integrated brain comes from several sources: the outer world of events and others within our daily lives, cultural rules of emotional display, our forebrain's reasoning power, and midbrain melancholy as we live our open-loop lives engaged with our social world surrounding us and the unfolding of history in the time that we're given.

I'll leave Jamison for now with this final quote from near the end of *Exuberance*. She says "Exuberance is an assailable thing, as is the hope that rides with it. Champagne will go flat, passion burn itself out, and optimism be trimmed by experience . . . . Savingly, nature teaches that joy can be replenished, life can succeed death, and joy find its way out of sorrow. Nature gives of its exuberance in remarkable, extraordinary ways."[20] For most of us, hope and vitality will surge back. For some given an exuberant temperament, they will surge back with an irrepressible force. For others of a more perhaps melancholy or introverted bent, a quieter healing will happen, "with joy and laughter seeping back in more slowly." But she concludes "even drops of joy make suffering more endurable."[21]

****

As I have said from the beginning of this book, where science leaves off, theology—or in my case, evolutionary theism—joins other fields of inquiry such as philosophy, in the quest for meaning beyond empirical discovery. And within this framework, I have cited in an earlier work[22] the prescient writings of the twentieth-century theologian Teilhard de Chardin. Although some of his later writings shade off into grand mystical vision, his training as a scientist and his theological probing into the mysteries of existence and the future of humankind have in many ways a contemporary ring to them.

---

20. Ibid., 259; 300–1.
21. Ibid., 303.
22. Levy-Achtemeier, *Flourishing Life*.

And one of his themes in his writing is that humans inherit a certain "zest" for life, a forward and upward thrust to their individual lives and the evolutionary life of our human species. In a book edited by Ilia Delio, titled *From Teilhard to Omega*, Ursula King contributed a chapter titled "The Zest for Life: A Contemporary Exploration of a Generative Theme in Teilhard's Work." Toward the end of Teilhard's life, he wrote a series of unpublished letters and finally a whole essay devoted to the topic of God-given zest for living which lies at the heart of our humanity. He used the French word "gout" meaning something like a taste, a joyful sense of appreciation, a preference for "upward" growth that activates human energies at the personal, social, and species level of existence—"a dynamic energy and movement, an aliveness that spurs us on, nourishes and sustains human attitudes, inspiring further action, growth, and development."[23] Although I have been focusing on experience and expression of joy in this chapter, I think a certain joyful savoring, a joy-filled flourishing lies at the base of Teilhard's concept of zest. And as King echoes his thought, our human flourishing is finally not possible without the evolutionary flourishing and development of environmental, economic, political, social, and spiritual flourishing of our entire species.

It is in the spiritual sphere that Teilhard brings together his understanding of Divine Spirit within the forces of evolutionary growth. That is, a truly human life in the fullest sense "requires physical, mental, moral, and spiritual care for body, mind, spirit, and soul." This means that "human life needs spirituality like the body needs breath and blood to flourish." Throughout Teilhard's writings, whether in his letters or in his essays and longer works, he expresses a deep faith in the goodness of life (to use King's expression). Whether we are blessed with positive events or faced with inevitable losses, Teilhard embraces a basic trust in our evolutionary development, reflecting a "deep belief in being held and enfolded by something greater, of being cared for and protected by God's presence and loving care."[24]

King also points out that this will to love and to live life to the fullest—contributing to the growth of not only our own individual lives, but also the growth of our entire planet's well-being—can be undermined by indifference, by boredom, by what is termed one of the seven deadly sins, by *acedia*, or by the attitude expressed by "I don't care ... I just ... don't care." She says then that enemy number one is "the loss of a taste for life, the absence of inner resources, and the danger of dropping out of all commitments by not taking responsibility for one's own life and that of others."

---

23. King, "The Zest for Life," 190.
24. Ibid., 192.

In the broadest sense, our zest for life, our joyful engagement as co-creators with Divine Transcendence—to use the most general term spanning religious practices beyond Christianity—evolves for each of us through the influence of our families and friends, our culture, and our communities that we join. Thus, on a wider scale, we evolve as human beings by the shaping of science, art—musical and otherwise—and for Teilhard, especially through the nourishing of our spirits through contemplation and prayer. Thus we connect with the "energy running through the whole evolutionary process," linking together and forging bonds between "mysticism, [scientific] research,"[25] and the biological, adaptive processes that continue to emerge within our species over time.

> Nurturing the human spiritual potential means the development of a spiritual awareness or consciousness, understood as a different, deeper way of "seeing," to which Teilhard de Chardin gave such emphatic witness. It is an all-embracing vision, a commitment to a depth dimension of human life, traditionally understood as a transcendent dimension. It enables human beings to see their experience in a larger context, having a greater vision by relating more widely, and responding more effectively, by taking "response-ability" toward themselves and others, the environment, nature, the earth, the human community, and Ultimate Reality, however named, often called the Spirit or, in theistic traditions, God.[26]

Despite the psychological fact that our joy-filled zest might blind us to life's realities and set us up for repeated disappointment when our hopes are dashed, I think there is something fundamentally true in Teilhard's theological insights concerning human growth potential. So perhaps Levitin's suggestion for betting on the side of optimism—not blind optimism but joy-infused hope despite life's losses—can open us up to what God or Divine Spirit is up to in both our daily lives and in the evolutionary growth of humankind.

Now I would like to introduce you to one of the most joy-filled persons in my own life, a living exemplar of rising above life's struggles and still expressing zest and joy despite sorrow that comes in the wake of loss. So please meet Patty as she describes her life back then.

---

25. Ibid., 195.
26. Ibid., 196.

Interlude I: Meet Patty

I have known Patty for the past decade and she is one of my dearest friends here in Richmond. Patty is what you would describe as "a fun girl!"—despite the fact that she is now in her fifties. Patty lights up the room when she enters, and she is one of those folks who has never met a stranger. More about her present and future expected life in the next section of this chapter when we turn to the "now" of our lives.

But she has filled me in a bit on her past—her "back then"—as a late Boomer. So let me share that piece of the picture with you, before we turn and examine our present lives—and what our future may hold in store for all of us in our generation.

> Being part of a military family, we moved every two to three years. I credit that lifestyle with making me the extreme extrovert that I am today. I had to act fast in a new school to make friends because I was never sure how long we would be there. Once we settled in Richmond, when I was in the eighth grade, I could relax. I knew we were going to be here at least until I finished high school.
>
> Surprisingly I didn't have a lot of close friends in high school. I ran around with the smokers and the Friday Morning Fun Club Gang. Every Friday morning of my senior year a group of us met in an undeveloped subdivision and drank before school started. That was our version of happy hour!
>
> When I was a junior in high school, my mother collapsed one evening after dinner and was hospitalized for close to six months. Being the oldest daughter living at home, it was up to me to run the household. That included getting up early to feed my dad breakfast and help him get dressed for work, keeping the house clean, doing laundry, and cooking dinner—plus keep up with my school work and try to have a normal social life for a sixteen- to seventeen-year-old.
>
> It was a stressful and emotional time in my life but it taught me how to cope with all that life throws at you. And it made me a better person—I was made to realize the importance of family and to appreciate every day that we are given.

In Patty's reminiscing, she credits her resilience and her extroverted tendencies to her life circumstances, and of course as we've discussed in these pages, that is true for us all. Our families, our homes, our school companions, our culture, and our time in the historical flow of events all shape us. We select from the menu of options that we are given, and we create our life story in the process. But Patty was also born with a certain disposition—an outgoingness, a certain *joie de vivre*, a certain disposition to engage with others and live intensely despite what life has thrown at her—from early childhood on.

Again, we'll revisit her in the next section of this chapter. There I can also add to her story, because this is the Patty I know and have come to love over the years. So let us proceed to take a look at our current and possible future lives as they are now unfolding.

THE SCENE NOW: LIFE IS PRETTY MEANINGFUL AFTER ALL

> ... and then
> the life I'd never been able to foresee
> would begin, and everything
> before I became myself would appear
> necessary to the rest of the story.[27]

****

As I already noted, I have a particular bedtime routine that I enjoy immensely. For the past couple of years my oldest son has given me for Christmas a subscription to the app Pandora One. I have loaded that app with many of my favorite "stations," but the ones I listen to at night before bed are first, the Simon and Garfunkel or Gordon Lightfoot menu of songs from the '60s through the '80s, and then I always end with the Fleetwood Mac station—dancing my way to bed as I then turn off the phone and charge it up for the next day. Again, it doesn't matter how lousy my day was, or what kind of mood I was in when I came upstairs. I end the day on an upbeat, happy note as I listen to songs of my youth and good memories come flooding back through the neural synapses in my brain.

Standing back a bit and in a stance of self-assessment, I would say generally that at the upper edges of middle age (a moving target, isn't it?), I am quite content with my life at this point. I have had times of recent sadness that we will get into a bit more in the chapters ahead, but my current life is a full one—filled with family, dear friends near and far, and my writing projects, along with exercising my clergy role and vocation through active

---

27. Raab, "My Life before I Knew It," 51.

church community involvement. So as I have mentioned earlier, along with Tom Hanks—if I were going to carry out a life review at this point—I do believe that I'm a better version of myself than in earlier decades. Wisdom comes along with the passing years, and we pull together our life story as the poet above observes, so that everything that has gone before appears "necessary to the rest of the story."

It turns out that this self-assessment is actually pretty typical of a wide segment of the population, not just in this country, but around the world. There is something fairly universal in making peace with the past and experiencing current life contentment in older age, a pattern found repeatedly in crosscultural studies in recent years. And since there is evidence that this pattern is also observed in our closest primate ancestors, apparently the root of such contentment is also biologically built into our species. If this is the case, then what is referred to as the "U-shaped curve of life satisfaction" is not unique to my Boomer generation. But much of the recent research into this phenomenon has been carried out with those of us who are currently post-fifty, and so I think it's appropriate to turn to this body of work and examine a bit more closely this source of the current scene.

The Source of the Current Scene: "Let It Be"

> The Boomers might have decided that as a prescription for a life-time of happiness, *All you need is love, love, love* was a bit hollow and a bit simplistic. But they are still inclined to cling to another tenet of Beatles philosophy:
>
> *Let it be . . . things usually work out for the best.*[28]

****

Jonathan Rauch wrote a timely article that came out recently in *The Atlantic* titled "The Real Roots of Mid-life Crisis." In it, Rauch quoted a close friend who once said to him—when Rauch was thirty and his friend was in his mid-sixties, "Midlife crisis begins sometime in your 40s, when you look at your life and think, *Is this all?* And it ends about 10 years later, when you look at your life again and think, *Actually, this is pretty good.*"[29] In the article, the author cites among other things what is referred to as

---

28. MacKay, *Generations*, 134.
29. Rauch, "The Real Roots of Midlife Crisis," 90.

the Easterlin paradox. Richard Easterlin is an economist who decades ago analyzed crosscultural data that showed that beyond a certain necessary subsistence point required for daily living (minimally decent health care, enough work available to provide food for eating and housing to protect from the elements)—beyond this basic base of life maintenance, "countries don't get happier as they get richer." That the old adage that money doesn't create happiness is, in the last analysis, true after all.

Admittedly this U-shaped curve of life satisfaction is perhaps easier to observe in wealthier countries where people tend to be healthier and live longer. Nevertheless there is adequate evidence that even controlling statistically for such factors as income, marital status, employment, and even health status, the age effect still holds. Rauch writes, "... there may be an underlying pattern in life satisfaction that is independent of your situation."[30] He quotes David Blanchflower of Dartmouth who, with Andrew Oswald of the University of Warwick, carried out international surveys of life satisfaction in the 1990s. Blanchflower told Rauch the following: "'Whatever sets of data you looked at ... you got the same things': life satisfaction would decline with age for the first couple of decades of adulthood, bottom out somewhere in the 40s or early 50s, and then, until the very last years, increase with age." Hence, again this pattern became known as the happiness U-curve.

As I mentioned in the opening to this section, this upward shift in happiness and life satisfaction in the mid- and post-middle years may simply be part of our genetic makeup that we inherit at birth, a shift that is both age-linked and adaptive to our species' survival. Rauch cites evidence suggesting the U-curve's evolutionary base in findings from studies carried out with chimpanzees and orangutans in several countries. Animal caretakers filled out well-being questionnaires rating these primates' "mood" displays and found the following:

> The apes' well-being bottomed out at ages comparable, in people, to between 45 and 50. "Our results," the authors concluded in a 2012 paper, "imply that human well-being's curved shape is not uniquely human and that, although it may be partly explained by aspects of human life and society, its origins may lie partly in the biology we share with closest related great apes."[31]

Toward the end of his piece, Rauch asks the question—given the apparent reality of this U-shaped happiness curve—why does it exist? If this is built into our genes, how is this possibly adaptive for our species?

30. Ibid., 91.
31. Ibid.

The author admits that part of the answer to this statistical phenomenon emerging from numerous studies is that those who are very unhappy for various reasons tend to die out sooner, and thus are removed from the equation. But he doesn't believe that is by any means the whole story. What he does argue—and we'll see this explanation showing up from several studies in the psychology literature—is that as folks age, they may in fact become a bit wiser through a lifetime of experience. Goals become more realistic as the future becomes foreshortened, and stress becomes lessened as unattainable ambitious goals become nonissues over time.

Rauch says "Midlife is, for many people, a time of recalibration, when they begin to evaluate their lives less in terms of social competition and more in terms of social connectedness."[32] In short, as we age, people begin to live more realistically, and as the Beatles' song of the '60s says, are much more willing to "let it be." Again, there is empirical evidence for such growth in wisdom. For example, Bauer, McAdams, and Sakaeda reported findings from a study carried out on a community sample with an average age of fifty-one years (Boomers, yes?) which showed that these older subjects reported living a happier, more fulfilling life than a younger comparison sample—partly because they interpreted their past difficulties in terms of growth in wisdom and self-understanding.

Finally, Rauch concludes—along with a psychiatrist he cites named Dilip V. Jeste—that perhaps the evolutionary-based, adaptive purpose of the U-shaped curve finally resides in the development of wisdom, that maybe we become wiser with age—even despite physical decline. Jeste says "All across the world, we have an implicit notion of what a wise person is." And Rauch responds

> The traits of the wise tend to include compassion and empathy, good social reasoning and decision making, equanimity, tolerance of divergent values, comfort with uncertainty and ambiguity. And the whole package is more than the sum of the parts, because these traits work together to improve life not only for the wise but also for their communities. Wisdom is pro-social .... Humans ... live for an unusually long time after their fertile years; perhaps wisdom provides benefit to our children or our social groups that make older people worth keeping around, from an evolutionary perspective.[33]

I found that thought intriguing. Because without a doubt—and I speak from my own life as well as from looking closely at the lives of those I've

32. Ibid., 93.
33. Ibid., 94.

interviewed—that an increase in equanimity does tend to occur with advancing years. I've also reviewed findings from studies such as those mentioned above, as well as others we'll look at later, that show there is an age-associated coming to terms with reality. That is, as we age we develop an increased appreciation of the time that we have been given and more importantly, the time we have left, with a focus on things that really matter. Actually the few things that *really* matter—like love and friendship and the life of the spirit. And giving back and giving generously out of gratitude for life itself. Rauch calls that wisdom. And so do I. Perhaps not everyone reaches that exalted wise level, but I believe most of us can write and rewrite our life story as we've talked about here—committing our lives to something beyond ourselves. And that benefits our communities and society in the end.

****

In Rauch's article, he describes the role of gratitude as an integral aspect of wisdom and well-being. He quotes a fifty-four-year-old friend of his who reflects on her current state and the upsurge of generosity out of a sense of gratitude in her life. She says "I measure my worth now by how I can help others and contribute to the community. I enjoy the relationships that I've been able to nurture over these years—longer-term friends, growing with those friends. It was always striving and looking ahead, as opposed to being in the now and feeling grateful for the now . . . . When I am in a situation when I can moan a little bit or feel bad about some of the difficult things that have happened, the balance sheet is hugely on the side of all the great things that have happened. And I think that gratitude has helped me be both more satisfied and more giving."[34]

I think this is a perfect reflection of the central theme of Rauch's writing: life on the whole is pretty good (growth in wisdom) and we are grateful for all the blessings along the way. And gratitude wells up within us and we find our life satisfaction increased by giving beyond ourselves to others and to our surrounding community.

In fact, there is a very large literature concerned with the expression of gratitude, its causes and effects,[35] as well as empirical studies examining under controlled conditions the effects of gratitude enhancement. For example, in a classic study by Robert Emmons and Michael McCullough,

34. Ibid, 92.

35. For example, Emmons and McCullough, eds., *The Psychology of Gratitude*; Leithart, *Gratitude*; Emmons, *Gratitude Works!*; and Visser, *The Gift of Thanks*.

these researchers found that when they induced feelings of gratitude in subjects—in both a university sample and a community-based sample of disabled older adults (average age, forty-nine years)—that a grateful outlook (elicited by paying attention to daily blessings) heightened a later report of well-being (rated by self and others) and joyful outlook or, in their terms, "positive affect." They also found that those who paid attention and counted their blessings reported becoming more likely to offer emotional support to others. They conclude that "a conscious focus on blessings may have emotional and interpersonal benefits."[36]

These authors define gratitude as "the perception of a positive personal outcome, not necessarily deserved or earned, that is due to the actions of another person."[37] That is, gratitude is experienced when you recognize a positive benefit or undeserved gift and you also attribute the source of that blessing or gift as coming from outside of you—primarily due to the generosity of someone in your life. Emmons and McCullough conclude their research report with the following summary:

> The experience of gratitude, and the actions stimulated by it, build and strengthen social bonds and friendships. Moreover, encouraging people to focus on the benefits they have received from others leads them to feel loved and cared for by others .... Therefore, gratitude appears to build friendship and other social bonds. These are social resources because, in times of need, these social bonds are wellsprings to be tapped for the provision of social support. Gratitude, thus, is a form of love, a consequence of an already formed attachment as well as a precipitating condition for the formation of new affectional bonds .... Gratitude is also likely to build and strengthen a sense of spirituality, given the strong historical association between gratitude and religion.[38]

Thus, on the basis of these findings, as well as findings from other studies of gratitude effects, it appears that in general, feeling grateful not only increases your sense of well-being, but also builds social resources for weathering whatever the future might bring, increasing the likelihood of viewing one's life as pretty good after all!

The roots to altruistic giving are both biological and cultural. That is, reciprocal benefit—giving and receiving "gifts" that enhance well-being for both the giver and the recipient—are found in subhuman species, from fish

36. Emmons and McCullough, "Counting Blessings versus Burdens," 377.
37. Ibid.
38. Ibid., 388.

to primates. But the *expression* of gratitude, as in all things human, is shaped by our context—our culture and the expectations built into our various social groupings. We are taught from cradle onward the mode of expressing all forms of virtuous behavior, including saying "thanks" for a gift.

In Margaret Visser's *The Gift of Thanks*, she notes that in addition to reciprocal "gift" giving found in animal studies, "reciprocal altruism is to be found in nearly all known human cultures . . . . People do come to each other's aid in times of danger. They often help the weak—the old, the young, the sick, and wounded; they share food and implements and knowledge. These actions are believed to occur because they meet the essential criterion of natural selection: that of 'small cost to the giver and great benefit to the taker.'"[39]

But again, our particular culture in which we dwell shapes the expression of this universal trait. There are *rules* of gift giving and receiving that must be followed. For example, for a gift to be truly a gift, it has to be freely given, not extracted under duress. And there usually is a surprise quality to the gift giving and so most gifts come "wrapped" in some way or another. And one who receives is to give thanks for the other's generous largesse, and not return the favor until some time has elapsed, in order not to appear to "pay for" what has been freely given. Gift-giving rules differ from east to west, and Visser's book is a lovely history of such gifting customs. But the rules have to be learned, because universally ingratitude is seen as a disrespectful disregard, an insult to the giver.

As Emmons and McCulloch demonstrated in their study cited above, gratitude essentially involves social bonding. We are grateful *to* another—someone who has bestowed a benefit on us, who has shown devotion or sympathy to us—"implying movement and binding to another—or to a group that includes the other" where the receiver "consents to entering into relationship with the donor."[40] Echoing Emmons and McCulloch's linkage of gratitude with spiritual growth, Visser concludes that "gratitude is of inestimable importance to all of society . . . it also contributes to the spiritual well-being of every person, but especially to those who are thankful."[41] We'll return to the role of gratitude when we turn our attention to the role that religion plays as we author the story of our lives.

---

39. Visser, *The Gift of Thanks*, 30.
40. Ibid., 374.
41. Ibid., 4.

Gratitude and Elevation: The Role of Biography

Author Gabrielle Hamilton, when asked who her favorite writer was, answered more generally, "the perfectness of reading is when a book hits you and you hit it and during those hours you are completed in a way you have never been before. The *you* you were when you started the book is no longer; you are changed forever after; you become somehow denser, more solid and yet clearer and cleaner and more organized in your heart and mind at the same time."[42] As I have tried to make clear in these pages, I believe this is true in the dynamic of reading, as well as listening to songs that move us profoundly. In general, if the story in the book—fiction or nonfiction—or if the song's lyrics touch the great questions of our life like love, loss, God, and death, the effects on the reader or listener can be profound.

Biography is of course within the genre of nonfiction (although as we said earlier, all biography—whether memoir or telling the life of someone else—is at best somewhat fictional, "truthy" because our memories are not perfect and we do tend to remember and fill in the blanks with imagined meaning). Jonathan Haidt is a psychologist who has studied among other things the moral effect of some biographical descriptions that he terms "elevation."

We visited some of Haidt's work in an earlier chapter when we discussed the evolutionary roots of moral intuition shaped by culture into virtuous behavior. In the case of elevation, he considers this an evolved moral sense we have inherited from our earliest ancestors—adaptive because our species became attracted to those who contributed to the well-being of their tribe—adaptive for the community that benefitted from altruistic behavior of some specially favored members. This is part of our inherited disposition then and now.

Haidt quotes Thomas Jefferson, who responded to a friend asking for Jefferson's advice about books he should collect for his library. Jefferson writes, "When any ... act of charity or of gratitude, for instance, is presented either to our sight or imagination, we are deeply impressed with its beauty and feel a strong desire in ourselves of doing charitable and grateful acts also .... Now every emotion of this kind is an exercise of our virtuous dispositions; and dispositions of the mind, like limbs of the body, acquire strength by exercise." Jefferson goes on to cite "the fidelity of Nelson, and generosity of Blanford ... [that] elevate [the reader's] sentiments .... Does he not in

---

42. Hamilton, "Gabrielle Hamilton."

fact feel himself a better man while reading them, and privately covenant to copy the fair example?"[43]

In a summary of empirical studies examining the effects of being "elevated" by exposure to acts of generosity and self-giving—for example, watching a film of Mother Theresa caring for the homeless and dying on the streets of Calcutta—those elevated by biographical sketches or other displays of generosity, seemed to be opened up, to "turn their attention outward, toward other people." Haidt links such pro-social effects with studies that show, in general, that such positive emotions tend to motivate people to build socially oriented skills and selfless giving to others that will then benefit the giver in the long run—again, adaptive all the way around, for both self and community.

In a summary table of his research findings, Haidt describes four features he and his colleagues have found associated with elevation: this moral emotion tends to well up in the face of "people moving up, blurring human-god divide"; motivating them to "open up, help others," causing them to feel emotionally "lifted up, optimistic about humanity"; and physically, reporting a "warm, positive glow." At the end of Haidt's chapter on elevation and its effects, he quotes an autobiographical excerpt sent to him by letter. In this excerpt, the author reflects on what moves him to what he terms "tears of elevation." He writes

> It's the kind of tear that flows in response to expressions of courage, or compassion, or kindness by others .... When John stood in support of the resolution [to welcome gay people into the congregation], and spoke of how ... he was the first gay man to come out at First Parish, in the early 1970s, I cried for his courage. Later, when all hands went up and the resolution passed unanimously, I cried for the love expressed by our congregation in that act. That was a tear of celebration, a tear of receptiveness to what is good in the world, a tear that says it's okay, relax, let down your guard, there are good people in the world, there is good in people, love is real, it's in our nature ... now the love pours in.[44]

When I read that excerpt, it brought to mind a similar moving experience in my own life. As I discussed in an earlier chapter, at one time I was very active in the anti-death penalty movement in Richmond, and am still quite opposed to state-sponsored killing of human beings. One year, I authored a resolution against the death penalty that went before our Diocesan

---

43. Haidt, "Elevation and the Positive Psychology of Morality," 275–76.
44. Ibid., 287.

Council—the annual gathering of clergy and lay people to discuss and resolve important church issues and offer guidance and advice to the bishop.

The son of one of the clergy present at the meeting had been murdered recently by someone now imprisoned for the killing. All knew how difficult the whole issue and subsequent floor discussion was for him, as speaker after speaker came to the microphone to support or oppose the resolution. Finally he stood and walked to the front. The entire two hundred or so gathered hushed so that you could hear the proverbial pin drop. In an emotion-laden voice he talked about his own struggle with the grief still in him. Finally, he concluded by saying that however, with God's help and grace, he now was speaking in favor of the resolution to do away with the death penalty in Virginia.

And with one accord, the entire body of the Council stood and started clapping—with tears running down the faces of many, including my own. It was an amazing, moving moment of witness to the forgiveness and goodness that we humans are capable of displaying. And as the writer of the above excerpt says, it gives hope that goodness is real and in the end, will outstrip evil that at times infects us.

My role in leading this fight against the death penalty was a direct result of having been "elevated" by the autobiographical account by Sister Helen Prejean in the book *Dead Man Walking*. Other autobiographies have played a shaping role in my past life—for example, the Trappist Thomas Merton's *The Seven Story Mountain* had a strong influence on me in my late teens as I struggled with the thoughts of a religious vocation. Currently, I have been deeply moved by the generosity displayed by Etty Hillesum in her collection of letters and diary excerpts entitled *An Interrupted Life*.

When I was ordained to the priesthood in 1996, a priest friend of mine gave me a copy of *An Interrupted Life*. It's the story of a young Jewish girl who grew up in Holland, and was gripped by the Nazi political influence and finally absolute control during World War II. Etty, along with her entire family, was confined to a prison camp near Amsterdam, and finally transported to Auschwitz where she was murdered at the age of twenty-nine.

I have recently reread this work. And I have again been as moved—or perhaps more so now than decades ago—by her courage and her compassion and deep love for not only her fellow Jews, but also for humanity as a whole. She showed great grace and dignity and generosity in the face of evil, and even when she knew for certain that she was headed for death, her thoughts were of others. It's a moving account, and in the end, brought "tears of elevation" to my eyes all over again with the rereading.

I recently included her story in a sermon delivered at St. John's and many eyes glistened with tears of elevation when confronted with her sheer goodness. Which brings me to the role of God in moving our humanity to such heroic acts of generosity and self-giving out of gratitude for life itself. As Gabrielle Hamilton said, the me that was there when I began reading that book became a different and in many ways, transformed me after the reading.

Gratitude and God

In her *The Gift of Thanks*, Margaret Visser finally links the expression of gratitude—the reaching out and gifting others beyond oneself—to grace-filled transcendence beyond borders. She says "from the smallest event that elicits a felt 'thanks' to an appreciation of kindness that totally opens someone's heart to another, gratitude is a transcending movement, one that 'rises to the occasion.'" This reaching out, this crossing of borders, can then "spiral upwards." "A moving spiral of giving replaces the static boundary line enclosing those 'in' and excluding those 'out.'"[45] In this sense, the giver reaches out and freely gives gifts, and the receiver receives what is given with gratitude . . . and they are linked finally by grace.

Because in the last analysis, all that is good is God's gift, starting with life itself. Visser quotes Dag Hammarskjold who wrote "Night is drawing nigh—For all that has been—thanks! To all that shall be—yes!" Visser says such gratitude is what Christians call grace—the unexpected and undeserved gift of life—"overflowing, supple, joyful, enabling, generous to the point of extravagance"—always enough and more than enough in our lives if our hands are open to receive it.[46] And of course as this author points out, the notion of "grace" is not particular to Christianity. Within Judaism there is the notion of *hesed* and within Islam is the notion of *baraka*—both referring to God's loving-kindness extended to all of God's creatures. The gratitude that can well up in our hearts reflects the grace we can receive in our daily lives.

And finally, Visser insists that such transcendent grace freely given by God can upset our human arrangements, calling us to reach out from our comfort zone to others who are not us but are also in need of grace-filled, loving gifts. And I suppose most amazingly is gratitude expressed for God's grace within life itself—even in pain and hardship. She says

> "All is grace" is the mystical insight achieved in those who reach full realization that, no matter what happens to them, they are

---

45. Visser, *The Gift of Thanks*, 375.
46. Ibid., 376.

creatures—children—of an all-giving, all-loving God. Such people are grateful even in hardship and sorrow—freely and profoundly grateful, incredible as it can seem to ordinary people who have not traveled the distance.[47]

And one who traveled that full distance is that Dutch Jewish woman, Etty Hillesum—who I spoke of a few pages back. Visser ends her chapter with a long quote (a prayer, actually) that Etty wrote while imprisoned at a Nazi transport camp, shortly before she was transported to Auschwitz where she knew, really, that she would die. And yet she prayed:

> [O God] you have made me so rich ... please let me share out Your beauty with open hands. My life has become an uninterrupted dialogue with You, Oh God, one great dialogue. Sometimes when I stand in some corner of the camp, my feet planted on Your earth, my eyes raised toward Your heaven, tears sometimes run down my face, tears of deep emotion and gratitude. At night, too, when I lie in my bed and rest in you, oh God, tears of gratitude run down my face, and that is my prayer.[48]

I included that prayer in the recent sermon that I gave at St. John's. It speaks to my soul—as it has over the years. Her life itself I believe is a gift to us all. Because despite the hell in which she wound up existing under Nazi occupation and imprisonment, she wrote again and again, that "despite everything, life is full of beauty and meaning."[49] Awesome and elevating to those of us who have not yet traveled that distance.

Interlude II: Patty Now

When I introduced Patty to you in the first section of this chapter, I indicated that we had known each other for about a decade and she is currently one of my dearest friends. So the "Patty Now" is the one that I know, and for the most part I'll let her speak for herself.

> I have never been the type of person to follow all the rules and stay "inside the box." I have always had an underlying zest for life and it has at times gotten me into trouble. I have also always been a passionate person—I attack everything in my life with this unbridled excitement. Mike [Patty's late husband] introduced me to the passion of cooking—and that is still one of my

---

47. Ibid., 378.
48. Ibid., 380.
49. Hillesum, *An Interrupted Life*, xx.

greatest pleasures in life. And since Mike's death I have been free to discover other passions. One of those is music and dancing. Any type of music instantly lifts my spirit and brings out the "bubbly, fun-loving" Patty.

My world was shattered when I heard the word "cancer" for the first time [when Mike was diagnosed with advanced melanoma]. I promised Mike that it would all be OK—was I ever wrong. Nothing was ever going to be OK again for the two of us. A little over nine months after being diagnosed with stage four melanoma Mike died peacefully at home while I was holding his hand. I can recount every detail of those nine-plus months—even now seven and a half years after his death. The experience of watching the person you love more than life die a little bit every day changes the very core of your being and I will never be the same again.

While Mike was sick and undergoing treatment, he and I both were able, somehow, to maintain a sense of humor. We actually referred to it as our "gallows" humor—which usually horrified those around us. But keeping laughter present in our lives at that time was an absolute necessity—we would have gone crazy if we couldn't have laughed at all that was happening to us.

Now I don't let the fact that I have no one special in my life stop me from enjoying all that life has to offer. I like to think that my exuberance for life is contagious and that those around me can feel my love and joy and that it helps them get through whatever challenges they face in their own life.

I have amazing friends who love me and support me in all that I do. I laugh a great deal every single day. I find joy in simple things, like cooking a meal for friends (or just myself), listening to music, going to the theater, grocery shopping, running errands, or relaxing with a glass of wine after a busy day. I have never met a stranger. I love to talk to people and to learn about their lives and how they got to where they are in their life. I love my job and look forward (most days) to getting up and going to work.

My past has taught me just how strong a woman I am. And it has also made me realize how precious life is and how important it is to be grateful for every moment, every breath. I don't take anything or anyone for granted and I thank God for my blessings and all that I have every day.

I hesitate to speculate on what my future will hold. If you had asked me this question ten years ago I would have known just what to say. But these past years have proven to me that we never know what lies around the corner and what challenges we will encounter along our journey called life.

Finally, as I have said, my faith and my faith family in my church are integral to my life. I hope that my relationship with God will deepen and strengthen as I enter my later years and that I will continue to grow spiritually.

So there is Patty, an example *par excellence* of someone who—despite some awful losses along the way—has lived her life exuberantly, with gusto, bouncing back for the next round, deeply grateful—like Etty—for all of God's blessings across her days. Lucky to have inherited the traits and stamina that have seen her through, but also shaped by circumstance and communal context to express her zest and live out her life well despite life's losses through the years. I give thanks for such a friend in my life.

Concluding Thoughts

In the introduction to this book, I quoted Oliver Sacks's piece in *The New York Times*—about how he was so looking forward to being eighty years of age. He viewed old age as a time of both freedom and joy in still discovering and relishing the good things of life. In this chapter we looked at some empirical research supporting the notion that indeed, as we age—found in both our near primate relatives as well as found perhaps universally in human samples from around the world—that there is something true about the U-shaped experience of increasing life satisfaction and joy-filled happiness, which then spill over into gratitude and blessing to others beyond our own private domains. Being grateful motivates us to transcend our own selfish interests and contribute to the greater social whole.

Finally, I traced the argument that this growth of wisdom and maturity reflected in the U-shaped experience of those growing older is itself adaptive and hence, possibly one root reason why such wisdom that comes with age is beneficial to humankind as a whole. In a recent op ed essay titled "Gray Hair and Silver Linings," Frank Bruni expresses beautifully what we have been saying here.

> [After about age fifty] more than before, you're able to find the good in the bad. You start to master perspective, realizing that with a shift in it—an adjustment of attitude, a reorientation of expectations—what's bothersome can evaporate and what only seems to be urgent really isn't. . . .

You get older and you let things go. You say goodbye to the most isolating parts of your pride and, if you're lucky, you slough off some of your pettiness.

You finally appreciate the wisdom of doing so, and you come to recognize that among multiple vantage points and an array of responses to a situation, you really can elect the most positive one.

There's truth to those old saws about clouds and silver linings and lemonade from lemons. But it can take a good long while to wake up to that: to divine the lessons beneath the clichés and embrace them without feeling like a sap.[50]

Miroslav Volf, a theologian on the faculty at Yale University and a recipient of a Templeton Foundation grant to study the theology of joy, recently published online an essay about his and his colleagues' initial findings. He defines joy as "emotional attunement between the self and the world—usually a small portion of it—experienced as blessing." He goes on to add that our experience of joy in our lives is usually not an all or nothing affair. But whether it's occasional or more chronic and enduring, whether it's felt as overwhelmingly strong or as a subtle undertow, it's usually blended with other emotions and reflects a life on the whole being well lived—again, with purpose and self-giving.

In that sense, Volf says "joy is best experienced in community. Joy seeks company ('come and rejoice with me') and the company of those who rejoice feeds the joy of each." Finally he stresses that for those who are religious, joy is indeed ultimately found in the "One Good that is both the source and the goal of our existence."[51]

Let me close this chapter on joy with the following observation. Samuel Wells wrote an essay for *The Christian Century* where he described sitting by the bedside and praying with a parishioner who was dying a very slow, painful death. And he asks the question, "Thanks for what?" in the face of such suffering. And he struggles to answer that question for himself.

He talks about our intercessions to God in such extremity, and says under such circumstances such intercession is standing face-to-face before God and demanding "Well, how about it? Show us what you got." But maybe this is true across the whole of our days as we pray for ourselves, our friends, our loves, for strangers who suffer. And then we live out the story of our lives, in both pain and blessing, responding to what God has given.

---

50. Bruni, "Gray Hair and Silver Linings."
51. Volf, "What is the Difference between Joy and Happiness?" para. 13; para. 18.

And so Wells asks "Thanks for what, exactly? Thanksgiving is the flip-side of intercession: God has answered the question, 'What you got?'—and we work out if it's too little—or too much. And I discover that the one who can find the grace to give thanks has been given the power to survive the worst that life can send."[52] It's in the working out of God's answer that we write and rewrite our story . . . filled with blessings for those with eyes to see. Which leads nicely into section II of this work as we examine how we are wired for religion, comfort, and love across our days.

---

52. Wells, "Thanks for What?"

SECTION II

Wired for Religion, Comfort, and Love

Continuing the Story

5

"My Sweet Lord"
God's Lure and the Life Well-Lived

> The power afforded popular performers: the power of communication, the ability—the privilege, really—to transmit the energy that humans require to maintain balanced psyches and to direct their lives in ways that benefit each other. (In spite of it all, I remain idealistic.) The artist can and should project *truth*—truth about feelings, truth about the world, truth about love and sex and relationships, and, if it's in them, truth about the Divine. When I'm onstage and I feel the sensation of being a conduit ... the energy comes from somewhere and feeds me, and therefore the audience, and back again ... a symbiotic loop, flowing amorphously and in perfect sync, when working right.[1]

****

It must have been about 1968. We had moved to Bloomington where my husband had just joined the faculty at Indiana University as an assistant professor. I was determined to finish my undergraduate degree in psychology—I firmly intended to then enter graduate school and earn a PhD in clinical psychology. I was already driven and that was the goal that I set for myself at age twenty-five—despite also having two little boys aged two and four to raise.

---

1. Cockburn, *Rumours of Glory*, 126.

So upon arriving in Bloomington, I immediately enrolled as a psychology major and I also elected religious studies as my minor area of study.

As may be clear by now, the Christian religion was deeply rooted in my bones from childhood forward. But I was also riding a tidal wave whipped up by my generation of Boomers who were fascinated and involved with all things religious of one stripe or another. At the time I was what is referred to as a "practicing Catholic," but I quickly found my way to an underground gathering of Catholic and Episcopal students as part of a home mass worship group led by a hippie priest with a guitar. I can still see him strumming and hear him singing the words to the Beatles' new song "My Sweet Lord." He led into the music with some comment about how he wanted us to learn and sing the song before it became a popular commodity and would lose its radical, inclusive meaning. The lyrics included shades of Indian mysticism. We sang/chanted "Hare Krishna"—not entirely sure who or what we were singing to but sensing the Divine beyond the lyrics.

Yes, those were the days of the underground church and the rise of such ecstatic worship styles as the Catholic Pentecostal movement, including such manifestations of the Spirit as speaking in tongues. Surprisingly this Spirit-led worship style sprang up from its roots at Notre Dame University—the home of the Fighting Irish and one of the rock beds of Catholic intellectual thought in this country.

A perfect reflection of the underground movement within the established churches was a little book that came out in paperback in 1965 (costing seventy-five cents!) titled *Are You Running with Me, Jesus?* by a radical, anti-establishment activist Episcopal priest named Malcolm Boyd. I bought a copy of that book and read the prayers within it. The topics mirrored the social concerns of the anti-establishment religious movement of the times. Prayers for a "free self," a "free society," for "racial freedom," prayers for the city and the campus, for "sexual freedom," and so on. The opening prayer from which the title was drawn is imprinted in my brain to this day. In part, Boyd prays:

> * I've got to move fast . . . get into the bathroom,
> wash up, grab a bite to eat, and run some more . . . .
> *Where am I running? You know these things
> I can't understand. It's not that I need to have you
> tell me. What counts most is just that somebody
> knows, and it's you. That helps a lot.
> * So I'll follow along, okay? But lead, Lord.
> Now I've got to run. Are you running with me,
> Jesus?[2]

---

2. Boyd, *Are You Running with Me, Jesus?*, 19.

Not only did I buy this little book and read it from cover to cover (or rather, pray it from cover to cover) around 1968, but I remember also buying my parents a copy—of all things. If I remember the scene, my dad had a slightly puzzled look on his face as I presented them with my gift on one of their visits to Bloomington. I have my doubts that they took it back home with them as a treasured collection of radical prayer/poems, but they took it with them anyway. They probably filed it lovingly on some back bookshelf as a gift from their "girl."

Like Pete Seeger, Boyd was on the left side of almost every social issue of the times. In one sense, he was ahead of his time. As a gay man and activist priest, he "came out" in 1977 and due to his extensive writing and social prominence, he became well known as an openly homosexual clergy person in the days when most remained in the closet. In 1968, Boyd edited another little book titled *The Underground Church*.[3] Again, like his prayer/poems in *Are You Running with Me, Jesus?*, the chapters—concerned with peace and freedom, civil rights, black power and the kingdom of God, the church as underground and "counter-sign," the "serving church"—mirror the activist church movement of the '60s and beyond.

So this is a little taste of the religious center to many of our Boomer lives at that time: a religious fervor that was restless, seeking, experimenting, and hoping for a new world order that my idealistic generation would bring about through not only social protest and street marches, but also through prayer and witness, expressed through ecstatic worship styles—embracing various forms of mysticism, both eastern and western. This restless movement and anti-establishment energy were reflected in the songs we sang and the books we read. Let's look a little more closely at the scene back then as we immerse ourselves in those decades of the '60s and '70s—searching for existential meaning, firing our imaginations and our communal lives.

THE SCENE BACK THEN: "THE SOUNDS OF SILENCE"

The courses I elected to satisfy my outside minor requirement were within the Religious Studies Department, which had been a Religious Studies Program at its founding. But the chair and faculty petitioned the faculty senate and other powers that be at the university to become a full-fledged, degree-granting academic department. I recall that there was a great deal of controversy and wrangling in that deliberative faculty body over the wisdom of granting departmental status to an area concerned with *religion*! Were they

---

3. Ibid., *The Underground Church*.

going to proselytize? I think it was those in the "hard" sciences (for example, physics) who voiced the greatest concern over such a move.

But in the end, departmental status was granted. And this was a sign of the times. It quickly turned out that the Department of Religious Studies had huge enrollments in its undergraduate courses—I being one of the hordes of students clambering for entrance into both lower- and upper-level class offerings. In fact, I not only took every class offered that I could squeeze into my schedule, but also—when I did finish my undergraduate studies and immediately entered the PhD program in psychology, my first year's teaching assistantship was in the Religious Studies Department. As it turns out, I wound up lecturing in the introductory religion class I had enrolled in a few short years earlier.

And of course there was the music. A religious and spiritual *zeitgeist* was in the air and in many of the songs we listened to and sang along with. As Dan Levitin puts it, "Some form of music accompanies every behavior that even remotely resembles a religious practice worldwide, from the Pentecost Islanders' male puberty ritual, to ancient Egyptian funeral services, to a contemporary Catholic Mass."[4] As we've seen in earlier chapters, music is the tie that binds communities together and shapes individual lives into a shared narrative. And the most inclusive and sweeping narrative of all is a transcendent one.

But something happened to community and traditional expressions of religion and thus its music in the '60s and '70s. In January of 1970, *The Annals of the American Academy of Political and Social Science* devoted a whole issue to the topic: "The Sixties: Radical Change in American Religion." In the opening paper introducing the topic, Sydney Ahlstrom comments about the increasing use of terms such as *postmodern* and *post-Christian* to describe the times. He says "the decade of the 1960s was a time, in short, when the old grounds of national confidence, patriotic idealism, moral traditionalism, and even of historic Judeo-Christian theism, were awash."[5] Ahlstrom concludes his paper thus:

> Because the national scene looks hopeless, and with so many hopeful leaders prematurely in their graves [for example, the Kennedy brothers, Martin Luther King, Malcolm X] the tendency to irrational destructiveness or withdrawn communalism is very strong. In any event, the yearnings that underlie these responses and these temptations provide the ground in which radical theology sends down its roots and draws its

---

4. Levitin, *The World in Six Songs*, 205.
5. Ahlstrom, "The Radical Turn in Theology and Ethics," 3.

nourishment, seeking to bring a measure of transcendence, hope, and community to those who are alienated from technocratic society generally, from the American nation-state in its present orientation, and from outworn forms of religious life and practice. The future of this theology, however, is unknown.[6]

As we shall see in the pages ahead, we are living that future now, and I believe it's important to try to understand its roots in our generation's search for transcendent meaning beneath the taken-for-granted social arrangements of the everyday surface—both then and now.

As Ahlstrom also noted and as I've described in earlier chapters, we were a post-war generation who grew up in an affluent culture, a television generation whose easy optimism went sour with the social upheaval of the times. Talk of "moonshots, nuclear testing, discussion of an ABM defense system, and the stark possibility of human extinction" all contributed to "old-time religion" malaise.[7]

And this stark and questioning malaise is reflected in the lyrics of many of our songs at the time. The last verse of Simon and Garfunkel's "The Sound of Silence" is bleak: "And the people bowed and prayed/To the neon god they made/And the sign flashed out its warning/In the words that it was forming/And the sign said, 'The words of the prophets are written on the subway walls/And tenement halls'/And whispered in the sounds of silence."[8] This tone of restless and searching darkness is also expressed in their *Bookends* album and the lyrics for "America." The words paint a picture of two kids boarding a bus in Pittsburgh to go find some meaning to their lives. The last verse's poem reads "'Kathy, I'm lost,' I said./Though I knew she was sleeping./'I'm empty and aching and/I don't know why'/Counting the cars/On the New Jersey Turnpike./They've all come/To look for America,/All come to look for America.'"[9] They were hoping to find something that would make sense of their lives.

If you listen closely to the lyrics of the Beatles' song "Eleanor Rigby," you will also hear the sounds of a dying church and the lostness of souls adrift in a meaningless life . . . all those lonely people . . . where do they all belong? And you have this vision of Fr. McKenzie sitting at night, darning his socks, alone and lonely with no one to come and no one to save. And after Eleanor Rigby died, Fr. McKenzie buried her and no one came. She died *in* the church—alone. "And was buried along with her name/Nobody

---

6. Ibid., 13.
7. Ibid.
8. Simon and Garfunkel, "The Sound of Silence."
9. Simon and Garfunkel, "America."

came/Father McKenzie, wiping the dirt from his hands as he walks from the grave/No one was saved."[10]

Bleak. But you could argue that, for one reason or another, humans inherit a religious impulse, a desire for religious transcendence, a pull toward worshiping a God by some name. In the '60s and '70s (and again, into today) this religious impulse turned toward untraditional sources—from Zen Buddhism and various other forms of Eastern theism—to other channels of mystical experience such as psychedelic drugs, communal experimentation, and the occult.

George Harrison of the Beatles, Cat Stevens, and Leonard Cohen (the Canadian singer and songwriter who wrote, among many other pieces, "Suzanne" and "Hallelujah") all turned toward Eastern mysticism, living out at least part of their lives in a monastic environment. Many of the songs on Harrison's two-album CD, *All Things Must Pass*—including "My Sweet Lord," "What Is Life?" "Art of Dying," and "Hear Me Lord"—are spiritually searching songs reaching out and in to find deeper meaning beneath the banality of our existence.

Bruce Cockburn is a Canadian song writer and singer whose life and lyrics perfectly reflect the Boomer years then and now. I did not know his music until I was introduced to his life's story in an interview of him published recently in the journal *Image*. The conversation centered on the 2014 release of his memoir titled *Rumours of Glory*. I immediately bought and read the book, and because his journey from his youth to middle age is so reflective of the radical decades when we came of age, I'm going to focus a bit on him here before turning to the biographies and fictional narratives that also played a large part in shaping me and others in the then of our lives.

In the introduction to *Rumours of Glory*, Cockburn reflects on the essential role that music has played in his life. He says "in a way we, and all living things, are made of music.... Music eased my searching and often angry adolescent soul. My grown-up wanderings, sometimes no less angry, are largely catalyzed by, and reflective of, music. Music is my diary, my anchor through anguish and joy, a channel for the heart."[11] Again, his whole life from then to now iconically captures the Boomer journey.

Cockburn's early music in the late '60s and early '70s was a spiritual/folk sound, which became more overtly religious after his conversion to Christianity in 1974. His conversion experience happened during the wedding ceremony with his first wife. He writes, "At that moment, when I held

---

10. The Beatles, "Eleanor Rigby," words and music by John Lennon and Paul McCartney, Copyright 1966 by Sony/ATV.

11. Cockburn, *Rumours of Glory*, 4.

Kitty's hand to place her ring, I became aware of a presence standing there with us—invisible to the eye but as solid and obvious as any of the people in the room. I felt bathed in the figure's energy. I shivered and said . . . 'it's got to be Jesus.' Who else would it be [in a Christian church]? He spoke no words, but the presence was real, male, and loving."[12]

Later, in part because of extensive foreign travel and exposure and adoption of protest politics, Cockburn's religious sensibilities turned toward more mystical expression and away from orthodox, fundamentalist Christianity. He noted that as often as you would find Christian influence in his lyrics, you'd also find elements of Buddhism—the Buddhists being great "technicians of the sacred." In addition, reflecting his Boomer disillusionment with big government and the military/industrial complex, Cockburn's music also turned toward what he refers to as "witnessing songs," songs of protest against injustice, and in particular against US military ventures in Central and South America. After witnessing a US-backed military attack on a Guatemalan refugee camp, Cockburn wrote the song "If I Had a Rocket Launcher" that became a Top 40 hit in 1983. The last verse goes: "I want to raise every voice—at least I've got to try/Every time I think about it, water rises to my eyes./Situation desperate, echoes of the victim's cry/If I had a rocket launcher/Some son of a bitch would die."[13]

Fairly early in his career, Cockburn discovered that his music had power over his audiences' embodied and emotional responses. At first he recoiled, thinking "things are getting out of hand. People want to dance at these shows. Oh my god, that's not me. I can't be responsible for inciting this sort of madness."[14] But like other rock artists he finally adapted to his audiences' enthusiasms, recognizing that music works on the body through the brain's chemical processes. You play with a beat and audiences are going to want to dance! As we've seen throughout these pages, that's the way the brain works. For Cockburn and others of a transcendent bent, the musician becomes a conduit for the Divine. What I'm going to take up in the science section of this chapter is what I have already referred to as God of the synapse. But I'll let Cockburn anticipate that discussion with this reflection.

> The Divine infiltrates our being and manifests, as it must, through the electrochemical processes in our brains . . . . Christianity is based on the Divine touching a human. So is Islam, so is Taoism or Shinto, and so are the animist beliefs that are all over Africa. The Divine is there in any case, no matter the

12. Ibid., 115.
13. Ibid., 226.
14. Ibid., 125.

> ism or structure that goes with it. It's as if God is the matrix in which we move, if we were only aware of it. The Divine touches us. We feel it as a species. We hunger for it.... We were made that way, devised and constructed to be in [the world] *and* of it. If you're not in your body, how are you going to hear the whisper of the Divine, the visceral nudge we call a hunch? How else but through the deepest feelings can we convince our ... minds to receive these boundless truths?[15]

Cockburn admits to being a Boomer through and through, suspicious of all things that smack of authority, focusing primarily on the individual, with a waxing and waning nod to community ties. He has no illusions about the evil and injustice and greed endemic to human institutions from local to national, from private to public. So he is clear-eyed about what he refers to as the distortions that occur "when the gifts of God are translated by cultural gatekeepers somewhat deaf for the Divine," as well as by the more extreme radicals in the world—the Talibans of the world who try to murder young girls who want an education, the brutal dictators who would rather starve their own people than give up power.

And yet in the recent interview published in the journal *Image*—now in his late sixties and looking back over a lifetime of singing and protest, Cockburn embraces a hope for us as individuals and hope for our species as a whole. He says:

> I have hope in God for us as individuals. I have hope that doesn't stand up to rational scrutiny. Of course, I still hope we get by as a species. I hope we don't kill ourselves off. I hope we don't destroy things to the point where life on earth becomes even more hellish for many of the people who currently live on it.
>
> I hope all those things, but what do I base that on? Not much. Just what my heart tells me that I need. But I believe that as individuals we have the ability to transcend that stuff through a connection with the divine. That connection can be nurtured and brought to life, or it can be ignored. That's a choice ... God is out there. God is in here. God is the flow of everything, and you can align yourself with that flow or you can stand in resistance to it, in which case it will flow right over you. If you are successful though at resisting it, you will just become collateral damage to the flow, I think. But maybe not. Maybe you just have to flow along further before you get redeemed.[16]

---

15. Ibid., 341.
16. Cockburn, "A Conversation with Bruce Cockburn," 49–50.

Bruce Cockburn has come a long way from the born-again Christian that he became in 1975. The religious sense that he now embraces is inclusive, with pluralistic influences from various world religions. Later in the chapter we'll see this Boomer embrace of "spiritual but not religious" openness to Divine transcendence as typical of our generation—including both those within, as well as those outside of mainline churches.

But for now, I want to focus on the early shaping and expression of our Boomer values beyond the music we heard and rhythmically moved to, to consider the books—primarily biographical stories—that shaped our brains, our values, and thus our lives. Interestingly, Cockburn also made clear the books he read in his early years that helped form his understanding of God and humanity. Two of those writers have also been important to me—one then and the other more recently in my own life.

One author we shared in our coming-of-age years and already mentioned in these pages was the Trappist writer Thomas Merton. I had converted to Roman Catholicism my senior year in high school, and as with most converts, I became quite devout in my religious practice, including the books that I chose to read. During my freshman year at St. Mary's College, Notre Dame, I embraced with a vengeance the idea of becoming a nun.

And for some incredible reason, I also decided that I wanted to join the Order of Our Lady of Africa—better known as the White Sisters. This necessitated my learning French (for some reason I don't remember), and I spent the summer between my freshman and sophomore years at St. Mary's attending Laval University in Quebec in order to take a summer course in conversational French. I boarded with an elderly French Canadian woman and her sister, and other than having a couple of adventures with men—one a waiter at the Hotel Frontenac, the other a law student I met at the university that summer—I remained determined, at least for that summer, to become a nun.

One of my most vivid memories from that summer was sitting on a bench in the square across the way from the Hotel Frontenac as I finished reading the last page of Merton's now classic autobiography, *The Seven Storey Mountain*. I have right now in front of me that original, first edition which was published in 1948. Merton ends on a meditation where he imagines God speaking to him.

> Do not ask when [your stripping of all ego investment and absolute solitude] will be or where it will be or how it will be: On a mountain or in a prison, in a desert or in a concentration camp, or in a hospital or at Gethsemani. It does not matter. So do not

ask me, because I am not going to tell you. You will not know until you are in it.

But you shall taste the true solitude of my anguish and my poverty and I shall lead you into the high places of my joy and you shall die in Me and find all things in My mercy which has created you for this end and brought you from Prades to Bermuda to St. Antonin to Oakham to London to Cambridge to Rome to New York to Columbia to Corpus Christi to St. Bonaventure to the Cistercian abbey of the poor men who labor in Gethsemani:

That you may become the brother of God and learn to know the Christ of the burnt men.[17]

Merton closes the book with the Latin words *Sit finis libri, no finis quaerendi*—"let this be the end of the book, not the end of the search."

Merton's whole life was a search, a pilgrimage, which took him from the places he imagines God to have recited to the Trappist abbey of Gethsemani in Kentucky. But his relentless search for God led him also to a hermitage on the edge of that property, and then to a wandering search over the years for the perfect monastic silence in other houses. Merton finally forged a searching engagement with Eastern Buddhism and then died an early and tragic death by electrocution caused by a faulty fan in a hotel in Bangkok.

In a sense, I grew up with Merton—at least I grew up spiritually with his writings. His books had a profound effect on me and on many others at the time and over the years since. In fact, *The Seven Storey Mountain* is alone credited with causing an upsurge of men and women petitioning to enter various monastic communities especially during the 1950s and 1960s.

In his *The Life You Save May Be Your Own*, Paul Elie notes that Merton's book was a best seller not despite the fact that it was religious, but because it was a profound account of one man's firsthand religious experience. He imagines Merton saying "here is what it feels like to be in the grip of God . . . God exists . . . . The way to seek God is first-hand, through religious experience. So I have done. Here is the story. Now go and do likewise."[18] Merton finally grasped his whole life as a monastic call from God, giving his life a wholeness, a story. As Elie sees it, Merton imitated the Christian story in his own life—"that of the individual soul's peregrination to God."[19]

Elie's book is a beautifully written biographical weaving of the lives of four Catholic religious writers—Merton, Dorothy Day, Flannery O'Connor,

---

17. Merton, *The Seven Storey Mountain*, 422–23.
18. Elie, *The Life You Save May Be Your Own*, 170.
19. Ibid., 151.

and Walker Percy. He cast each life as a pilgrimage, with these major religious writers creating masterful works within the story of their own life's pilgrimage. In the introductory pages to his book, Elie defines what he means by pilgrimage: "A journey undertaken in light of a story." Each of these writers he examines created works that are "set on the border between life and art, between faith and doubt, [describing] that experience with rare clarity and power.... At its best, it is writing that one reads into one's whole life, testing the work against one's own life and vice versa."[20]

Of course thinking back over the chapters in this present book, this is exactly the kind of response to story—whether told in a song's lyrics, in a profound novel, or in an autobiography such as Merton's or in the other works that Elie considers—a reader or listener response that matters as we shape our own life story. As Elie says, you test the work against your own life experience and examine your life against the biographical pilgrimages captured in important works like these four authors writing on the edge between art and life.

Dorothy Day, a second author that Elie weaves into his pilgrimage theme, was also one writer cited by Bruce Cockburn as having an important effect in his own radical journey. A founder of the Catholic Worker Movement, a convert to Catholicism, a social activist who told the story of the urban poor from the inside, Day embraced poverty the way that Merton embraced monastic solitude and silence.

The image I have in my memory about Day's writing is sitting with a bunch of fellow Catholics—"underground" free thinkers in my Bloomington years—discussing a long biographical sketch and interview of her in some issue of *The Catholic Reporter*—a liberal Catholic newspaper then as well as now. We were all inspired by her life and sat around our living room talking about what it would be like to embrace poverty in such a radical way. We never did, of course. But Day's living out of her solidarity with those who had little or nothing had an impact on us just the same. As I remember, her voluntary poverty also raised feelings of guilt and wonder and admiration for such a way of life.

Elie notes that because postwar America was on the whole prosperous, the abject poverty of failed farms, closed mines, and impoverished mill towns, and the stark poverty found in the underbelly of cities where the rich did not venture, divided our society into haves and have-nots, which of course persists to this day. Dorothy Day and her co-workers in the Catholic Worker Movement voluntarily lived that poverty, dwelling in blighted neighborhoods, sharing what they had with neighbors in need.

20. Ibid., x; xiii.

Dorothy Day was a prolific writer and tireless champion of the poor. She died penniless. William D. Miller ends his biography of her with the question, "What was her legacy? It was nothing material, for the New York archdiocese felt it appropriate to pay for the opening of her grave. Her legacy was vision—a vision of ending time with its evil nightmares by bringing Christ back on Earth"[21]—by hoping to usher in the kingdom of God with justice and plenty for all.

I can't close this section without at least mentioning one other autobiographer that meant a great deal to me back then. At about the same time we were admiring Dorothy Day's life, I was also reading and listening to Viktor Frankl's lectures about the existential therapy he called "logotherapy," which aimed at helping patients discover meaningful and authentic lives as human beings. I have an image of lying on the floor of our living room in Bloomington, absorbed in these lectures recorded on reel-to-reel tapes. This was probably around 1969 or 1970—as I was finishing my undergraduate studies and absolutely enamored of all things existential. Frankl lectured about his experiences surviving a Nazi death camp and how while in that place he both witnessed, and himself gave witness to, what it meant to be human under inhuman conditions.

In a revised edition of *From Death-Camp to Existentialism* combined with an introduction to logotherapy under the title *Man's Search for Meaning*, Frankl was lyrical in his description of the possibility of a noble life even in the face of extreme cruelty and hardship. Allow me to share a bit of his writing with you because even today, I find the words quite inspiring.

> The way in which a man accepts his fate and all the suffering it entails, the way in which he takes up his cross, gives him ample opportunity—even under the most difficult circumstances—to add a deeper meaning to his life. He may remain brave, dignified and unselfish. Or in the bitter fight for self-preservation he may forget his human dignity and become no more than an animal. Here lies the chance for a man either to make use of or to forgo the opportunities of attaining the moral values that a difficult situation may afford him. And this decides whether he is worthy of his sufferings or not.[22]

As to the question of religion and where God might fit into all of this, Frankl was Jewish and was swept up into the Holocaust atrocity. It isn't clear how observant a Jew Frankl was, but in one place in his book he says "in a last violent protest against the hopelessness of imminent death, I sensed my

---

21. Miller, *Dorothy Day*, 518.
22. Frankl, *Man's Search for Meaning*, 67.

spirit piercing through the enveloping gloom. I felt it transcend that hopeless, meaningless world, and from somewhere I heard a victorious 'Yes' in answer to my question of the existence of an ultimate purpose."[23]

Still amazing to me was the religious practice that continued to flourish in such deathly circumstances. Frankl notes that there existed in many prisoners a depth of religious piety that was heartfelt and often amazing to new arrivals. He says, "Most impressive in this connection were improvised prayers or services in the corner of a hut, or in the darkness of the locked cattle truck in which we were brought back from a distant work site, tired, hungry and frozen in our ragged clothing."[24] And yet. They prayed.

At the end of Paul Elie's book, he speaks of our (whatever you want to call it) postmodern, post-Christian condition as we are the products of protest against authoritarian institutions of all kinds—social, political, or religious in nature, living in a pluralistic and in many ways, essentially secular culture. We are thus thrown back on our own. He says all religious belief exists on the cusp between revelation and projection of our own profound needs in the face of frailty and finitude. But the burden of belief, as he says, rests finally on the individual believer and perhaps this is where it rests all along. Keeping in mind the roles that tradition and community still play, nevertheless, "There is no way to seek truth except personally. Every story worth knowing is a life story."[25]

Maybe there is no better way to end this section than with Elie's own words. "Like it or not, we come to life in the middle of stories that are not ours. The way to knowledge, and self-knowledge, is through pilgrimage. We imitate our way to the truth, finding our lives—saving them—in the process. Then we pass it on."[26] Along with Elie, I think that the writers I have cited here—whose work shaped my own story in one way or another—saw religious meaning in the depths of their own stories; they believed in God's call in their own lives as they lived them out in their pilgrimage. With readers in mind, they put their stories in writing for us to test our own lives against. And we are better for it.

Our Brains, Culture, and God: "Amazing Grace"

There we were—a clergy colleague and me—officiating at a final service in a funeral home for a woman that neither of us had really known. The

23. Ibid., 39.
24. Ibid., 33.
25. Ibid., 472.
26. Ibid.

deceased's daughter-in-law was a faithful church member at St. John's and since the mother-in-law was not actually a churchgoer, we were asked if we would conduct this last service for the poor woman.

Toward the end of the service the Episcopal liturgy (as well as other Anglo-Catholic liturgies) calls for the most solemn of ritual words and gestures referred to as the commendation. At that moment, the clergy take their place usually in front of the altar area where the coffin or ashes within an urn are waiting, and the celebrant begins to intone the prayers, beginning "Into thy hands, O merciful Savior, we commend thy servant _____. Acknowledge, we humbly beseech thee, a sheep of thine own fold, a lamb of thine own flock, a sinner of thine own redeeming . . ."

But before we could get that far, the sound system began blaring out Tom Jones's rendition of "What's New Pussy Cat"! I called out "cut, no, not yet!!" making the cutting-throat sign with my right index finger. Someone in the gathering mumbled "Jane [the deceased] just played the last joke!" and everyone broke out laughing.

At any rate, we finished the solemnities, and then after the blessing, the clergy proceeded down the aisle accompanied by Jones's song.

Now, what is wrong with this picture? In Dan Levitin's discussion of religious songs, he says that songs that have religious meaning are tied to a specific belief story and are bound to ritual displays that participate in that world of meaning. He says that binding of ritual and song is the hallmark of religious music. "Ritual and religious songs are . . . bound to particular times and events, and for the explicit purpose of accompanying, guiding, or sanctifying a specific spiritual act."[27]

So what was wrong with the above picture is this. We were engaged in a solemn ritual, a religious performance in the sense of a performative ritual participating in a world of Christian religious meaning—our story if you will. And Jones's song was simply a shocking and jarring insertion of secular fun into an otherwise solemn occasion. As Levitin points out, we probably all at some level have a sense of what's fitting to the occasion—religious or secular in nature. As he notes, somehow "Pomp and Circumstance" would not be fitting when you're having a romantic dinner date, but "Jingle Bells"—not a religious song but associated with the holidays—is okay to play, even in July. However it would not be fitting to hear a solemn mass sung as elevator music. Just wouldn't fit. Wouldn't be fitting, even if we couldn't say exactly why.

If you remember our discussion of the notion of "affordance" in an earlier chapter, religious music of all kinds—monastic chants, Propers of the

---

27. Levitin, *The World in Six Songs*, 204.

Eucharistic Mass, and so on—afford a sense of the holy, culturally embedded in a religious myth or story encompassing a whole world view. When it is inserted into secular music, the effect is one of jarring shock. That can be an effective device to get the listener's attention and move the hearer to other levels of meaning. But still such practice is shocking because . . . well . . . it's just not fitting.

Nor was Jones's song at the time of the commendation at the close of that funeral. (An aside: I went along with it because the dead woman herself had requested "What's New Pussycat" to be played at the end of her funeral. And since I assumed the solemn ritual would be completed by then, as a pastoral accommodation I saw no harm. But I drew the line when the young staff member at the funeral home made a mistake and interrupted the ritual before it was time. Just not fitting!)

Universally, religious ritual almost always involves music of some kind, including rhythmic chanting. Although other animal species display ritual behavior and "sing" songs for various purposes—to sooth young, to attract mates—only humans sing songs of religious, spiritual meaning, hope and yearning. Levitin points out that all human groups sing such songs and move in prescribed fashion as their tradition embedded in their sacred story dictates. "The musical brain brought a new hum of neural activity between the brain's rational and emotional centers, along with all the billions of new connections possible with the enlarged prefrontal cortex."[28] We became self-reflective creatures, asking questions, trying to understand our living and our dying. Children as young as two years of age grasp some sense of magic or the supernatural in their lives, and ask questions about ultimate concerns like "where was I before I was born?" and "what does it mean to die?" Paul Harris, a developmental psychologist at Harvard, has spent his career studying the development of religious ideas and beliefs in children. He has found that even very young ones do have a profound sense of the Unseen, from the Tooth Fairy, to Santa Claus, to angels that hover. And again, he has found that by as young as two years of age, children engage in various ritual behaviors with spiritual meaning.

As we have seen throughout this book, music binds a community together. And if that community has gathered for a religious purpose, then the ritual and music bind the group in a way that induces trust and comfort by the release of neurochemicals such as "brain-soothing" oxytocin. The whole integrated brain becomes activated in response to religious ritual and song.

The prefrontal cortex responds to patterned input, making sense of sensory stimulation; the emotional centers are activated, in this case with

---

28. Ibid., 220.

soothing, comforting and joyful effects; and the motor centers of the basal ganglia and cerebellum bind "an aesthetic knot around those different neurochemical states of our being, to unite our reptilian brain with our primate and human brain, to bind our thoughts to movement, memory, hopes, and desires."[29] As Levitin points out, the "big idea" of religion is that ultimately, things will work out, life will be better, and in the end, perhaps all will really be well.

Levitin ends his chapter on religious music with a description of his grandmother's funeral. Gathered at her graveside, his family intoned the ancient Aramaic Psalm 131 that begins "Lord, my heart is not haughty, nor mine eyes lofty . . ." and ends with "O Israel, hope in the Lord from this time forth and forever."[30] That music coupled with the ritual of last rites moved all gathered there at her grave to tears.

Religious music has a way of doing that: bringing closure, bringing comfort by tears shed, binding the past, motivating us to hope for what is to come. As one rabbi scholar put it, God doesn't need our songs; we do. From ecstasy-inducing drums that can open up experience of Divine Transcendence to the sweep of Handel's "Messiah," to the singing of "Amazing Grace," we participate in an ancient story with our embodied minds, binding ourselves to that story that in the end gives us hope. There are certain hymns we sing on a Sunday morning at St. John's that can bring me to tears—not because God needs them but because I do.

In addition to comfort, of course, other emotional states are aroused by religious music bound to embodied ritual. In his *Music, Modernity, and God,* Jeremy Begbie cites an amazing quotation from a passage written by St. Augustine in the fourth century. Augustine is commenting on Psalm 32:8, where he likens singing well to God as singing in jubilation. He says, "It is to realize that words cannot communicate the song of the heart . . . then as if bursting with a joy so full that they cannot give vent to it in set syllables, they drop actual words and break into the free melody of jubilation . . . and to whom does that jubilation rightly ascend, if not to God the ineffable? . . . Sing well unto him in jubilation."[31]

Begbie comments about the ultimate limits of speech and the overflowing of meaning beyond words into embodied expression in song, "saying the unsayable." Not that that relieves us from speech, from trying to say what ultimately is beyond our grasp. But there are ways to "say" with our

---

29. Ibid., 226.
30. Psalm 131:1–3.
31. Begbie, *Music, Modernity, and God,* 205.

bodies, our rituals, and our songs that reach the heart and bind us to one another as community of story and belief.

In her book, *Exuberance*, psychologist Kay Redfield Jamison—who we met in the previous chapter when we talked about joy—also focused a bit on religious ecstasy and musical activation of the brain. She cites William James's observation that some who are religious practice as if in a high fever. In religious passion, such religious experiences "add to life an enchantment." In this same vein, Anthony Storr notes "music exalts life, enhances life, and gives it meaning . . . . Music is a source of reconciliation, exhilaration, and hope which never fails . . . an irreplaceable, undeserved, transcendental blessing."[32]

Along with Levitin, Jamison writes that music activates the same neurochemical reward systems in the brain that are activated by play, laughter, sex, and even drugs of abuse. She says that "pleasurable music creates patterns of change in the dopamine and opioid systems similar to those seen during drug-induced euphoric states."[33] If subjects are given an opioid inhibitor such as Naloxone, they report a significant reduction in pleasurable response to musical input.

When discussing his music of the '60s and beyond, Bruce Cockburn mused about how God "infiltrates our being and manifests, as [God] must, through the electrochemical processes in our brains."[34] Recently I posted a blog post with the title "A Taste of Heaven: God of the Synapse." Within that blog, I ask the question: "Is God always present—a Transcendent Presence, impinging upon us and within us in sustaining Spirit—but our incarnate consciousness normally veils God's Presence?" Then I offer the following thoughts.

> After all, in the Christian tradition as well as in other religious traditions, worshipers are admonished to become selfless—to let go of the ego—that can eclipse our experience of the Divine. And if this is the case, does God's Spirit engage us—among other ways—at our most basic neurochemical level in the brain at the neural synapse—that space between brain neurons filled with neurochemicals that inhibit or potentiate cell communication at the base of consciousness?[35]

32. Jamison, *Exuberance*, 160.

33. Ibid.

34. Recommended reading related to God's potential impingement on our brains include the following works: Blum, "The Science of Consciousness and Mystical Experience"; Green, ed. *What About the Soul?*; Newburg and Waldman, *How God Changes Your Brain*; and Trimble, *The Soul in the Brain*.

35. Levy-Achtemeier, "A Taste of Heaven," para. 4. Read this blog and others in their

As we have seen in these pages, scientists have shown that trance-like states can be induced by various means, from music with a beat, drumming, dancing with exuberance, and agents such as psychedelic drugs. I concluded that blog posting by assuring my readers that I was not encouraging the use of illicit drugs!

But there are healthy ways of opening up the mind's receptors to God's impingement. If we are receptive to Divine engagement by various means—music, dance, ritual, silent "mindfulness," and meditative practice—God engages at the very level of our brain cells to inspire and shape our life stories. I will return to this fundamental point in the conclusion to this work.[36]

There are different ways to slice the brain. In Iain McGilchrist's *The Master and his Emissary*,[37] he considers our human brain from left to right hemisphere, rather than from "top to bottom" as we have done up until now. In brief, the right hemisphere (the Master) is the seat of aesthetics, intuitive knowing, and engagement with the particulars of the world—able to grasp the whole of things, the center of musical responsiveness, the emotional, holistic engagement with the world around us.

The left brain (the Master's Emissary) is the practical and useful seat of abstraction, categorization, mechanistic objectivity, in short, of language and scientific method. And it is the left brain that has taken over our world of reality, gaining prejudicial superiority over our more intuitive selves. The result is that in our postmodern worship of science, we live in an increasingly alienated world of abstract fact—divorced from our incarnated wholeness and spiritual/emotional depths. And in the process, argues McGilchrist, we have lost our I-Thou engagement with both our world and with God. The result is that we are in danger of our spirits, of our religious sensibilities "withering away."

Like all of the scholars we have called upon here, McGilchrist pleads persuasively for an integrated brain. To give back to our right hemisphere functions the honor they deserve. To nurture our right brain centers—including the right frontal area's neural network controlling our imaginative powers, religious awe, musical attunement, aesthetic appreciation, moral reasoning and humor: all those powers that make us uniquely human. The

---

entirety at www.sandralevy.net.

36. With this thought of God's spirit engaging us at the level of the brain's synapses, I have come to understand that beautiful New Testament passage in Romans 8:26–27 in a new light: "Likewise the Spirit helps us in our weakness; for we do not know how to pray as we ought, but that very Spirit intercedes with sighs too deep for words. And God, who searches the heart, knows what is the mind of the Spirit, because the Spirit intercedes for the saints according to the will of God."

37. McGilchrist, *The Master and His Emissary*.

left hemisphere should, indeed must play its supporting role, enabling us to control and manipulate the world about us. But the right brain "knows" more than can be counted. Our happiness in the end resides there.

****

To reiterate: From the micro level of the synapse to the integrated brain centers extending from forebrain and emotional centers to motor movements of ritualized behavior, we both create and participate in the stories of our lives. And at the level of fiction—in the sense we have used it here, as imaginative narrative that gives shape and meaning to our lives—our stories provide answers to our most fundamental questions regarding life and death. As Jonathan Gottschall says, we are not only *homo fictus*—a species wired for story—we are also "spiritual apes," wired for a sense of the sacred and an inborn sense of moral order.

In his *The Storytelling Animal,* Gottschall along with others[38] argues that there is a good evolutionary argument that we are born to be "religious"—whether we name our god as God or as science or as art or as humanistic virtues. He says that there must be some reason for the religious impulse to have expressed itself from earliest, prehistoric times because religious rituals and all that goes with them are not practical. It took time and energy to practice cave art, to carve sacred images and so on. Thus, religious belief and practice were either evolutionary adaptations (for example, engendering trust through brain soothing rituals, bonding communities together, reducing intra-tribal discord) or a social by-product of chance mutations that allowed our human brains to generate answers to questions of ultimate concern.

In fact, it was likely both. But in either case—adaptation or by-product—a religious belief system helped define a group of like believers; provided rules to live by, controlling and punishing social offenders; and thus promoted group bonding and solidarity.

As psychologist Jonathan Haidt has shown, there does seem to be inborn moral senses that we all share and weave into the stories we read and tell. Gottschall says "fiction preaches." Maybe you could argue, as he does, that modern fiction is a bit more morally ambiguous than our narratives used to be. Still, there is a sense of righteous justice when the bad guy gets caught and indignation when he gets away with murder. Certainly the stories we read in Scripture, as well as many of the stories in the novels we read today, "preach" religious morality broadly conceived. Gottschall concludes that "story . . .

---

38. See for example, Brian Boyd's *On the Origin of Stories.*

continues to fulfill its ancient function of binding society by reinforcing a set of common values and strengthening the ties of a common culture."[39]

To sum up this section on going deeper beneath religious ritual, song, and communal expression, we are multilevel creatures, embodied and complex selves, essentially socially bound to other humans. We have enormously developed brains from which our minds have emerged, giving us the power to self-transcend, reflect, imagine, remember, and hope. Out of our minds we have created a culture that provides a menu of meaning—stories, songs, rituals, symbol displays, scientific discoveries—all dynamically impinging on our brains, sculpting them to the end of our own individual lives.

Throughout all of these multiple levels, from the brain synapse to the most sweeping story given by our inherited traditions, we are I believe touched and inspired by God. Ultimately, the well-lived life is one of coherence among all of these levels. Echoing the psychologist Dan McAdams, Haidt says "if your lower-level traits [mostly gene-driven and inherited] match up with your coping mechanisms [goals and strategies culturally learned over a lifetime of shaping], which in turn are consistent with your life story [which you continue to author until nearly your last breath], your personality is well integrated and you can get on with the business of living."[40] And of course, this is the aim of this present book—to assist you in that very process.

Well, enough of the abstraction—that left hemisphere exercise that my written words have expressed as I've attempted to lay out before you a feel for the Boomer '60s and '70s, our religious impulse during those years, and what research suggests as to what we were and how we got that way. Now I want to express a bit of particular engagement—a bit of right brain

---

39. In considering the power of virtuous displays to inspire and "elevate," Haidt details an interesting series of studies that he and his students carried out at the University of Virginia. In brief, experimental subjects who were shown uplifting displays of goodness (for examples, personal testimonies of generosity and redemption vs. humorous TV or sports reruns) reported feelings of being uplifted and "warmed." They also showed evidence of increased vagal nerve activity and the probable release of oxytocin—that hormone known to be "brain-soothing," with communal binding effects eliciting feelings of trust, love, and well-being. In short, the subjects in the elevation condition experienced a significant increase of love for others, even strangers. They were inspired to love in return.

In my own life, as I read Frankl, Merton, Etty Hillesum, Dorothy Day, Sister Helen Prejean, and others, I also have been warmly moved and felt exactly what Haidt described in his research findings. Of course, this says nothing directly about God's role in any of this. But in the major religious traditions we have been considering here, God is a God of love and mercy, and loving others in return is part and parcel of living out a religious story in your life. By definition.

40. Haidt and Joseph, *The Happiness Hypothesis*, 226.

exploration—as I introduce to you Dave, a "typical" but unique Boomer in his own right.

Interlude I: Meet Dave

I have known Dave for the better part of four decades. Known him, liked him, and admired him. I asked him to be part of this book's story because I do think he's a typical Boomer in terms of his individual drive, perfectionism, and spiritual quest. So for the most part, I'll let him speak for himself.

> I graduated from college with a degree in English and a strong interest in literature, journalism, and politics. I moved to Washington, DC, and took a job on Capitol Hill working for a Colorado congressman. Although the congressman was not a lawyer—he had a PhD in education from Stanford—most of the people handling legislation on his staff were lawyers. I was surrounded by them. They had a credential that seemed almost like a union card. They were members of what seemed like a special club and spoke a special language and wrote in a special, precise way. They used language and logic to solve real world problems large and small. It seemed like good training, no matter what career path I ultimately chose. So I enrolled.
>
> During law school I found myself more drawn to courses dealing with the courts, evidence, trials, and constitutional law and less drawn to courses dealing with transactions, tax, will,s and business organizations. There is a wonderful human element in conflict resolution. It has drama, tension, absurdity, and humor. It also has an honored tradition.
>
> When I started practicing thirty-one years ago, I didn't think I could ever be a good legal strategist and courtroom lawyer, but I soon found that I had the tools and talents to be better than most. So I set about to develop those skills, handling a broad range of civil cases over the years, including complex commercial disputes, environmental torts, crop damage claims, personal injury and wrongful death cases, claims related to the wrongful withholding of insurance benefits, and more.
>
> These cases have brought me into contact with many wonderful, intelligent, and interesting people—clients, experts, other lawyers, and judges. I've been blessed to be able to use my skills to address real world problems (micro, not macro) and to have had the opportunity to help some clients through the hardest days of their lives. I've also had an unusual practice that has enabled me to appear in jurisdictions—including two tribal

> courts—throughout the western United States and elsewhere, something that I continue to find fascinating.
>
> I worked tenaciously at the law—on weekends and nights and sometimes on holidays. I wanted to be more than an average lawyer. I wanted to be a good one. I'd come from a clan of achievers, and I wanted to not be left out.

At this point, Dave started to reflect on his personal life—his family and spiritual life—and to consider what else was going on back then as his past story unfolded.

> I also wanted to be a good provider for my family. I wanted my daughters to be able to attend the best colleges and universities. When our daughters were growing up, my wife [who was also trained as a lawyer—they had met in law school] worked full time or part time. We both took on numerous civic and political commitments, she more than I. Gradually, more and more on evenings and weekends, she was gone, attending meetings, volunteering. And my parents were living in town and needed attention. And the dogs. Life was too regimented for too long. And too impoverished.

For all the decades that I have known Dave, one of the bonds that has always tied us together is our hunger for the transcendent. As you'll see here, he was raised Roman Catholic, but as they say, "fell away" from the church of his childhood. Still, throughout his life, he has been on a spiritual quest, a pilgrimage in Paul Elie's sense, a search that has taken him to the Eastern practice of Buddhism. His search also intersected with his personal life dissatisfaction, and like so many other Boomers, he wanted more from marriage than his was able to give. In his own words:

> I was raised in a Roman Catholic family and attended Catholic schools until I was fourteen years old. To my father's dismay, I stopped attending mass during my high school years. I had lost faith in the church's teachings and its politics.
>
> The world to me seemed random, disorderly, and at times very harsh. It was like Tom Stoppard's *Rozencrantz and Guildenstern Are Dead*. You're dropped into a life and then swept along by currents without any orientation, explanation, or roadmap. You fumble your way in search of meaning while you head toward an inevitable end.
>
> I never ruled out the existence of a caring God, I just couldn't make contact with him, her, or it. This didn't stop me from

praying sometimes, like sending a message in a bottle down a river or shooting a time capsule into space. I did it very privately.

Meanwhile, there were people in my life who were dead certain that God does not exist. I was never at all like that. I never had enough confidence in our powers of perception or our individual or collective intellectual capacity to be sure of anything on that scale. And I gradually began to think to myself that there's too much beauty in this life—in the side canyons of the Colorado River, in my daughter's face, in a Chopin Nocturne—for it all to be godless and random.

One of the people in my life who disavowed all religion of any kind was my wife of twenty-seven years. We tried going to her temple a few times when our daughters were young, but it didn't work. And at my urging, we also tried the Unitarian Universalist church, but were both put off—she more than I—by a church and a congregation who together seemed to embrace no particular belief. She decided she wanted no part of any religious organization. Sunday mornings were then for other activities—hikes, the newspaper, talking on the phone to parents and siblings. I acceded.

So we drifted along. We raised our children without any religious orientation. And without any active spiritual life of our own. I felt quite empty.

When our marriage was ending, I turned to meditation for healing and refuge. My readings at the time included Jon Kabat-Zinn and Pema Chodron, whose works are infused with Buddhist thought. I credit these writers with changing fundamentally, and for the better, my approach to life. They prompted me to consider seriously for the first time such notions as that I and we may be inherently good and worthy—if only I could recognize it—rather than fallen and marred by original sin.

In a way, Dave's past—the then of his life—is an example of many of the themes we have already covered in this book: striving for individual perfection, idealism, unwillingness to settle for mediocrity in marriage or career, and directly to the point of this present chapter, a searching for God or spiritual experience outside the borders of conventional religion. We'll revisit Dave at the end of the next section, as we turn to Boomers' religious lives in the years of the new millennium.

THE SCENE NOW: "HALLELUJAH"

One word, charged with centuries of meaning, delivered ironically or solemnly or both. It serves as a prayer, perhaps the great prayer of the modern age, regardless of one's relationship to God. One look at the tears streaming down the faces of a sea of kids singing along with Leonard Cohen at the Coachella Festival demonstrates the ability of this song, with one age-old word at its center, to transport listeners in a way that organized religion has largely failed to do for this generation.[41]

****

There was a knock on my office door in the late afternoon sometime in mid-January, 1995. I had just been ordained to the Episcopal priesthood on Saturday, January 7 of that year—in the midst of an ice storm that caused all kinds of havoc for those driving and flying in for the service and celebration afterwards. The knock on the door to my office at R. E. Lee Memorial Episcopal Church that day in Lexington, Virginia, was delivered by the town photographer.

Turns out that during the ordination service he had stationed himself in the back balcony, where he had a good shot at capturing the action at the moment the Bishops and clergy laid hands on me to pronounce the words: "Therefore, Father, through Jesus Christ your Son, give your Holy Spirit to Sandra; fill her with grace and power, and make her a priest in your Church." And that was it. The moment of transport, the words that would change my life and my identity forever . . . at least in this world. The photographer now presented me with two framed and enlarged photographs of that exact moment of ordination. Today, one of those photos hangs on my kitchen wall, amidst framed handprints of two grandchildren; the other hangs on a wall in one of the bedrooms upstairs that also serves as a study.

The day after that Saturday, the day after a rehearsal dinner and two party celebrations following the service, when all the out-of-town guests had flown or driven away, I remember sitting with my husband, Leo, in our living room in Lexington, saying to him and to myself, "It doesn't get any better than this!" I was euphoric, because it had been a long journey from that Saturday morning when as a seventeen-year-old, I had wandered into St. Isidore's Roman Catholic Church in Nappanee, Indiana, to the Saturday morning in Lexington, Virginia, where two bishops and ten Episcopal

---

41. Light, *The Holy or the Broken*, 228.

priests encircled my kneeling figure and pressed their hands on my head or shoulders and intoned that prayer.

Clearly I was an early Boomer who had maintained her grounding in an orthodox, traditional form of worship and belief. And there are a surprising number of us who have done so, despite all the current noise about the disappearance of organized, traditional forms of religious expression. Yet, even for those of us who have clung to traditional ways, there is an independence of thought and a wariness of authority that still permeates our religious sensibilities.

Several recent books are concerned with contemporary Boomer forms of worship and theological belief systems. Examples include Hoge, Johnson, and Luidens's *Vanishing Boundaries*, Wade Roof's *Spiritual Marketplace: Baby Boomers and the Remaking of American Religion*, and more recently, Linda Mercadante's *Belief without Borders* and Nancy Ammerman's *Sacred Stories, Spiritual Tribes*. In my discussion that follows, I'm going to draw principally from Roof's analysis and Ammerman's fleshing out of today's practice in everyday life.

But before examining the current scene of Boomer practice and looking a little more closely at the rise of "spiritual but not religious" self-identity, I'd like to spend a little time talking about the music and lyrics of Leonard Cohen—who died this past year but whose music captures for me the Boomer questing and questioning spirit. Born in 1934, Cohen—a Canadian poet/songwriter—was of course not technically a Boomer, and most of his music never reached mainstream status here in the United States. But two of his songs—"Suzanne" and "Hallelujah"—were major hits, sung by others like Neil Diamond and Jeff Buckley. I think these two songs capture a sacred and incarnational meaning that rings true to the very depths of our ensouled, holistic selves. At least they ring true to me.

Cohen was Jewish—his grandfather was a rabbi—but he grew up in Catholic Montreal. In a recent piece about Cohen's music that appeared in *Image*, the author Bill Coyle notes that Cohen was always drawn to the figure of Christ. "What appeals most to Cohen about Christianity, and about the figure of Christ, is its insistence on the power of powerlessness, of victory rising from defeat . . . and the desire for brokenness goes through nearly every poem, novel and song that Leonard Cohen has written."[42]

Sometime in the 1990s, when we were living in Pittsburgh—before I up and left academia for the seminary—I discovered the song "Suzanne." I fell in love with it. It transported me as I danced to its music and sang its lyrics—having deep emotional and religious significance for me. I believe

---

42. Coyle, "Heart's Companion," 88.

it was Neil Diamond's rendition that impressed itself on me. I still hear his voice when the song plays. But the lyrics are iconic.

> And Jesus was a sailor/When he walked upon the water . . . /
> But he himself was broken/Long before the sky would open/
> Forsaken, almost human . . .
>
> And you want to travel with him/And you want to travel blind
> . . . /For he's touched your perfect body with his mind.[43]

Much of Cohen's poetry put to music was a blend of the sacred and of human sensuality—in the deepest sense incarnational and whole—seeing all of life as holy in some deep sense. The other work of his that I want to mention here is his song "Hallelujah." I must confess that I have "discovered" this song only of late, although it's made its way through music charts and even in films for decades.

In his *The Holy or the Broken: Leonard Cohen, Jeff Buckley and the Unlikely Ascent of "Hallelujah,"* Alan Light quotes Salmon Rushdie's description of the song's lyrics. Rushdie says that the lyrics are "joyous and despondent, a celebration and a lament, a juxtaposition of dark Old Testament imagery with an irresistibly uplifting chorus. 'Hallelujah' is an open-ended meditation on love and faith."[44] One of Cohen's most famous lines was this: "There is a crack in everything/that's how the light gets in."[45] We're all flawed, and God still flows in through the breaks and cracks in our lives. And his last verse to "Hallelujah" that Cohen retained, despite the reworking, the adding and subtracting in other renditions by other artists, goes like this: "I did my best; it wasn't much./I couldn't feel, so I learned to touch./I've told the truth, I didn't come to fool you./And even though it all went wrong/I'll stand before the Lord of Song/with nothing on my lips but Hallelujah."[46] As we saw in the quotation that opened this section, there is something iconic about that word, something ingrained deep in our brains, something absorbed from millennia of tradition that conveys a sense of holy for those who hear and sing it.

To end this little excursion into Cohen's life and music, let me just mention again here that he followed his sense of sacred right into a Buddhist monastery, the Mount Baldy Zen Center in California, and was there

---

43 Words and music by Leonard Cohen. Copyright 1967 by Sony/ATV Music Publishing LLC, 8 Music Square West, Nashville, TN 37203 and all rights administered by Hal Leonard Company.

44. Light, *The Holy or the Broken*, xvii.

45. Cohen, "Anthem."

46. Words and music by Leonard Cohen. Copyright 1984 by Sony/ATV Music Publishing LLC, 8 Music Square West, Nashville, TN 37203.

ordained a Rinzai Buddhist monk, taking the name of Jikan, meaning Ordinary Silence. His music, like his life, was a blending of Old Testament promise, New Testament passion, and a spiritual quest that took him to the heart of silence. An extraordinary talent and a prefiguring of Boomer pilgrimage today.

Going Deeper: "Here Comes the Sun"

In a recent *New York Times* op-ed piece, Nate Cohn commented on a Pew Research Center report from last year that showed a marked decline in the number of Americans identifying themselves as Christian. The report states that "the decline is taking place in every region of the country, including the Bible Belt."[47] Apparently, a significant proportion of this decline can be attributed to unchurched Millennials. But across generations—Boomers, Gen Xers, and Millennials—there is a significant increase in those willing to check the box of "none" when asked about religious affiliation.

Hence, this cultural phenomenon has been the recent focus of a number of books about our changing and shifting religious scene. Because my main interest is in what is happening now to our Boomer generation in this regard, I was particularly interested in another article appearing last year in the *Times* (yes, I read it religiously!) titled "Examining the Growth of the 'Spiritual but not Religious,'" by Mark Oppenheimer. He reviews a number of recent books on the topic—some of which we will take up here—and says "at the very least, we might conclude that 'spiritual but not religious' isn't necessarily vague or wishy-washy. It's not nothing, although it may risk being everything."[48] In short, if all is included in your spiritual narrative, it has no center of meaning that focuses, grounds, and expresses its essence.

One of the books that Oppenheimer includes in his review is Linda Mercadante's *Belief without Borders: Inside the Minds of the Spiritual but not Religious*. The author is particularly interested in what has become of the religious life of Boomers since the 1970s. She notes that by the late 1970s, there did occur a steep rise in the number of Boomers willing to say they professed "no religion." And many who continued to claim a traditional religious label, still rarely crossed the thresholds of their identified churches. We'll see that for many who still enter the sanctuaries, they do it their way—questioning authority, entertaining doubts, selecting what rules they will follow and what dogmas they will reject.

---

47. Cohn, "A Big Decline in Americans Identifying as Christian."
48. Oppenheimer, "Examining the Growth of 'Spiritual but Not Religious.'"

Mercadante also points out that much of this change was spearheaded by white, middle-class, mainstream Boomers. The picture is more complex when considering other population subgroups such as immigrants, non-whites, and the disadvantaged overall. Still, there was and is a *zeitgeist* in the land, and as she says, no group has been completely able to hold the traditional line against the revolution at their doors. From Post-Vatican II revolts within the Catholic Church laity as well as clergy, to black, feminist, Latin American, and other liberation movements, to the young evangelical "emergent" movements today, "the times they are a-changin'" to quote Bob Dylan. What began in the '60s and '70s has drastically affected the religious landscape today, both inside and outside of religious structures.

Referring back to our discussion in the last chapter, around middle age most humans begin to feel satisfied with their lives, have overall a sense of well-being that tends to increase as they age—that life becomes increasingly meaningful in its second half. In fact, considering life as meaningful is associated with many good things including superior self-reported health, decreased mortality, slower cognitive decline, richer social lives, and adaptation in the work environment.

In earlier chapters of this work, we saw that many writers have characterized the generation of Boomers—among other ways—as searching for and embracing a purpose in life, seeking an authentic self-identity, and expressing an idealistic zeal in their project of self-invention. This is a generation of "me making myself"—in short, as a cohort creating a meaningful life into middle age and beyond. From recent work studying the self-report of meaning in life from large population samples, the authors conclude that life is both pretty meaningful for most people and that having a sense of meaning already does not preclude a continued quest for deeper meaning in one's life.[49] In short, a sense of meaning gives us a sense that our life matters, that it not only makes sense, but that the whole is greater than the sum of years lived.

Now one would expect that by extension, finding life meaningful might be positively correlated with a religious and/or spiritual quest. While it seems to be part of our human nature to journey on a quest for meaning of some sort, this quest imperative has been heightened among the Boomer and Gen X cohorts due to our postmodern, shifting world of pluralistic values—made more immediate through globalization and by the constant presence of the Internet and the use of mobile devices for instant messaging.

49. Heintzelman and King, "Life is Pretty Meaningful." The authors define a meaningful life as "one that has a sense of purpose, and second . . . that possesses significance . . . . The meaningful life makes sense to the person living it, it is comprehensible, and it is characterized by regularity"(562).

As we have seen, many Boomers—and I am one—remain an integral part of an organized, traditional religious institution. In fact, as Nancy Ammerman notes from the results of her own recent research, the majority of Christians, Muslims, Jews, and Buddhists not only remain engaged with their local congregations, but are different in a number of ways from those Seekers and others outside of organized religion. They tend to be more consistently "spiritual," have a richer worship life beyond the church doors, and also tend to be more engaged in group efforts to improve civic life in their communities.

On the other hand, for Seekers, their spiritual quest is more eclectic as many piece together a narrative of belief and practice that they create—not just on their own, since humans by definition are communal creatures, but through what Wade Roof refers to as the "evolution of new structures: to small groups, to extended networks, to informal gatherings and celebrations, to renewed activities within families and businesses, to direct marketing agencies that offer spiritual services in exchange for fees, to reliance on the media and emerging forms of electronic communication."[50] However, as Ammerman says regarding this Seeker group, "when people do not have regular sites of interaction where spiritual discourse is a primary *lingua franca*, they are simply less likely to adopt elements of spirituality in their accounts of who they are and what they do with themselves. If they do not learn the language, it does not shape their way of being in the world."[51]

One interesting effect of our contemporary culture on religious communities—including mainline traditional houses of worship—is that their members tend to be products of the '60s and '70s' quest for individual and authentic meaning. Both Seekers and long-term "Dwellers" question authority, raise doubts, have conversations within small groups and in after-service coffee hours where they debate what has just been said in the sermon, where they question what was just discussed in the Adult Forum. Roof sees this tendency to question and probe as a healthy dynamic in the life of faith. He also sees this as a problem of religious institutions because in fact, if you actually probe what the folks in the pews really believe, you will find that there is little agreement about core beliefs and practices.

Thus, religious spirituality both within and without traditional structures is nourished by what is found on shelves in Barnes & Noble, on radio and TV stations, in musical lyrics, and in retreat centers of various stripes. But the maintenance of a spiritual consciousness is primarily sustained through conversation. Citing Peter Berger and Thomas Luckmann's early work on reality maintenance, Ammerman says:

50. Roof, *Spiritual Marketplace*, 298.
51. Ammerman, *Sacred Stories, Spiritual Tribes*, 301.

"Spiritual narratives are produced in interaction, carried by conversants from one place to another, and redeployed and reworked in each new telling .... There is an intertwining of individual and communal. Religion is found in the places where individual agency and shared symbols intersect, where elements of socially recognized tradition meet the everyday situations of ordinary people ... where sacred consciousness is being socially created and sustained."[52]

Recently I was sitting at a table in one of my favorite restaurants in Richmond, having lunch and doing some work while sipping a glass of Pinot Grigio. I couldn't help overhearing a conversation at the next table and it was distracting me from my work. Apparently a number of women had met for lunch—coworkers who were primarily there to do business. All of them finally got up and left except for two women who stayed behind. And I then heard them talking about some woman's health, and how the church had prayed for her. And then there was another one on their list of concern. Finally they agreed that they would also pray for these two to be healed. They whispered a soft prayer and then collected their coats and handbags and also left—presumably to return to the workplace for their afternoon projects.

I thought of this scene when I was reading Ammerman's conclusion to her work. She notes that "spiritually inclined" persons sense a bond between them, they find each other somehow, they recognize this basic meaning in their own lives and in one another—even in the workplace. She says "it is surprising that two-thirds of work-based friendships were described to us as religiously homogenous—not necessarily people sharing exactly the same religious tradition but people who think of each other as religiously similar"—as roughly of the same tribe.

Ammerman concludes that a "sacred" awareness is produced both within "institutionalized spiritual tribes" (that is, traditional places of worship), and in the "bonds of conversation" between spiritually and religiously inclined folks who sense and find each other. She concludes that our world for the most part is still an enchanted one. Still she insists that these two ways—one a communal way with roots in symbols and practices of an ancient tradition; the other more eclectic and "extra-tribal"—profoundly matter in our everyday lives. Thus again, spiritual quests matter in our practices in home and workplace, in our ideas of God and God's engagement in our human lives, in our reaching out to others and our civic engagement for bettering communities.

52. Ibid., 300–1.

Seeking within or outside of a traditional community matters in terms of the stories we author of our lives. Roof notes that Boomer stories are on the whole the most complex and diverse and thus distinctive of any past generations in American life. "Treasuring story-telling as they do, the narration of life experiences is itself elevated to something only slightly less than an art form; it might even be said that in some respects, this generation is held together by its stories."[53]

I think with all this as background this would be a good place to revisit Dave, whom we met in the first interlude of this chapter—because he represents a lifelong quest for spiritual meaning, a Seeker who has made his own way and is still crafting a life narrative shot through with Divine presence.

Interlude II: Dave Revisited

Dave is now in his early sixties and I asked him to talk about his current life, to talk about what's important to him—especially in terms of his spiritual and religious life, his everyday practices. He says:

> Just last year I lost three beloved friends to cancer—Dan, a retired economist who turned his vast energies to his art (sculpture) and to community action to raise awareness of the perils of climate change; Bob—my longtime mentor, a public interest lawyer and law professor with a highly contagious laugh and an unmatched curiosity about the inner worlds of the people around him; Judy—a retired Park Service ranger, who knew Rocky Mountain National Park like the back of her hand, and loved the wildflowers, wilderness, and her friends with power and much insight.
>
> As you mention, I of course miss my dad. My relationship with him was complex and challenged me greatly over the years. Would I ever measure up? Did he respect me? Could I ever penetrate that aloof veneer? I'm very fortunate that in his final years (he died at ninety-four) we finally made our connection and formed a strong and wonderful bond.

I asked Dave specifically about the books he reads—what he reads that's important to him, and how his reading might fit into his spiritual life in some way.

> I love fiction and nonfiction, both. At the moment, I'm reading Ben Fountain's *Billy Lynn's Long Halftime Walk*, an irreverent

---

53. Roof, *Spiritual Marketplace*, 313.

novel that deals with a young Iraqi war hero and the spiritually challenged America to which he returns. I'm also finishing George Packer's troubling and provocative nonfiction work *The Unwinding*. Packer, a journalist, borrows narrative techniques used by John Dos Passos in the USA trilogy to portray a contemporary America in which key institutions are faltering and the society is fraying. I mentioned earlier Kabat-Zinn and Chodron, whose works I read and reread like user's manuals.

I also asked Dave to elaborate a bit on these last two writings and, more generally, how that reading fits into his own spiritual life at this point.

Chogyam Trungpa Rinpoche founded the Shambhala Center and Naropa University in Boulder in the 1970s . . . For years, I was aware of the Center and knew that it was respected as a place for meditation instruction and spiritual learning based on Buddhist traditions. When my marriage . . . was failing, a therapist recommended to me that I consider meditation to restore my mental health. He recommended readings, including two works by Jon Kabat-Zinn. These proved meaningful to me, and inspired me to read more widely about meditation. I read a number of works by Pema Chodron, the Buddhist nun and prolific author, who for many years worked at the Shambhala Center. These too, became important to me, and prompted me to look into the offerings at the Center.

I considered starting the Way of Shambhala training very late in the marriage. My wife asked me not to, as she had no interest in the programs and she worried that they would distance us even further. I respected her wish but continued to read. After we separated, I soon began attending some of the free, walk-in meditation classes at the Center and signed up for the first Way of Shambhala weekend programs.

One of the things that I found most remarkable about Rinpoche's writings and the Center's meditation training is that they are based on the radical idea that . . . "every human being has a basic nature of goodness which is undiluted and unconfused . . . . There is something basically good about our existence as human beings." Imagine that. If we can somehow tap this goodness, he argues, we can, in our own unique and individual ways, help this tired, hurting world. In a way, this notion turns the Catholic teachings about original sin with which I'd been raised on their head . . . . Shambhala's core tenet was also in keeping with my long-held interest in serving the community. In short, my experiences at the Center provided me with a footing for a start on a new path, an individual path, informed by the Shambhala teachings, which has involved some disciplined, daily looking inward in order to better serve the world around me.

In terms of spiritual practices, meditation is the basic foundation of all activities (or non-activities) at the Boulder Shambhala Center. This meditation is rooted in the simple but revolutionary premise that every human being has the ability to cultivate the mind's inherent stability, clarity, and strength in order to be more awake, and that by being more awake, we can develop the compassion and insight necessary to care genuinely for oneself and the world.

My meditation practice involves, among other things, at least fifteen minutes a day of sitting. It is a time to stop, breathe, observe my thoughts, and feel my body. It is a time to remind myself that this day is really all I have in an uncertain and ever-changing world. The objective is to wake up to life. As Thoreau said, "only that day dawns to which we are awake."

In addition, I sometimes take part as a volunteer assistant or participant in training programs at the Shambhala Center called "The Way of Shambhala." These courses and weekend retreats offer an experiential overview of practice, teachings, contemplative arts, and physical disciplines rooted in the tradition of Shambhala and Vajrayana Buddhism.

My spiritual practice also involves reading. For example, last December, I had my sixtieth birthday. Of course, this milestone served as a disturbing reminder that my soul is, as William Butler Yeats says, "fastened to a dying animal." It caused me to turn again, as I have before, to one of my favorite books, Philip Simmon's *Learning to Fall*, in which Simmons writes: "When we learn to fall, we learn that only by letting go our grip on all that we ordinarily find most precious—our achievement, our plans, our loved ones, our very selves—can we find, ultimately the most profound freedom. In the act of letting go of our lives, we return more fully to them." In short, in my own awkward, faltering way, after sixty years on the planet, I'm trying to learn to wake up and let go—so that I might live more profoundly and fully. It is a daily challenge. I cannot do it on autopilot.

In terms of God's lure in my life, it stems from my gut sense that there are mysteries in this life—made more palpable in recent years by the death of family members, loved ones, and mentors—that are beyond our ken and the reach of our intellects. To use the words of another wonderful writer, David Wolpe, I have a growing sense that there is an unseeable order in life and in the universe, the detection of which is not possible, even with more refined instruments.

I sense that God's hand is in the unseeable order. I do not presume to know God or to comprehend his ways. I simply sense and respect the presence.

We live in this astonishingly beautiful, but sometimes dark and sordid world. And then we die. And our loved ones live here too. And then they die. We all do. It's still more than I can fathom. There are answers that I will simply never know. And my loved ones will never know them either. And I'm not sure we need to know. As Wolpe says, "Acceptance of mystery is not an act of resignation but humility."

As I said earlier, Dave's life now in his aging years reflects many of the themes we've traced in these pages: A growing contentment and adaptation to the facts on the ground of his life, a spiritual quest that is quite unconventional, but typical of our Boomer generation in its relentless search for authentic meaning.

I want to return now, at the end of this chapter about God's lure in our life, to ask again the question whether God tells stories, if in some unfathomably deep sense, we are part of God's unfolding story as God continues to author all of creation to some purposeful end.

Van Gogh, Jack Miles, and God

Dave talked about books that he read and has reread like spiritual manuals. I have long thought that some books—fiction, nonfiction, especially biographies—find their way into our hands as gifts of providential grace.

In my middle and later adult years (as a Boomer I would say "middle-ageless" years), I would list in this providential category Tolstoy's *The Death of Ivan Ilych*, Gail Godwin's *Father Melancholy's Daughter*, Etty Hillesum's *An Interrupted Life*, Frederick Buechner's memoirs and essays, and Oscar Hijuelos's *Mr. Ives' Christmas*. From all of these writings, I have learned about the profound complexities of our human lives as we live them out in the days we're given.

From Tolstoy I saw the real possibility of a vacuous life redeemed in the end through the kindness of a poor servant boy—a saint, a Christ figure in the story. Gail Godwin's book came into my life as I was preparing to leave the academic world and head for seminary. Her Father Melancholy who "offers himself daily . . . [and who] lives by the grace of daily obligation"[54]

---

54. Godwin, *Father Melancholy's Daughter*, 199.

inspired me as I felt called to active ministry. Etty Hillesum's life as revealed in her diary kept while she was in a Nazi concentration camp moved and astonished me as she showed forth the greatness that humans can rise to even in the depths of evil circumstances. Frederick Buechner's writings for me and many others have always stripped away human pretense, and with humor and irony shown us to be such clay-footed saints with—in the end, as he puts it—purpose and promise too good not to be true.

And finally *Mr. Ives' Christmas*—an unforgettable picture of human suffering, of grief, of being eaten alive with sorrow and hatred for a man who shot an adult son in the prime of years. Mr. Ives's life, his marriage, his friendships, his whole existence was absorbed for years in this past tragedy. And then there was the gradual dawning of grace and the final act of forgiveness that seared itself into my soul and has remained there to this day.

These are some of the books that have shaped my life and I expect that you might be thinking of some in your middle and later years that have also imprinted themselves on your brain, in your character, in the way you view the world around you. As I have said across these chapters, we weave together our own narrated lives, piecing together and authoring our story, selecting from the menu that our culture offers. This is the way we are wired.

But here is the question I will raise again at the end of this chapter and will return to as we close out this book. If it is true that we are made in the image of God, does God then also tell stories? A great majority of Americans have some sense of God as creator of what is. That of course is the grand story in Scripture, from Genesis to Revelation. But as I said before, I'm asking the question from a different slant.

I haven't done a careful study, but I'm struck with the frequency of cartoons in the *New Yorker* magazine with God as the central figure—despite the fact that we're supposed to be an increasingly secular nation. The one I'm thinking of now shows God standing on a cloud, looking forlornly at the earth down below. And God says, "What the hell was I thinking?" Funny in a way, but also somewhat poignant. I mean, we get the cartoon and then laugh . . . ruefully . . . because we realize that the joke's on us.

But I ask again, since our tradition has it that we are made in the image of God, is God as creator still telling an ongoing story? And if so, despite the limited freedom we have as human beings, are we all playing our parts in God's narrative while on the stage of time? The artist Van Gogh wrote a series of letters to his brother, Theo. And in a letter he wrote in 1888, he made the most astonishing observation.

> I feel more and more that we must not judge of God from this world, it's just a study that didn't come off. What can you do

with a study that has gone wrong? If you are fond of the artist, you do not find much to criticize—you hold your tongue. But you have a right to ask for something better. We should have to see other works by the same hand though; this world was evidently slapped together in a hurry on one of his bad days, when the artist didn't know what he was doing or didn't have his wits about him.[55]

More recently, in his *God: A Biography* and *Christ: A Crisis in the Life of God*, Jack Miles treats the Old and New Testament narrative as pieces of literature. He analyzes the story authored by God as a dynamic, ongoing creation where God in a sense rewrites the Old Testament character of himself as a fierce warrior God. His revision portrays God incarnate as a sacrificial Lamb, redeeming humanity and his own character in the end—sacrificed for the whole world he came to save. And because that victory is assured through the Lamb's sacrifice, death, and resurrection, "even the poor, even the meek, even the grief-stricken and scorned who in this world must hunger and thirst for justice may count themselves blessed. Theirs, because he made himself one of them, is the kingdom of heaven."[56]

So I ask again. Does God tell stories? Is God still authoring a grand narrative, engaging with human characters in an ongoing, evolving story in time? Many artists along the way have understood God and creation in this way. From Teilhard to Van Gogh, from the contemporary theologian, John de Gruchy, to the musician Bruce Cockburn. As de Gruchy says, "we are active agents [along with God] in our evolution."[57] So in answer to my own question about God as storyteller, I will say yes. God is still telling stories and we are part of the plot as God's story unfolds. To that end, you and I are persons with character, created in God's image, living out the grandest story of all. Let us play our own parts as well as we can.

---

55. Van Gogh's letter #490 to his brother, Theo, quoted in Edwards, *Van Gogh and God*, 70–71.

56. Miles, *Christ*, 253.

57. de Gruchy, *Led into Mystery*, 165.0

6

"Take Me Home, Country Roads"
The Comfort of the Familiar

> Whatever it was that was making us so unhappy pulled us toward the street. It was the only way out and it was completely open. The street was the place to meet kindred souls of every physical description, the place to score dope, the place to hang out and find out what was happening.... It was where we lived, learned, worked, played, taught, and survived; it was where you oriented yourself among it all. Naturally, it was the best place that anyone who wanted to could find and play and make and go to hear music.[1]

****

There I was, hunched over at my desk in a high school civics class—I think it was maybe in the fall of my junior year—with tears streaming down my face. Everybody was pretty much ignoring me and I wasn't making a scene. Just quietly crying in Nasty Nierste's class. He was the coach of the B basketball team and also taught this really boring class that everyone had to take.

I sat there with my heart broken because somehow I had learned that the guy I really liked (despite the fact that I was supposed to have been going "steady" with a guy in a downstate college—I was a bit precocious in that

---

1. Sander, *Trips*, 9–11.

regard) had been seen at a party the night before holding hands with a girl a year behind us in school. So I had "lost" him and I felt bereft. If you can remember back to those teenage years, you might indeed remember what such loss felt like—like it was the absolute end of the world.

Well, that's it. That's the extent of the losses that I can recall in my early years. I got over that boy loss, and I did my share of breaking up (for example, with that college boy who I no longer cared to date), going steady with others, breaking it off, giving rings back, and so on. The usual teenage stuff.

But that is it as to loss memories for me. As you know from earlier chapters and snapshots of my life, I grew up in a fairly loving, intact family that was financially secure by the time I came along. I had a typical small-town childhood in the 1950s and early 1960s—home, church, school, after-school clubs, basketball cheerleader my freshman year, riding in our cars all around town and to nearby towns when we reached that magical age of sixteen and got our licenses. Typical nurtured childhood and adolescence. This of course is not the story of many in my generation, including some of my friends that I went to school with—those who lived on the "other side of the tracks." And we'll look at some of those intra-generational differences later in this chapter. But in terms of remembered loss episodes from my own past, my report here is going to be pretty thin.

At the beginning of this chapter dealing with loss in the Boomer generation back then and now in our lives, I want to make two preliminary and I think important points. First, with some major social and economic class caveats just alluded to, loss is primarily a phenomenon of aging. As we live our lives, losses tend to accelerate in our middle and later years. Therefore, in contrast with earlier chapters in this work, the "Back Then" section here will be relatively shorter. It isn't that loss wasn't on our minds back then. With war and the threat of nuclear annihilation, with visions of Armageddon and death just over the horizon, the existentialists we read and particularly the songs we sang spoke of darkness and loss that we experienced as a generation nonetheless. Still, this first section will be relatively short.

Second, there is an essential link between this chapter focusing on response to losses in our life and the next one concerned with love. I debated about folding them into one chapter. In fact, you could argue that you can't feel loss for something—spouse, friend, health, freedom, work, and so on—unless you love or at least highly value what has now slipped from your grasp. However, and as I think you will see, the human experience of loss and grief, and the experience of love in all its forms can be viewed as distinct—closely tied together in experience, but nevertheless, two human ways of being in the world and so deserving separate treatment.

Someone has said that we are indeed born to loss. That's life. So let us now see where this topic of loss takes us as we remember our past and deal with our current lives as we are living them out to the end. Turns out it's quite a journey made up of both anguish and accumulation of wisdom along the way.

BACK THEN: "THE EVE OF DESTRUCTION"

Let's start with remembering those fitful days of existential unrest in our '60s and '70s lives. We covered a lot of the protest ground in chapter 2 of this volume, so there's no need to repeat that here. But along with the protest against the Vietnam War, racism, and gender inequality that drove us to the streets—at least for those of us in undergraduate and graduate school in those days (as well as the hangers on around campus life where the action was)—along with all that protest, there was also an undertow of phenomenological *angst*. Or in plain English, an underlying mood of impending doom among many of us at that time.

The cultural ground was rapidly shifting beneath our feet, accelerated by the bloody war and daily body count abroad that spilled into our living rooms every evening via television. In Watts, Newark, and Detroit violent riots erupted. "In the summer of 1967 alone, there were 90 killed, 4,000 wounded, and 70,000 arrested in America's inner cities."[2] During 1968, much of this turmoil was in response to the assassination of Martin Luther King. I remember visiting my parents in Thomasville, Georgia, the day King was shot. We watched the footage on television in my parents' living room that evening, and I remember my mom saying "Now we got trouble!" And how the trouble came.

The year that King was killed was the year after my husband and I moved to Bloomington, Indiana, with our two little boys. In an earlier chapter, I described the campus scene and the turmoil after the Kent State shootings, as well as the general atmosphere of unrest on campus. So I won't repeat that here. But the years following that move—my years of undergraduate and graduate school shaping—were also years of tremendous personal growth and change for me—as well as for many of us in those years of protest. A song that stands out in my memory—as I left one marriage that I had outgrown and entered another that more closely matched my academic lifestyle—is "The Dangling Conversation." Remember? "And we sit and drink our coffee/Couched in our indifference, like shells upon the shore."[3] I

---

2. Lipsitz, "Who'll Stop the Rain?" 220.
3. Simon and Garfunkel, "The Dangling Conversation."

had been there, and the song still brings back all the personal tumult of my life at that time.

In his chapter on youth culture and social crises of the '60s, George Lipsitz points to many of the song lyrics of those times as reflecting both rage and despair at the direction our country seemed to be heading. There was a sense that the future held nothing good for our generation that was just emerging onto the stage of life—that we were staring instead at a world gone amok. He says that the lyrics of songs like "Eve of Destruction" "expressed the rage, frustration, and despair of people who felt that they had no future while at the same time projecting utopian fantasies about community, cooperation, and pleasure within a deeply divided society that routinely resorted to violence to advance its objectives."[4]

Songs from back then that I love and still listen to on my Pandora station come to mind. For example, "Reach out in the Darkness" by Friends and Lovers; "The Night They Drove Old Dixie Down," sung by Joan Baez; Bob Dylan's line, "When you ain't got nothing, you got nothing to lose"[5] in his "Like a Rolling Stone"—all spark memories of that youthful time. Lipsitz insists that such fatalistic lyrics reflected resignation in the face of America's aggressive and oppressive empire, and a desire to just "get out the way" before it was too late to do so.

And where did we want to go? Well, many fled eastward—far eastward to embrace Buddhist or Hindu spiritual practices. Or to the countryside to establish idealistic communes where peace and harmony could reign. Or into the psychedelic drug scene, to drop some acid and drop out of it all into some kind of nirvana—seeking alternative lifestyles rather than taking on the power establishment in any confrontational way.

Interestingly, Lipsitz points out that such alternative "solutions" were no solutions at all for other marginalized, poverty-ridden subpopulations in our culture. He notes that the influx of flower children into East Village or San Francisco's Haight-Ashbury did nothing for the local inhabitants but raise rents, upset existing community institutions, and increase "oppressive" police presence in their locales. In fact, despite embracing a gentler way of flower power, the movement did nothing to stem the violence of our war machine or police force at the community level.

But still, many of the song lyrics we listened to had a ring of truth to them, an uncovering of something sacred that was being lost in the face of bloody violence seen in images of burning cities, the photo of a naked child

---

4. Ibid., 221.

5. Words and music written and performed by Bob Dylan. Copyright 1965, published by Special Rider Music. Copyright administered by SESAC.

running down a foreign street with burning flesh from a napalm bomb, or the firing of a pistol point-blank into the face of a Vietnamese captured in the war. But in fact, Lipsitz does note that despite a strong countercultural movement in the 1960s, most of the country supported the Vietnam War, and most also harbored racist and unexamined sexist sentiments.

In an earlier chapter I drew from Christopher Partridge's *The Lyre of Orpheus: Popular Music, The Sacred, and the Profane*. If you recall, Partridge's main point was that many protest songs and earlier folk song lyrics uncovered sacred truths that had become buried beneath the normative societal tolerance and even embrace of injustice and other forms of social evils. Partridge saw protest songs as "transgressive" in their willingness to subvert the reality of evil that holds the dominant community together. He says "in so doing, it threw into sharp relief key sacred forms (such as the sanctity of life), which had become subjugated in the taken-for-granted everyday world that had come to tolerate injustice."[6]

In thinking about such transgressive lyrics, the song that comes to my mind is titled "In the Year 2525"—the lyrics written by Richard Lee Evans. Remember it? The whole song is about a bleak future of test-tube babies, living on pills, robbing the earth of all it has, giving nothing back. And very explicitly, there's a sense of God's coming judgement—either satisfied by what humans have wrought, or tearing the whole thing down and starting over. It's an incredible song of judgment on where humanity is headed, terrifying in its own way.

Lipsitz does assert that most citizens wanted urban violence—racial unrest reflected in, for example, sit-ins and marches—and drug use to be stopped at whatever brutal cost. Nevertheless he also sees that the youth counterculture of the '60s and early '70s did make a difference in eventual cultural awareness of injustice in our midst. Specifically, in the values embraced by crossing racial barriers, expanding the notion of family beyond biological limits, celebrating peace in a society too comfortable with violence, and exposing materialism as greed gone amok, the counterculture made its contribution to a better society.

In the decades since, a certain nostalgia has grown in remembering that time of turmoil and change. I think one of the best examples of nostalgia for the way it was are the songs of Bruce Springsteen. Lipsitz cites his "My Hometown" hit of 1985 as a nostalgic recall of our past, a certain romanticizing of our memories of our youth and times. We'll see in the next section of this chapter how a replay of the songs from our past taps rosy remembrances of the days that are past, when we were young.

---

6. Partridge, *The Lyre of Orpheus*, 113.

Still, in all, despite such contributions to our culture, our utopia never materialized. Despite resisting a corporate culture of materialism that dominated our landscape post World War II, our generation never created a truly viable counterculture where one could live outside the larger social order or map out some way forward for meaningful future change. While our Boomer generation created art forms such as music and its lyrics that conveyed the protest we wanted to express, we never "figured out a way to reconstruct society to make it look like the visions [we] conjured up in culture."[7]

But then, standing back, on reflection, given our ultimate limits and flaws as human beings, and given the final failure of most if not all utopias across human history, I suppose it isn't very surprising that our visions never became cultural reality. But as Lipsitz concludes, our push back against the prevailing taken-for-granted culture, and our generation's embrace of unconventional forms of family life and sexual expression, our inclusive ideologies and our spiritual quests are still playing out in today's social agenda.

Going Deeper: "Rainy Days and Mondays"

Thinking back on my life—and maybe as you reflect on your own past over the course of your adult years—we have all probably had many failures along the way. Even those of us who have done reasonably well, having launched and established ourselves pretty well in a career that we have more or less enjoyed, had a successful marriage (or two), made lifelong friends from grade school onward, and are still making overall a pretty good life. Nevertheless, we have probably had many failures along the way.

I mean, we've all been there at one time or another. And the songs sung by the likes of Bruce Springsteen have a message that goes like this: Hang in there. You're not alone. We've all felt like that when we're down, and somehow, it's all gonna work out in the end. If rainy days and Mondays get you down, well tomorrow's Tuesday and so another day and maybe the sun will come out and the whole world will look different. When I was a little girl, my grandmother had a small plaque on her dressing table that said "And if perchance a cloud or two, should hide the sun a spell or two, keep smiling still and don't feel blue. You know it'll shine tomorrow." Or something like that. And many of our songs also affirmed beneath the lyrics the same hopeful message.

In *The Longevity Project*, Howard Friedman and Leslie Martin reported findings from a multi-decade longitudinal study that followed a cohort

---

7. Ibid., 231.

of individuals from their early childhoods in the 1920s into the twenty-first century. They examined this huge body of data for clues to long life. One of the major findings from that work was that those who were conscientious and persistent in pursuing both careers and friendships lived longer than others in the study. They say that such individuals "had the persistence, the motivation, and especially the support of a spouse or a close friend to come back each time they faced a challenge. Resilience was not a trait they were born with, nor an inner insight, but a process of perseverance and hard work."[8] And when you are faced with those challenges, when you are weighed down, Dan Levitin would argue that music can not only soothe your brain, but can also assure you that you are not alone in your loss or suffering. In fact, the neurological effects of comfort music can assist you in keeping on, persevering in hard or challenging times.

Take my dentist, for example. Charlie always has a soundtrack going when he's doing something in my mouth. And when he starts to hum along, I know he's in a tough spot. But not to worry. The music will carry us both through. In fact, soundtracks help employees get through the day. And surgeons operate with music in the surgical suite. Mothers know that lullabies sooth babies to sleep. "Lullaby and good night . . ." has a simple, predictable rhythm to it, stimulating the primitive levels of our brain with its repetitive cadence, soothing the brain in the process. And so it has been since our pre-human ancestors vocalized melodies to comfort their offspring.

As Levitin points out, comfort songs—songs like "Take Me Home, Country Roads"—can calm us down even in the face of danger or death. My former spiritual director, a Roman Catholic priest named Chet who died in his nineties, grew up in the mountains of West Virginia. Over the years we used to sing that song made popular by John Denver. When Chet was on his death bed and I visited him for the last time in the hospital, I wasn't sure if he could hear me. But I sang the words to him again. "Take me home, country roads, to the place where I belong."[9] A fitting song to comfort his sense of "going home" for the final time.

Levitin reported a fascinating fact regarding sorrow, music, and the brain. Prolactin—a "tranquilizing" hormone—is released by deep centers in the brain at certain times (for example, during lactation by females). One of those times is when a person experiences sadness. And it turns out that a chemical analysis of tears shows that only tears of sadness—not tears of joy or tears released when the eye is irritated—contain prolactin. And again, tear release containing that chemical hormone soothes the brain.

8. Friedman and Martin, *The Longevity Project*, 211.
9. Denver, "Take Me Home, Country Roads."

Upon hearing a sad song—stimulating emotions and memories with sad meaning—tears shed at that time "trick" the brain into releasing prolactin and thus providing comfort to the listener. In an earlier chapter, I talked about the lyrics to the song "MacArthur Park." The lyrics inevitably make me sad because of the story I hear within them—of irretrievable loss. I remember and link such losses to my own life—and I shed tears I'm sure contain prolactin, soothing me in the process. Levitin also points out that such felt "sorrow does have an evolutionary purpose, which is to help us conserve energy and reorient our priorities for the future after a traumatic event."[10] This is how our marvelous brain has developed to enable us not only to persevere, but even to thrive despite losses and setbacks.

On the experiential level of human meaning-making beyond the neurochemical, sad folks who have had painful loss often feel alone in their sadness. You would think that at times of losses in their lives those who are sad would actually prefer to listen to joyful, happy music. But research shows something quite different. In fact, the *last* thing they want to hear is happy, clappy music. That just makes them feel more isolated because it's not where they are at, so to speak. They can't share the emotion. But hearing a song about loss, hearing a song that fits their mood, makes them feel that they are not alone in the world, that someone shares their feelings, understands their world. "A sad song brings us through stages of feeling understood, feeling less alone in the world, hopeful that if someone else recovered so will we, and we feel ultimately inspired."[11] As with many truisms, misery loves company is in the end true. Music binds us to others, and ultimately binds us to meaning beyond ourselves.

Music as therapy has a long history. In fact, music's role in aiding us through periods of adversity may also be older than the human race. In his *The Singing Neanderthals*, Stephen Mithen—whom we have visited in previous chapters—has the following to say:

> There is unlikely ever to have been a population of humans—modern, Neanderthal or otherwise—for whom the creation of a social identity to override that of the individual was more important. For that, music is likely to have been essential. This is the case for modern humans: when living in conditions of adversity, they make music. Such music enables intense social bonding and facilitates mutual support. I have no doubt that the Neanderthals behaved in exactly the same way.[12]

---

10. Levitin, *The World in Six Songs*, 133.
11. Ibid., 134.
12. Mithin, *The Singing Neanderthals*, 236.

So music making and responding, creating social bonds, and aiding us to get through the tough places of life, is in our genes. There is, in fact, a growing body of evidence demonstrating that music as therapy can play a role in both mental and physical health enhancement.[13]

As with most trait characteristics—dispositions that we are born with—it may not be too surprising that there are individual differences in musical responsivity. That is, some of us are more responsive to musical rhythms than others. In the study mentioned earlier by two psychologists, Chris Loersch and Nathan Arbuckle, these investigators did find that musical reactivity independently predicted who was more likely to value social connectedness and express a need for belonging. In three separate studies, including both a nationwide and international sample, those who were rated as more responsive to musical input were significantly more likely to express motivation to belong to various social groupings. Loersch and Arbuckle conclude that "the pleasure we derive from listening to music results from its innate connection to the basic social drives that create our interconnected world."[14]

Plato is reputed to have said "music and rhythm find their way into the secret places of the soul." And sometimes music has been known to save our very lives. Alice Herz-Sommer, who died in 2014 at the age of 110, was thought to be the oldest living survivor of the Holocaust. She survived for two years in a Nazi concentration camp at Terezin near Prague, where she was made to perform as a highly gifted pianist in a camp set up as a grotesque propaganda front for the war's atrocities. Many of the camp's inmates were artistically talented, and music and theater flourished there until many were murdered or died of disease.

At the time of Herz-Sommer's internment, she lost both her mother and husband. She and her young son survived until the war's end, and she credited the music of Chopin for their survival, despite hunger, cold weather, and death all around. Before her death, Herz-Sommer was interviewed by a journalist from *The Guardian*. During that interview she insisted that "rich people are ridiculous. They think they have everything, but they have nothing! . . . We who survived the ghetto have our suffering, and the music that lifted us out of suffering, and that makes us richer than any wealthy man."[15]

The New York Times ran a lengthy obituary at the time of her death. In it, the writer also pointed to the sustaining and saving power of music that Alice Herz-Sommer credited with her survival. Herz-Sommer was

---

13. Novotney, "Music as Medicine," 46–49.
14. Loersch and Arbuckle, "Unraveling the Mystery of Music," 777.
15. Villiamy, "Terezín: Music from a Nazi Ghetto," para. 30.

quoted from an earlier source as saying "these concerts, the people are sitting there—old people, desolated and ill—and they came to the concerts, and this music was for them our food . . . through making music, we were kept alive."[16]

Certainly the story of Alice Herz-Sommer's life is a story of survival with trouble deep down in the center of it. Trouble and the overcoming of horrendous loss. It and stories like it I believe inspire those of us who hear them, inspire us, awe us that such spirit can overcome such hardship. Such stories also call us to search for deeper meaning, to ask questions about why, and what for, and where to in the end.

Which brings me to the story of Forrest Church. In contrast to previous chapters, the biography that I sketch out in this chapter concerned with loss is not a sketch of someone I personally know or interviewed directly. Instead I have turned to a biography that has made a great difference to me and to others who have read his account. Let me turn now to the early experience of Church as he tells his story in his book, *Love & Death*.

Interlude I: Meet Forrest

Forrest Church was born in Palo Alto, California, in 1948, when his father, Frank Church—later Senator Frank Church—was a law student at Stanford. Forrest also later graduated from Stanford and then received a PhD in early church history from Harvard University. For many years, he served as senior minister of the Unitarian Church of All Souls in New York City and was author of several books during his tenure there. He died on September 24, 2009.

The year before Church died, he authored *Love & Death*—an autobiography he wrote when he knew that he was dying from esophageal cancer. As is true of many memoirs, the book covers episodes in his past life that marked his journey through life. It's not just another "death and dying" book about facing life's end. I think he attempted in its writing to describe his philosophy concerning how to live. There are images and stories in it that have become part of my own struggle for meaning in the face of loss. Early in his book, he says that "the courage to love is nothing less than the courage to lose everything we hold most dear . . . . Love is grief's advance party."[17]

The episode in this "back then" section recounts an early and profound loss in Forrest's life that marked him until the end. The central account of his loss I have incorporated into at least one sermon, and I have told and

---

16. Fox, "Alice Herz-Sommer," para. 24.
17. Church, *Love & Death*, 9.

retold the story to countless others over the past five years or so. So here it is, a paraphrase of his early story along with letting him speak for himself.

One of the people that Forrest Church came to love was his closest friend at Stanford, Dalton Denton. He says that Dalton was great fun to be with, serious about life but not "somber." They spent much of their free time together when not in classes. Forrest says that Dalton struck him as a true sophisticate, introducing him to scotch and Beethoven. They had been dorm mates freshman year, and grew into best friends from that time. He says that more than once they stayed up all night, discussing the great issues of the day, sharing their ideas and their lives.

During the middle of their sophomore year, Dalton died of pneumonia while on a skiing vacation at Vail. Church says:

> He had been out on the slopes just the day before. That morning he felt a little tired and somewhat congested, so he stayed in the cabin while his friends skied. When they returned home later in the afternoon, Dalton was dead . . .
>
> A week before he died, I told Dalton that I did not believe I would live past the age of twenty-five. This romantic, melodramatic flourish didn't impress my friend. He simply said, "Lighten up, Church. You've been reading too many existentialists. Besides, six years from now is a fantasy however you cut it. Today's the day. Don't ruin it."
>
> He was right. And then he was dead.[18]

Church goes on to talk about the aftermath of Dalton's death. He took it very hard. In fact, for weeks he seemed lost. He says "Only after he was gone did I realize how much I loved him, how achingly I needed and missed him. I would walk down the street and hear people blathering on about nothing and go temporarily out of my mind."[19]

At the time, Church hadn't developed enough of life's wisdom to be able to deal very well with his friend's death. What he felt instead was just emptiness. He threatened to leave school but apparently his father the senator stepped in and that was the end of that. He finished school, made a life, learned some things along the way, and put together a philosophy and theology of life that allowed him to integrate all the blessings and losses of a lifetime into a very good story.

More of that will appear in the next section of this chapter dealing with the Now of our mature lives. But to end this early reflection and looking back on that early loss, Church concludes his story of this sad episode

18. Ibid., 10.
19. Ibid.

thus: "What I know now about Love & Death, but didn't know then, might well have helped me negotiate my pain over Dalton's loss. Love & Death are allies. When a loved one dies, the greater the pain, the greater love's proof. Such grief is a sacrament. Sacraments bring us together. The measure of our grief testifies to the power of our love."[20]

Forrest Church couldn't have known all of that at the age of nineteen. No, such wisdom and perspective only comes with the experience of living and aging and digging for deeper meaning in our lives as we move through time. And that is just what we are going to turn to now as we look at what life is like for us Boomers and others who have been able to amass a bit of wisdom despite—or rather because of—the losses we have faced and surmounted.

THE NOW OF OUR LIVES: "THOSE WERE THE DAYS MY FRIEND"

What a wonderful life I've had. If only I had realized it sooner.[21]

****

My husband and I were just getting back from a Caribbean cruise and had flown from Barbados to Miami where we spent the night before flying home to Richmond. It had been pleasant enough sailing—calm waters, first-class ship, touristy, but slightly interesting ports of call. However, our last evening in Barbados had bordered on catastrophe.

At that point, my husband, Bud (nickname to family and friends), was in the advanced stages of prostate cancer. On Barbados, we had several hours' wait to get into our rooms. But once we got into them, they were lovely. We had a great dinner in the hotel's elegant dining room where I discovered that I liked tuna steak after all. But after dinner, when we went back to the rooms, my husband had a bleeding incident that turned out to be relatively trivial. But we thought that night that he was going to die right there in Barbados—or at least need to be hospitalized. We just wanted to get back to Miami, where we knew the university had a great hospital—if we could just get through the night.

---

20. Ibid., 10.
21. Colette.

So we kept our fingers crossed, prayed, and hoped for the best. The bleeding did slow overnight. We got to the Barbados airport the next morning and were very happy indeed to board the plane for home.

After an uneventful night spent in Miami, the next morning we headed for the airport and decided to have a second breakfast or brunch in the restaurant before boarding our plane. Now it was spring break time for a lot of colleges, and of course, Miami attracts lots of students for a spring fling. At the next table from us sat about eight of them—they must have been around nineteen or twenty years of age. They looked like kids, which they were. And they were having a terrific time joking, laughing, kidding around, despite the fact that they had apparently been up all night partying.

I looked across the table at Bud and remember saying, "They know nothing. Nothing at all about life, about what's really real, about suffering that comes along with living. They know nothing."

For some reason, that episode sticks in my mind. Maybe because it's so true. As I said to my middle-aged son recently, there are some truths about life that come with age, truths that lead to wisdom as we get older, truths that cannot be taught—even by Mom. They can only be lived and that comes along with living life in all its joys and sorrows, in loving and losing, and finally letting go at the end. Bud died nine months later.

In her memoir titled *Lots of Candles, Plenty of Cake*, Anna Quindlen says much the same thing about knowledge, wisdom, and aging. When her twenty-two-year-old daughter asked what message Anna would give to herself if she could travel back to that age, Anna said that she would have to break the bad news: "that she knew nothing, really, about anything that mattered. Nothing at all. Not a clue." She says "you don't know what you don't know when you're young. How could you? People who are older nod sagely and say you'll learn—about love, about marriage, about failing and falling down and getting up and trying to stagger on toward success, about work and children and what really matters, in general and to you."[22] Sounds like the development of wisdom that often comes with the post-middle age U-shaped curve of life satisfaction that we talked about in an earlier chapter.

In her introduction to this delightful book, Quindlen says about the passing time and our passing lives that "first we were so young and then we were so busy and then one day we awoke to discover that we were an age we once thought of as old."[23] Isn't it all amazing? Yet she also makes clear that she wouldn't be twenty-five again "on a bet!" Not even forty-five. Because in many ways, as she cites Carly Simon, "*These* Are the Good Old Days." We

---

22. Quindlen, *Lots of Candles, Plenty of Cake*, 3.
23. Ibid., xi.

are not only older and wiser, but in many ways—given reasonable health and resources to get by—not only are we contented, but also excited about our lives as we face the future challenges that we know await us all.

So with that, let's look at aging Boomers and our lives—those middle-ages that we've followed through our excursions into the great existential concerns laid out by Levitin's and others' work—friendship, knowledge, joy, religion, and now loss, sickness, and dying—along with the songs and stories that helped shape the story of our lives.

****

Toward the end of her book, Quindlen talks about growing up as a Boomer and living a life of choices, of choosing our own way, doing it our way come hell or high water. She says "the great hallmark of my life, my generation, my time, has been choice. We've been a wandering breed, we Americans straddling the twentieth and twenty-first centuries, changing jobs, changing homes, changing spouses, religions, political parties. We've had more options than any generation before us, to marry those of different races or religions, to marry those of our own sex, to not marry at all but live together without legal obligation or live without a lifelong partner."[24] She contrasts our lifestyle with her grandfather's—who lived in the city where he was born, stuck with the same job all his working life, and expected his children to do the same. And divorce was rare. Of course even then there were exceptions. My grandmother Pauline who married my grandfather Louis (whom I never met) at age sixteen finally divorced him in mid-life because he was a "philanderer." Understandable grounds even in her day, but still unusual for her generation.

In his 2012 book concerned with the increasing phenomenon of "going solo"—not just among Boomers but in the population at large—Eric Klinenberg reports that "more than 50 percent of American adults live alone. He refers to the "cult of the individual" that has overtaken the Western world, not just the United States. He asks, "What makes it so compelling for the young, the middle-aged, and the old?"[25] One answer Klinenberg offers is that in a society running and striving and on call twenty-four/seven, living alone can provide a needed solitude, a place for individual freedom and personal control. And he also argues that living alone is by no means the same as being alone. Ideally, there are friends to go out with when you want to socialize, lunch or dinner out alone with the morning newspaper

24. Ibid., 175.
25. Klinenberg, *Going Solo*, 17.

or iPad when you prefer your own company, but want to be around other humans nevertheless.

During the seven or so years I was on the faculty at the University of Pittsburgh, my husband was chair of the psychology department at the University of Maryland in Baltimore County. He usually came up to Pittsburgh on weekends, but during the week I was on my own for the first time in my life. My mom said I had the best of both worlds—a stable, happy marriage, time to myself, and a career on the move in a great city. I loved it!

The challenge comes when one has to age alone. And of course, statistically this happens more often to women than men. On the upside, Quindlen notes that for many women who become widows, solo life is surprisingly freeing. She says it's "a terrifying thought, and sometimes, for a woman who has always been surrounded by others, a liberating thought as well. There is so much obligatory generosity to being a good mother, a good wife, and good friend. Solitude is an acceptable form of selfishness."[26]

Nevertheless, risk factors of solo living remain for many. Those who are poor, in increasingly fragile health, depressed, or physically limited and less able to get around to doctor's appointments, and so on are at risk for greater morbidity. Klinenberg points to findings from one study of elderly living alone that showed that for those who are also living below the poverty line, one third saw neither neighbors nor friends for as much as two weeks at a stretch. You read horror stories in the paper about someone noticing mail piling up in a box only to discover that the one for whom it was intended had died in their apartment alone days if not weeks before. Overall, risk factors for social isolation (which in turn is a major predictor of morbidity and mortality across populations) are being an unmarried male, growing old childless or without children nearby, being sick and homebound, being mentally depressed, and of course, being too poor for adequate health care or other personal services.

In a previous chapter, I mentioned Ross Douthat's 2013 op-ed piece that appeared in *The New York Times* titled "All the Lonely People." In it he offers some rather depressing statistics. He notes that the suicide rate for Americans aged thirty-five to fifty-four rose nearly 30 percent between 1999 and 2010. For men in their fifties—late Boomers that is—it rose nearly 50 percent. He also reported that more people now die from suicide than from car accidents, and suicides by the use of guns are almost twice as common as homicides by gunfire.

Douthat links these troubling data with the fact that one third of our citizens over the age of forty-five report being lonely. So he asks the obvious

---

26. Ibid., 84.

question: "With Baby Boomers reaching retirement age at a rate of 10,000 a day ... the number of lonely Americans will surely spike."[27] And without the comfort of community that neither Facebook nor Twitter can provide, what are the risk implications that such statistics raise?

Even if many of us do cherish a certain amount of solitude in our lives, and even if we actually like living alone, we do in fact wither without some attachment, some engagement with our kind. There was a story in *The New York Times*[28] a year or so back about the police raiding a McDonalds in the Queens neighborhood of the city, evicting some elderly Korean customers who tended to linger there beyond the permissible time limit. The restaurant for those elderly represented a place in the neighborhood close by where they could exercise their choice of association independently, that was inexpensive, and basically provided a place where they could socialize and not be alone.

At about that time, Stacy Torres wrote a think piece in the same newspaper concerning that police action event in which she quoted an old Italian saying, "At the table, you don't grow old." She asserts "all of us, of whatever age, need to socialize in public places to feel connected and alive."[29] Since I very much look forward to similar outings, I was delighted with her piece. Torres referred to "third places" aside from work place and home where such engagement with our kind happens: bookstores, cafes, and yes, restaurants like McDonalds. Such gathering places foster community, especially for those like the retired and the elderly Koreans in Queens. In fact, such places can be lifelines to those who are at risk for social isolation and worse.

Like Anna Quindlen, there came a time when I needed reading glasses, and then some time after that, I started taking a minimum daily dosage of a blood pressure medication—I became just a wee bit borderline hypertensive. And then after a while I started having my hairdresser put "highlights" in my hair to camouflage the gray. Quindlen says "I hate my glasses because they were the very first thing that alerted me to the notion that I was on a slippery slope of losing—my hair color, my jaw line, my bone mass, my vision."[30] Like her, I was also highly offended when a ticket seller at the Art Institute in Chicago asked me if I wanted a senior citizen discount! I said of course not!

As I have said before, we who are of that generation inhabit the world of middle-agelessness. We work out (I also have a personal trainer), lift

---

27. Douthat, "All the Lonely People," para. 5.
28. Kimmelman, "The Urban Home Away from Home."
29. Torres, "Old McDonald's," para. 1.
30. Quindlen, *Lots of Candles, Plenty of Cake*, 91.

weights, stay in shape. But nevertheless, we age. And things happen. Grandparents die, parents die, good friends die, sickness happens. Quindlen says then one day, something bad also befalls us and we join the ranks of those who suffer loss, who drop through that trap door that has swallowed those before us. She says we then become amazed, "not by our own strength but by that indomitable ability to slog through adversity, which looks like strength from the outside and just feels like every day when it's happening to you. [And] the older we get, the better we get at this."[31]

Near the end of Landon Jones's book about the Boomer generation, he notes that as Boomers age, we will represent a formidable interest group, demanding to be cared for and supported medically and financially, turning youth priorities into elderly priorities. From his vantage point in 1980—three and a half decades ago—he saw our demands at the center of national debate. Boomers will link "the fertility of our past with our future, and [the country's]. And [Boomers] will never go gently into that good night."[32]

A similar point was made by Greg Easterbrook in the *Atlantic*. He points out that society is dominated by the old—most of our political leaders, our Supreme Court judges, and others occupying positions of power in this country. And in his piece, titled "What Happens When We All Live to 100?," the elderly—made up increasingly of the Boomer generation—demand benefits for which the young have to pay. And while our life span increases, if our "health span" doesn't also extend into healthy old age, then economically the future will be grim for our children and grandchildren's generation.

Easterbrook does end on an optimistic note, an ideal picture of increasing health into very old age, with the elderly continuing to thrive in their communities, continuing to learn in university and other educational settings, and—with the benefits of wisdom that comes with increasing age—society itself can become more peaceful with less crime and aggressive war adventures.

In the meantime, however, we have the reality of gaps in health care, inadequate resources for in-home community services, and "retirement" communities financially out of reach for most Americans. As Quindlen noted earlier, we Boomers are not only an independent lot, but we are also mobile creatures and so, if we married and now are alone—or if we chose the solo life all along the way—then any extended families we might have are possibly both thin, as well as scattered around the country.

---

31. Ibid., 110.
32. Jones, *Great Expectations*, 386.

Of course the "retirement community" phenomenon has become a growth industry in this country. When my grandmother and grandfather on my mom's side got too old to continue living in their own house, they simply moved in with my Aunt Vi—my grandmother's sister—who owned a big farmhouse on the outskirts of New Albany, Indiana, and had a bit more means and room for them to move in. I don't think anyone asked them how they all liked the arrangement, because that's what one did in those days—just move in with the relatives who could house you for the rest of your time. And they did all die, one by one, in that common living arrangement. They made do with a common home until the end.

As Quindlen points out in her chapter about future expectations, today many of us have our own home, bigger houses comparatively speaking than our forebears. But of course we imagine there is no room for any parents to move in. And as she says, nor would they probably want to. She herself imagines an idyllic arrangement for herself when she can no longer live as she has in the past. Quindlen envisions perhaps winding up in a kind-of communal arrangement with a number of female friends, pooling resources and living together in one household. I can't pass up quoting her here because the arrangement sounds so ideal—if you like the idea of living with others around you.

> My plan is that a group of us will move together into our house in the country, with a crackerjack cook and a couple of aides. We'll repeat the same stories, trash the same absent friends, secure in the knowledge that none of us will notice the repetitions. Our children will call, male and female alike, working, busy, with too much to do, and we'll say, "Fine, dear. Nice to hear from you. Have to go."[33]

An observation that Quindlen made early in her work about female friends has stayed with me since I read her words. She says "friends are what we women have in addition to, or in lieu of, therapists. And when we reach a certain age, they may be who is left."[34] And when the chips are down, it's usually those friends we reach out to and say "I'm drowning here! Help!"

So we face our own aging and, unless we are hit by a Mack truck somewhere down the line, no matter how much we work out, jog, lift weights, watch the carbs—some day in the future we are going to get more frail, we are going to not dodge one of those bullets, we will hear that dreaded phone call that comes in from our doctor saying "Uh . . . I'd like to repeat that blood chemistry once more because . . . uh . . . I didn't like the looks of some of the

---

33. Quindlen, *Lots of Candles, Plenty of Cake*, 131.
34. Ibid., 35.

values." And then the follow-up. "I'm sorry to have to say this, but . . . not good news . . . ." This will happen, folks, somewhere in the future—hopefully at age ninety-plus, or even Easterbrook's one hundred year mark.

There have been a number of studies concerned with the need for "fictive kin" such as close friends who are listed as "next of kin" to be notified in case of emergency, who are even given health power of attorney when the solo Boomer is unable to make decisions for him or herself. Lawyers of course are frequently named as "health fiduciaries" having legal power to make health decisions for those who are widowed, divorced, or never married. Because many of us married more than once, usually stepchildren are simply not going to have the same affectional ties as biological offspring. So many of my generation have the need for professional caregivers when significant physical loss occurs. And the industry hasn't kept up with the need that is increasingly out there.

In an excerpt from her memoir titled *Downhill Almost All the Way* published in *The American Scholar* and available online,[35] Doris Grumbach has some slightly acerbic observations about retirement community living. She points out that these communities are usually set in lovely, landscaped parks, with cottages built for independent living and then graded living arrangements in community housing ranging from apartments, to assisted living spaces, to locked "memory floors" for those suffering from dementia, to nursing centers for end-of-life care.

Many if not most of these communities are expensive to buy into, and thus provide living space for mostly well-to-do, mostly white, college-educated, and Christian residents. The Richmond Westminster-Canterbury facility is a magnificent institution, with a grand performance theater and even a cocktail lounge off the lobby.

There are exceptions to this luxurious picture, of course, and as a clergy person, I have seen the inside of many such facilities. My mother wound up in a small-town nursing home for the last few years of her life. So did my late husband, Leon, who spent the last year of our thirty-five year marriage in a nursing facility, chosen because it was near our neighborhood for my daily visits—on the locked "memory" unit because of increasing and severe dementia. So there are facilities and then there are facilities—some with much better staffing than others. In this case, you probably get what you pay for—and the more you can pay, the better the staff-to-resident ratio and the more resources available to care for residents who can "age in place."

In Klinenberg's writing about solo life, he considers the current plight of the elderly in terms of finding adequate housing to meet increasing health

---

35. Grumbach, "The View from 90."

needs. He, like Grumbach, also points out that high-quality assisted living facilities are prohibitively expensive. Even when Medicare and Medicaid guarantee funding for a spot in an assisted living facility, it is usually in a lower quality institution, with a bed in a shared room.

This isn't the place to address public policy regarding such issues that do loom ahead for Boomers of my generation. But it would be comforting to know that there might be other options available beyond Quindlen's communal ideal, or an exclusive and expensive private apartment, or a second-rate, depressing nursing home. Such public policy options as public support for in-home caregivers, community programs that provide transportation options, affordable housing equipped to meet the needs of elderly inhabitants (for example, with handrails and grab bars in bathrooms, ramps for wheelchair easy access, and so on) should be on the political legislative agenda. Decent salary support for retirement and nursing home staff beyond minimum wage would likely increase the quality of caregivers and reduce staff turnover.

In personal terms, I have absolutely no interest in moving out of my home—too large for one person, but it is my home for the last eighteen years, my home that I have lived in longer than any other place in my life. Plus I have lots of room for family and guest visits! I have adequate support to maintain it, and the thought of group living—even of Quindlen's idyllic communal dwelling with old friends—has no appeal for me. As I have said repeatedly in these pages, I am by trait somewhat of an introvert. I love my friends, I socialize as much or even at times more than I want. But I also like my privacy.

On the other hand, unless I can achieve what Easterbrook ideally projects for future seniors—maintenance of health span to match my life span—living a full and vigorous life until the day I simply drop in my tracks—then I suppose the day will come when I have to think of other living arrangements. And when and if that day comes (we Boomers just don't quit, do we!), I have I guess some vague idea of moving into one of those upscale assisted living facilities, and making the very best of it—near one of my sons, of course. But, as Scarlet O'Hara famously said, "I'll worry about that . . . tomorrow . . . or some other time down the line . . . or . . ."[36]

****

I hope that death will lift me

---

36. *Gone with the Wind*, directed by Victor Fleming.

by the hair like an angel
in a Hebrew myth, snatch me with
the strength of sleep's embrace ... (Tim Dlugos)

This bit of imagery is from a longer poem quoted by Meghan O'Rourke in her own essay concerned with the current spate of "death and dying books."[37] She suggests that the flood of such works in recent years is one result of the modern way of dying in our contemporary society. At least in our developed world, most no longer die quickly from pneumonia or influenza, but we die more slowly from heart disease and cancer, giving the dying—with inclination to chronicle their demise—the opportunity to do so.

O'Rourke asks why the rest of us who are not yet dying read such memoirs—in newspaper essays, detailed obituaries, or book form. And she answers her own question thus: such reading "calls us to our senses, reminds us that even if we are not believers we may wish to approach the apportioning of our days with more profound awareness."[38] None of us, of course, will be able to finish our own life story to the end (and beyond). But as I will discuss further in the next section, by reading others' stories of what their dying is like, and by reading biographies of the survivors who witness the death and make a new, but bereaved life in its wake, we can learn vicariously the art of coping with loss and the art of dying.

I began the very first pages of this book with a reference to Oliver Sacks and his writing concerned with the joy of getting old. Sacks died on August 31 of 2015 from metastatic ocular melanoma. Of course, as a prolific writer, he wrote about his dying in an op-ed piece. He writes, "Over the last few days, I have been able to see my life as from a great altitude, as a sort of landscape, and with deepening sense of the connection of all its parts. This does not mean I'm finished with life." In fact, Sacks goes on to assure the reader that he still feels intensely alive. He knows that he is dying and that his days are quite numbered—after all, he is a physician—but he now wants to deepen his friendships, say goodbye to those he loves, write, travel if he can, and "achieve new levels of understanding and insight."[39]

In her book *Necessary Losses*, Judith Viorst writes of the possibility of growth and change even while dying. She, as well as others, have suggested that at least for some, when the end of life is in sight, those dying can view themselves and their life as a whole with humility and forgiveness, with greater insight concerning the futile trivia that so many of us allow to consume our days until they are all past and our living is done. That quotation

37. O'Rourke, "Deadlines."
38. Ibid.
39. Sacks, "My Own Life."

from Colette offered earlier comes to mind here: "What a wonderful life I have had; I just wish I had realized it sooner."

In the op-ed piece cited above, Sacks clearly recognizes that he no longer has time for the unessential. Of course I suppose that is also true beyond that post-middle point for us all. In a lengthy obituary honoring Sacks's life, the writer ends the piece with a quote from Sacks's "valedictory essay" titled "Sabbath," published shortly before his death. It is a beautiful statement, and worth quoting here—as sort of a bookmark that ends the life of a remarkable man.

> And now, weak, short of breath, my once-firm muscles melted away by cancer, I find my thoughts, increasingly, not on the supernatural or spiritual, but on what is meant by living a good and worthwhile life—achieving a sense of peace within oneself. I find my thoughts drifting to the Sabbath, the day of rest, the seventh days of the week, and perhaps the seventh day of one's life as well, when one can feel that one's work is done, and one may, in good conscience, rest.[40]

It doesn't take a lot of imagination to grasp the suffering that Sacks must have been undergoing, despite his uplifting words.

Tremendous losses, as well as dying, usually sweep the sufferers up into a maelstrom of pain and struggle. Apparently Walker Percy—Southern novelist and essayist—viewed the catastrophes that occur to us humans from time to time as nevertheless having great value. Percy saw our everyday routines miring us in the mundane, alienating us from one another and leading to a certain malaise. But when catastrophe strikes—losses caused by hurricanes, war, disease, and so on—such evils that befall us at one time or another trigger a search for meaning. Such suffering triggers a need to make deeper sense of what has occurred, and further, prompts a reaching for community as fellow sufferers are in the same boat and we are therefore not alone.

Pico Iyer, one of my favorite writers, recalls that in his Indian culture it was thought that you should pray for suffering because suffering, itself, can produce many blessings. Like Percy, Iyer sees suffering in fact as a privilege prompting a search for meaning, shaking us out of everyday complacency, binding us together in our humankind-ness. Ultimately, we are all in the same boat. So let us be kind to one another and learn from each other's wisdom as we pass through this life.

---

40. Cowles, "Oliver Sacks, Neurologist Who Wrote about the Brain's Quirks, Dies at 82."

> [Story writers] cannot rest because they are human, and all of us need to speak into the silence of mortality, to interrupt and ever so briefly stop that quiet flow, and with stories try to understand at least some of it.[41]

Robert Pinsky, a former United States Poet Laureate, said that "poems of loss and death can please the reader mightily." In fact, we have talked in these pages about the centrality of trouble, including loss and death, embedded in the stories we tell, read, and sing—stories in the form of poetry, fiction, nonfiction, fairy tales, songs of loss and longing. So what Pinsky says about poetry is also true in fiction and nonfiction narratives alike. If there's no trouble embedded in the tale, then the story is boring and we are likely to set it aside or maybe save it for the beach.

We are attracted to stories about life's big troubles—homelessness, rejection, poverty, injustice, illness, dying, and bereavement. By reading such stories and vicariously experiencing the losses and aftermath through the lives we have come to care for—the biographies and fictional characters who struggle with the trouble—we learn alternative strategies for dealing with our own life losses. As Jonathan Gottschall says, "The human mind was shaped for story so that it could be shaped by story.... When we experience fiction, our minds are firing and wiring, honing the neural pathways that regulate our responses to real-life experiences."[42]

Richard Gerrig develops the metaphor of being "transported" into and out of the narrative worlds that we enter when we become absorbed in a story, entering into a state of intimacy with the writer, contributing our own meaning in the process. While reading, we travel into a world that differs in many ways from our everyday lives, but in some basic sense conveys some truth about our humanness, about life's predicaments and their aftermaths. We learn something from the "trip" and thus come back changed from the vicarious experience. As Gottschall reminds us, we become changed from our brain wiring to our perceived options for coping strategies that we can call upon when we face our own life's challenges.

There are some very special books that I have read, and then put in an honored place on my bookshelves—either to draw from in an occasional sermon or just to run my fingers and eyes over once in a while and recall the wisdom I found between their covers. As I have said, examples include Oscar Hijuelos's *Mr. Ives' Christmas*, a story of grief and forgiveness; Anne

---

41. Dubus, *Broken Vessels*, 92.
42. Pinsky quoted in Gottschall, *The Storytelling Animal*, 56; 65.

Tyler's *A Patchwork Planet*, about the worth of all lives in serving the frail and lonely elderly in a small community; and all the novels of Kent Haruf, including his last one, *Our Souls at Night*—the story of two elderly people who had lost their spouses years before, and of a love that developed between them, as well as the aftermath of choices made within one family's life. There are so very many more; these are just examples of fictional stories that have meant a great deal to me.

And then there are the nonfiction, autobiographical accounts of life's losses and struggles to reach some meaning beneath the horrendous suffering that such losses brought in their wake. Examples in my own reading life include Nicholas Wolsterstorff's *Lament for a Son*, his grappling with the question of God and evil in the aftermath of his young son's death in a climbing accident; Kay Redfield Jamison's *Nothing Was the Same*, the account of her bereavement at the death of her husband who had also been her mentor through much of her life; Philip Simmons's *Learning to Fall: The Blessings of an Imperfect Life*, a beautiful series of essays written as Simmons was dying from Lou Gehrig's disease; Luci Shaw's *God in the Dark: Through Grief and Beyond*, another story of a widow's grief—read in the midst of my own; and John de Gruchy's *Led Into Mystery*, written following his son Steve's accidental death by drowning. Some of these later works we'll return to in the last section of this chapter. There we'll turn to the question of God's presence as we struggle to make meaning when horrendous evil and loss befall most, if not all, of us at some point in our lives.

I'd like to mention one more book here before we go a bit deeper into current research having some bearing on coping with loss. Andre Dubus, whom I quoted at the beginning of this section of the chapter, was a prize-winning writer known for his short stories. He died in 1999 from a heart attack, but his personal losses actually began in 1986 when he stopped to help a stranded motorist by the side of a highway outside of Boston. He and two others were hit by a passing motorist; one of the others died, and Dubus suffered massive injuries resulting in the loss of one leg and the use of the other. He spent the rest of his life in a wheelchair.

In 1991 a series of autobiographical essays by Dubus—written between 1977, before the accident, and 1990—was published under the title *Broken Vessels*. In the introduction to this collection, Tobias Woolf wrote: "Andre has made of his wheelchair a place to see the world more clearly than ever. I was struck again and again by the range of his vision, by its depth and compassion, and by the music by which he gives it voice." At the end of the introduction, Woolf quotes Dubus: "After the physical pain of grief has become, with time, a permanent wound in the soul, a sorrow that will last as long as the body does, after the horrors become nightmares and sudden daylight memories, then comes the transcendent and common bond of human suffering, and with that comes forgiveness, and with forgiveness comes love."[43]

These are some of the soul-making books I have read in recent years, books from which I have learned something about life, from which I have gathered some wisdom from others making meaning of their own losses. I have had my own losses accumulate over the past same years, and these books have been my companions. I have also shared whatever wisdom I could glean from them with friends, with family, and with anonymous others through my blog and other writings.

I think of the lyrics to the song, "Those Were the Days" sung by Mary Hopkin. The song brings back memories of my youthful graduate school days, but also is a poignant reminder of passing time that I couldn't have fully understood back then. But the last lines of the fourth stanza, "Oh my friend we're older but no wiser/For in our hearts the dreams are still the same,"[44] is only partly true. Yes we still want to sing and dance. We still want to fight and in the end, not lose. But I do think most of us have developed a bit of wisdom along the way. If we are very lucky, we can share the meaning we've found beneath life's losses with others in a similar stage of life who—through reflection and dialogue—are ready to create some common truth between us.

****

Going Deeper: "Help!"

> The past is always with us, in the form of our photographs which we feel as we might a rosary, wearing them smooth with the fingering of our eyes.[45]

Most folks are remarkably resilient in the face of life's awful catastrophes. Among the most awful include the loss of one's own health to life-threatening disease and the death of a spouse or child. Many examples in my own life come to mind. As I write this, I'm thinking about a close friend named Charlie who over a decade ago—at the peak of his career as

---

43. Dubus, *Broken Vessels*, xviii–xix.

44. Written by Eugene Raskin, performed by Mary Hopkin. Copyright 1962/1968. Administered by Essex Music Inc. (Tro Essex Music Group).

45. A. D. Coleman, writer and critic.

a historian and director of the Virginia Historical Society—was diagnosed with Parkinson's. This past summer, his beloved wife was diagnosed with a potentially deadly form of cancer. But they have both rallied to these challenges that they face and will face in the coming months and years. Sometime after Charlie was diagnosed, he wrote an essay titled "Keep Your Hand Tightly on the Wheel as the Journey Becomes More Difficult."

In it he talked about his coming to terms with his disease, fighting that "enemy" with all his energy, and passing on advice to others who suffer with chronic disease. He suggests being open about what has befallen you, but don't obsess over it—and don't bore others around you with constant reference to your condition. Stay active and productive as long as you can (sounds like Oliver Sacks's determined response in the face of his terminal disease), and especially cultivate your sense of humor to ease the burden of your condition. Charlie lives his advice and his spirit has carried him thus far—eleven years past diagnosis—in remarkably good shape.

In looking at predictors of long survival in the longitudinal data from *The Longevity Project*, Friedman and Martin conclude that in large part, resilience in the face of life stressors became cultivated over a lifetime of grappling with challenges and overcoming them during early and later adult years. Summarizing their findings, they also conclude that when those who survived the longest did face traumatic events in their lives, they called upon a lifetime of learned strategies to deal with the trauma, refusing to let the setbacks and losses consume them. In sum, they were "motivated, persistent, and prudent. They [took] care of themselves, avoiding catastrophizing thoughts and working hard at life's challenges . . . and most important, they [turned] to the good social relationships that are the hallmark of their healthy life pathways."[46]

Although this longitudinal study was carried out on pre-Boomers, Friedman and Martin report that a graduate student in their lab has carried out a meta-analysis—combining data from many studies into a single summary research project. In short, their overall findings in terms of mortality predictors have been confirmed in twenty additional studies. The take-away message for us then is that if you are conscientious and prudent as you live your life, then your habits and strategies you have developed for problem-solving, your brain chemistry and emotional stability, and your social network are likely to work in your favor in forestalling morbidity and early death.[47]

46. Friedman and Martin, *The Longevity Project*, 200.

47. Examples of additional research reports that show the survival advantage of hope, optimism, social support, and wisdom are the following: Weir, "Mission Possible"; Kim et al., "Culture and Social Support"; Shallcrois et al., "Getting Better with

Help me get my feet back on the ground/Won't you please, please help me?"[48]

But death comes. Sooner or later in all our lives. To parents, to friends, to classmates, to spouse perhaps, and in the end, to you and me. In his edited book, *Meaning Reconstruction & the Experience of Loss*, Robert Neimeyer refers to the "death awareness movement" of the 1960s. As a graduate student, I subscribed to a journal titled *Thanatology* concerned with studies of death awareness and anxiety, and as an undergraduate, I read Heidegger's *Being and Time*, where he asserted that as humans, we are free to be anxious in facing our death.[49]

And of course, the topic of death is of more immediate salience for me because in 2001—right before 9/11—my father died; in 2010 both my husband, Leon, and my mom died, and then in 2013 Bud died at home, with hospice care. This past year I have lost two additional dear friends—one the husband of a couple in our immediate friend circle, the other a past parishioner who was in some ways a father figure to me. So the topic of death is an immediate one in my life. As is the topic of coping with loss and rewriting one's life story in order to create a coherent sense of life as a whole post-loss.

As I reflect a bit on some of the wisdom found within the pages of Neimeyer's book and summarize some selected research findings from the narrative psychology literature, I can't help but personalize some of my observations. The topic lies too close to the bone not to weave in my own reflections and experiences.

One of the chapters in Neimeyer's book was authored by Lawrence Calhoun and Richard Tedeschi. They had previously published a book based on their research titled *Postraumatic Growth: Positive Change in the Aftermath of Crisis*. In this chapter, they reaffirm the major findings from their work: That following trauma comes a change in the sense of oneself—as

---

Age."

48. "Help," Written and performed by The Beatles. Copyright 1965 and all rights administered by Sony/ATV Music Publishing LLC, 8 Music Square West, Nashville, TN 37203.

49. My first-year research project as a graduate student was showing a group of undergraduates a film I came across—produced to help train physicians—titled "Death." It was the documentation of the dying and death of a guy named Albro, who lived an empty life and died a lonely death. The last scene was the image of his body being put into a refrigerated drawer in the hospital morgue. I remember doing before and after assessments of the students' anxiety levels, but I don't remember the findings. Apparently it wasn't worthy of publication!

both vulnerable and stronger for having weathered the loss and moved on in life. In addition, relationships tend to be embraced more fully, along with a willingness to self-disclose and a sense of greater empathy, especially with fellow sufferers. A deeper sense of spirituality in the sufferers' lives also seems to develop following major loss.

Calhoun and Tedeschi raise certain caveats along the way. Not everyone benefits from traumatic loss and they are careful not to paint a rosy picture of suffering. Pain is real and sometimes long-lasting. But you can also learn to live with the sad undertow of life that comes with wisdom and experience. In fact, a number of studies have been carried out in recent years that do identify positive outcomes following the death of a loved one (for example, bringing family closer, taking "time to smell the roses," seeing the self as stronger in the end, and so on).

Neimeyer's own research has been carried out in a clinical setting. Not surprisingly, since meaning is primarily constructed and reconstructed in dialogue with another, therapeutic approaches to helping the bereaved include therapeutic writing of one's life story to include the loss event, retelling the life in extended conversations with a therapist, and visualizing techniques to help overcome and incorporate troubling images into a more manageable and meaningful memory. In what Neimeyer terms a "constructivist"[50] approach, he emphasizes that we humans are motivated to create and maintain a coherent self-story. In his work, he focuses on various strategies to help the bereaved re-write their master narrative in order to re-establish a coherent and consistent sense of storied self in the midst of seismic change.

For me the most affecting chapter in the whole edited volume was the one by Thomas Attig. A philosopher by training, Attig views bereavement as a process of "relearning the world." He sees the functions of grief as twofold: To relearn our worlds of physical space, temporal events, and social networks; and to struggle with the pain, anguish, and residual grief that death leaves in its wake.

Faced with being alone for the first time in my life when Bud died, I had to deal with the concreteness of being alone in the house, dealing with his clothes and other personal effects (I actually waited over two years to clean out his closet and drawers), salvaging papers, journals, and books from his office at the seminary. Everywhere I looked, every place I drove to locally, all the restaurants and the park where we walked—everywhere I looked memories came flooding back. I spent a lot of time in the first six to twelve months with tears in my eyes.

50. Neimeyer, "The Language of Loss."

In terms of time, the first Christmas was the hardest. I went to California to spend that holiday with my youngest son and his family, but it was a bittersweet, sad time for me that year. In fact, I did a lot of travel the first year after he died, until I finally realized that I couldn't run away from my life. And so I settled down into my home and new world routine, and reached out a great deal—as I still do—to close friends. In fact, now—almost three years after his death—I go out more often during the week with one set of friends or another, much more than I ever socialized when my life companion was with me in the same house.

As to Attig's second function of grief, after the deaths in my life, there is always a certain residual sadness that I just live with. As he points out, it is entirely possible to be both joyful in your life and, at the same time, carry around your life's sadness within you. Interestingly, Attig says that in some real sense, living with the one who has died need not entirely stop—at least in terms of their felt presence. There is a kind of transition to a lasting love as he puts it. Examples he gives of ways to maintain that sense of "lasting love" include—in a very practical sense—the way my late husbands have provided for me. But this sense of ongoing love is also maintained by my honoring their memories in promoting their values and interests, by keeping a place in my heart for those I have lost—treasuring all my loved ones' photographs on my refrigerator— "fingering them with my eyes" like fingering my rosary beads on the table beside me.

Attig sums up his thoughts with the observation that finally those who relearn their worlds and deal with the pain and sadness of grief, also develop the wisdom of living into mystery. That some things cannot be understood this side of the grave, that change and impermanence become more tolerable when we come to realize that love and the meaning we found in our loved one's life remain after death. "Imperfection becomes more acceptable as we forgive them their shortcomings, sense that they forgive ours, and find consolation in the lasting good we found in our imperfect love. Not knowing and uncertainty become more acceptable as we find ways of continuing in faith and hope even in their absence."[51]

God and Suffering: "Wayfaring Stranger"

> If you've been around for a while, you know that much of the time, if you are patient and are paying attention, you will see that God will restore what the locusts have taken away.[52]

---

51. Attig, "Relearning the World," 51.
52. Lamott, *Help, Thanks, Wow*, 50.

****

On the afternoon that we finally got into our Barbados hotel rooms—before the bleeding episode and the nightmarish next twenty-four hours until Bud and I got back to the States—I was sitting on our balcony, admiring the palm trees before my eyes. Out of nowhere, the lyrics of the song "Wayfaring Stranger" came to my mind. And I sang that old spiritual softly to myself: "I am a poor, wayfaring stranger/Traveling through this world alone/And there's no sickness, toil,or danger/In that bright land to which I go/And I'm going there to see my mother/I'm going there no more to roam/I'm only going over Jordan/I'm only going over home."

Actually, in the rendition I heard in my head, one chorus said "father," alternating with the next chorus "I'm going to see my mother." The song brought back my lost parents to me in a very immediate, almost tangible way and also brought those comforting tears to my eyes. After Bud died nine months later, all those losses by death have colored my memory of that balcony experience.

So where *is* God in all this loss? It's the eternal question, isn't it—at least for many of us? In the last chapter, I attempted to answer at the micro level—speculating that God's Spirit impinges on our brains at the level of the neural synapse. And at the macro level, I've talked about evolutionary theism, opening up the possibility of God's creative purpose working through evolutionary mechanisms to call forth human beings in God's image as well as calling forth the human race toward Teilhard's Omega Point or the eschaton of a new creation.[53]

But at the level of our anguish, at the level of our grief and struggle for meaning, the question remains. Where is God in the middle of horrendous pain and suffering? Many who suffer grief and have the skills to write about it—to work through their sorrow by writing their questions out for the world to see and maybe fashion some kind of answer for themselves in the process—have comforted others who are suffering their own losses in life.

One of the books that I began to read when Bud entered hospice and continued to finish after he died was one written by Luci Shaw and titled *God in the Dark: Through Grief and Beyond*. It was hard to read because it was the story of her own husband's dying and aftermath. She described so many of the same experiences that I was going through such as recognizing herself in her new identity as widow. "I am a widow, a social symbol, my face smiling to the family, my friends, with a sharp superficial brightness that glares like an unshielded light bulb. I am alone." And when she walked

---

53. See Newberg's *Principles of Neurotheology* and Green's *What About the Soul?*.

away from her husband's fresh grave, she asked where he was. She says "This was my husband whom I was leaving under the gray sky. Or was it? Where was he?"[54]

After reading Shaw's observation that she was not just sorry for herself, she also grieved for her husband's loss. And she grieved at the loss of their marriage—"for the union we've woven of moments and years. Death is tearing at it, will tear it, like a ripped cloth."[55] A few months after reading those words, and about three months after Bud died, I was visiting my youngest son, Kevin, and his family in California. During lunch one day, I looked at Kevin across the table and said that like Shaw, I felt sorry for Bud's loss because he so wanted to live and continue being with me in our common life. I felt sorry for the bonded companionship that we lost through his death.

I couldn't do anything about his or our loss in my life. But I could do something about grieving for myself—feeling sorry for myself—by practicing smiling and by being grateful for the loves in my life that remain. I'm still working at it. It's a slow healing process. But I've also come a long way on the road to healing. As many reports and empirical studies show,[56] among the most important factors in struggling with loss through death are significant relationships with others and some sense of meaningful work to do. I have been blessed with friends near and far, and I find great satisfaction in my writing life, as well as exercising my priestly office at St. John's.

Again, being part of a religious tradition, a community of faith that provides an overarching story with hope and mercy at its core, can comfort. Such stories, symbols, and rituals of embodied meaning can also aid the one who is grieving to rewrite their life story into a coherent and meaningful whole. And I do believe that God is in the middle of such healing, from our brain synapses as we experience our world of work and others, through our communities, through our culture within which we live out our days.

In his *The Healer of Shattered Hearts*, David Wolpe writes about how through faith, God can touch a life, altering our vision. There are very few things other than such faith that can "ease the ache of loneliness, the terrible fear that we are spinning blindly through the universe."[57] And yet, as Matt Fitzgerald counters in a dialogue with the poet and theologian Christian Wiman, while faith may be like "water on parched lips, it is also sheer,

---

54. Shaw, *God in the Dark*, 169.

55. Ibid., 152.

56. For example, Currier et al., "Bereavement, Religion, and Post-Traumatic Growth"; and McIntosh et al., "Religion's Role in Adjustment to a Negative Life Event."

57. Wolpe, *The Healer of Shattered Hearts*, 172.

unanswered longing."[58] That is, for many God is both Mystery and silence. Perhaps, as Tom Fate says, "the point of faith is not answers, but meaning. Live in the questions, in the Mystery."[59]

Maybe there is no better way to end this discussion of God and our suffering and grief in life than to turn to John de Gruchy's discussion of faith and Mystery. After the death of his son Steve at the height of Steve's career as a fellow theologian, John de Gruchy wrote of his struggle with the meaning of our life with God after such evil had befallen him and his wife, Isobel. He admits that faith is not easy. No, it's a daily struggle to "affirm that there is purpose and meaning in life, that love does endure and ultimately conquers, that miracles do happen, and that there are signs of hope that keep budding."

De Gruchy says that at the end of the day, either there is nothing out there and thus no ultimate meaning to our lives, or there is something that gives it all meaning, an end that ultimately matters. In the final analysis, de Grunchy opts for ultimate meaning. He says, "We believe that in the end God is the ultimate mystery that gives everything coherence and significance. But faith in God remains a questioning faith; a journey into a mystery that embraces us, yet remains greater than we can fully grasp."[60]

I have circled around through these various authors that I have cited to try to express as clearly as I can my understanding of where God is in all of this, in the sorrow and joys of my own life, and in the sorrow and triumphs of the world's history. I live by hope and daily prayer to a God I do believe hears me in some sense, and forms and informs my being at all levels of experience. I face the mystery of my parents' loss, my husbands' deaths, and believe that somehow, in God's mystery, they still are. Beyond that, Mystery remains.

Interlude II: Meet Forrest Again

We met Forrest a few pages back as he recounted in his book *Love & Death* his youthful experience with loss in the death of his friend, Dalton Denton. As I said before, his book has been a significant one for me and I have drawn from it for a sermon or two, and have referred it to friends who are suffering loss of one kind or another.

There are two excerpts from his book that have become part of my memory store that I recall from time to time when experiencing some

---

58. Wiman and Fitzgerald, "Embrace and Abandonment," 23.
59. Fate, "The Presence of Absence," 31.
60. de Gruchy, *Led into Mystery*, 97.

rough patch in my own life. First, let me let Church speak for himself as he told his parishioners at All Souls Unitarian Church in New York City that he had just been diagnosed with a likely terminal disease. On October 17, 2006, he wrote this letter:

> Dear Friends,
>
> With apologies for sending this word out so impersonally, I'm writing to share with you the news that I have esophageal cancer. A bank of tests conducted over the past two weeks has confirmed the existence of a malignant tumor high in my esophagus, and we shall determine a protocol for treatment (radiation and chemotherapy or surgical removal) before the end of the month. Unhappily, this is a particularly fierce form of cancer.... More important than any of these cold medical facts, I am in good spirits and more grateful than ever for the gifts of life and love. All four children have descended on the household, and Carolyn is girding herself for the struggle ahead. She'll be the general, I'm relieved to report; I'll simply be the battlefield.

A few pages further on in his book, Church reflects on the clear fact that all of our lives end in the middle of the story that we are not able to finish ourselves. He says we leave the stage before knowing how our entire story will end. But still, in order to help ensure a good "exit," the one thing that remains within our power is to take care of all unfinished business—make peace with others, reconciling where need be with loved ones; make peace with ourselves, forgiving ourselves for perhaps loving deeply but not always well; and finally making peace with God.

One bit of wisdom that has stayed with me is what Church refers to as his "mantra." He says:

> In each of our lives not only will some rain fall, but fires will burn, the ground will shake, and one day, life itself will be exacted in payment for the gift of life bestowed. By wanting what we have [that is, not envying others but being content with your own accomplishments], doing what we can [living for others in community as much as you can manage], and being who we are [living your own talents and gifts, as well as forgiving your own shortcomings] our cup will forever be half full, not half empty. Do these same things with reverence, humbled by awe, and our cup runneth over... I call this thoughtful wishing—wishing for what is ours, here and now, to have, do, and be.

One metaphoric image of Church's that I used in a sermon of mine at St. John's was the image of our looking out on our world as looking through a stained glass window. The world is multicolored and bright as we survey the richness of our life. But then one day, one of the panes of glass becomes clouded over—we are diagnosed with something awful or a loved one becomes dreadfully sick or we lose our job unexpectedly or a child is in an accident. He says the tendency is that we "press our nose up against that one window pane, desperately trying to see through it. When we do this, we lose all sense of proportion. Our entire world goes black." And we lose sight of all the blessings that are still there in the richness of the world around us. Our entire life becomes bleak.

Church hastens to insist that there's nothing wrong with attending to that cloudy pane, to do everything we can to get well, to polish it up. But he says, what concerns him is this: "Even as we do everything in our power to get healthy again, we may obsess so on our sickness that we lose appreciation for all those things in our life that we would dearly pray be returned to us if someone suddenly snatched them away." Things like joyfully embracing lifelong friends, truly seeing a loving spouse, enjoying your child's triumph at school, and appreciating the music and art that surround you.

After extensive treatment for his esophageal cancer, Church experienced a pause in the disease's aggressive progression. But the pause did not last. And when it returned, it returned with a vengeance. And near the end of his book, he wrote a short chapter titled "Where Is God?" and of course, he recites the usual questions that many if not most raise when faced with horrendous suffering: Why me? Why didn't God answer our prayers for a cure? He asks "Why fate me, a relatively young man, never to meet my grandchildren and not to grow old beside my darling wife?" And as he notes, once you start to ask the "Why?" question, it doesn't stop. Why the Holocaust? Why 9/11? Why the suffering of the current Syrian refugees? Why whole swatches of a town wiped off the map by earthquake or tornado? Within all religious traditions there are answers given that always remain incomplete.

As John de Gruchy observes, the final answer is Mystery. In faith we cling to our understanding of God that in the end, in the end of it all, God is all-loving and all-merciful. Church concludes that "when love dwells in our hearts, we dwell in God's presence." He admits that this conclusion does not answer the "why" question. He says "Final answers to ultimate questions lie far beyond the ken of human understanding. We keep asking, of course. It's the nature of our being, the nature of our quest. We keep climbing up to reach the stars even as God comes down to share our tears, each to the other like a vanishing pot of gold at two ends of a rainbow." Near the end of this beautiful book Church offers this sage advice:

> One thing I do know is that we can't say goodbye to those we love either too early or too often. "I love you" should end every farewell, howsoever briefly we plan to be apart. Death can pounce in the middle of the night or interrupt the most uneventful day. When this happens, what a relief it is that the last message we imparted to our love one was "I love you." . . .
>
> For now, I bid you farewell. Go forth into this fragile, blessed world we share with laughter and tears at the ready. Love, work, and serve to a fare-thee-well. And then, when your own time comes, let go. Let go for dear life.[61]

Those were the last words in the book. Forrest Church died on September 24, 2009, at the age of sixty-one.

****

To paraphrase Leonard Cohen, all of our lives are finally cracked by loss and frailty—that's how the light gets in. Let me end this chapter on loss and story with another image from a story. Andre Dubus, whom we met earlier in this chapter, struggled mightily following the hit-and-run accident that cost him both legs. A former marine, a physically fit man struck down in mid-life and at peak career, he worked with a physical therapist to regain some mobility using only his right leg and a walker. Dubus kept working and while he was struggling to move, he cried. Cried tears for the pain and for the suffering and for all his loss.

When he was finally up on the massage table and the very wise and comforting physical therapist worked on his one leg with her strong hands, she recited something from the book of Jeremiah in the Old Testament. She said "the potter is making a pot and it cracks. So he smashes it, and makes a new vessel. You can't make a new vessel out of a broken one. It's time to find the real you."[62]

As Church says, be who you are. Accept who you are. You have a whole new life to live and so your story has to be rewritten after such loss. We all have or will have that opportunity post-loss—with a little greater wisdom about what really matters, continuing to weave together the sometimes

---

61. Church, *Love & Death*, 32–33; 42; 77; 94; 112–13; 131; 140.
62. Dubus, *Broken Vessels*, 172.

broken pieces of our lives into a coherent and hopeful whole to the very last chapter.

7

"Imagine Me and You..."
The Many-Splendored Thing Called Love

> "Anything worth thinking about is worth singing about."
> Which is why we have
> songs of praise, songs of love, songs
> of sorrow.[1]

****

I found out after bicycling home late that afternoon that my parents had had the Bremen police out looking for me. I had left home late that morning to ride out to the local Lake of the Woods and didn't return on my bike until around 4:00 PM. It was the summer after my eighth grade year and I had just happened to meet my first real boyfriend out by the lake and we rode our bikes around most of the afternoon.

I also remember our stopping occasionally to kiss, discovering this fantastic new thing that for some reason we kept doing, off and on, throughout the afternoon. At one point, we got off our bikes at some little local cemetery near the lake and held hands, and kissed a bit more. This afternoon wasn't the very first kiss between us. No, the *first kiss* was downstairs in my parents'

---

1. Bob Dylan quoted in Oliver, "And Bob Dylan Too," 17.

recreation room while we were sitting close together on the couch. Apparently we decided that that was a great thing to do, because we showered numerous kisses on each other that afternoon by the lake.

But here's the thing. Those kisses were absolutely innocent ones, little explorations into a new world that I, as a thirteen-year-old and Bill as a fourteen-year-old had not ventured into before. I realize that that sounds pretty quaint given our current cultural "progress" in this regard, where kids in junior high are now counseled in the art of birth control. But this was then, and innocence prevailed. Nevertheless our respective parents were not happy about this afternoon's disappearance and Bill's parents made him call my dad and apologize for keeping me out for so long and alarming them in the process.

But what I remember is the magic of it all. I remember lying on my bed that evening, sensing that something magical was happening inside of me, some sense, some feeling that was warm and rising up like sap in the limbs of a young tree. I couldn't have put a name to it, couldn't have really described the sensation. All I knew at the time was that the feeling was new and good. And I liked that feeling a lot.

So that was the beginning of my first "puppy" love. Bill's and my playful attraction had begun that same year—I remember his selling popcorn during basketball games and my hanging out nearby, and once he thrillingly held my hand across the counter. It didn't last of course. Bill pulled away from me sometime during our freshman year. Never did know why, but I moved on to other boys and other heartbreaks, some of my own making, some that happened to me. We covered a bit of that early ground in the last chapter.

Of course, before there was puppy love that came along as the hormones coursed their way through our adolescent bodies there were other loves in my life. First and foremost was the love I had for my mom and dad, and the love within the family circle. My one brother, Joe, was seven years older than me and in a sense, grew up as part of an earlier generation. But I idolized him. He was my hero. There was the well-worn family story about the day that I showed up to wait for him at his school bus stop, all outfitted up in my Hopalong Cassidy outfit, complete with holster and guns—apparently embarrassing him in front of his friends. But I just wanted to greet him because I did indeed adore my big brother! And still do, by the way. And I always admired my grandmother Pauline—the one who was married to that philanderer and finally divorced him before it became a socially acceptable thing to do by the time I had entered my Boomer twenties.

So I was one of the lucky ones, surrounded by a family who loved and nurtured me, and learning to love by seeing it done. As the title to this chapter suggests, love is in fact a many-splendored thing, the capacity we all have to one degree or another that finally makes us human. As we will see in the pages ahead, we are not the only species that forms family and tribal attachments. But in us humans, our capacity to give ourselves over to others—not only to offspring and spouses and early family members, but to community and country and abstract ideals such as freedom and justice and human rights represents our highest perfecting attainment.

None of us loves perfectly or even at times very well. But across our lifetimes, beginning at birth and ending at the end of our story, I believe we can learn to love better and again, as Tom Hanks said, to become a better version of ourselves in the process. So let's go back to our early Boomer selves and examine our life back then, learning to love as we experimented with the myriad forms its expression took in the '60s and '70s.

BACK THEN: "HOOKED ON A FEELIN', HIGH ON BELIEVIN' THAT YOU'RE IN LOVE WITH ME"[2]

> It is the love of our existence that is the highest love of all, the love of humanity with all our flaws, all our destructiveness, all our petty fears, gossip, and rivalries. A love of the goodness that we sometimes show under the most difficult stresses, of the heroism of doing the right thing even when no one can see us doing it, of being honest when there is nothing to gain by it, of loving those whom others might find unlovable. It is all this, and our capacity to write about it—to celebrate it in song—that makes us human.[3]

The Scene: "If You Could Read My Mind"

Near the beginning of his chapter on love songs, Dan Levitin notes that in our Boomer youth, we learned all about love from our songs. There were the early ones: "Unchained Melody," a song expressing the forever kind of love we dream about, and Johnny Mathis crooning "The Twelfth of Never"— ideal love that yearns and lasts into eternity, as infinite as the stars in the sky. In fact, a large percentage of the songs of our youth were all about love in all its manifestations. As Levitin points out, all these songs then and since are about one or more of the four stages of love: The "I Want You, I Need

---

2. Thomas, "Hooked on a Feeling."
3. Levitin, *The World in Six Songs*, 269.

You" longing stage; the "I Got You Babe" joyful, celebratory stage; the "Oh my love, my darling, I've hungered for your kiss,"[4] missing you stage; and finally of course the "something inside has died . . . and I just can't fake it,"[5] it's over stage.

The '60s and early '70s of course are known for the mantra "make love, not war." Those were the heady days of "free love," the pill, the idea of "open marriage"—which turned out to be not such a good idea, though many did enthusiastically decide to experiment with swapping partners for casual sex. Remember the movie *Bob and Carol, Ted and Alice* and the two couples' frolicking stay at the "growth" center Esalen?

I was in graduate school during part of that time and Indiana University was home to the Kinsey Institute and the scientific investigation of human sexual response. Sex therapy was on the rise (no pun intended), and clinical training centers such as the one at IU were equipping us to treat all manner of sexual dysfunction.

In fact, sex was in the air in those days. And our songs—like Bob Dylan's "Lay Lady Lay," Gary Puckett's "Young girl get out of my mind/My love for you is way out of line/Better run girl/You're much too young girl,"[6] and Simon and Garfunkel's "Cecilia" where someone "Got out of bed to wash my face/When I came back to bed someone's taking my place"[7]—all hinted at raw sex. Not that that equated with the search for love, but once in a while the two probably intersected.

I will note right here that along with not joining the drug culture at the time, I also did not participate in the free love scene. But I knew many peers who did. There are probably several reasons why I didn't—including the fact that I was about five years older than my peers, I had two little boys and another life beyond the boundaries of the clinic and social scene. And it also I suppose had something to do with how I was raised and an ingrained moral compass caused me to reject casual sex.

I don't want to paint myself as a goody two shoes. If you remember, I did slide out of one marriage into another at the end of my graduate student days. I was certainly part of the '60s scene as we've covered in earlier chapters—from miniskirts to barefoot flower child to the embrace of liberal political ideas to my parents' horror, to falling hard for a middle-aged

---

4. The Righteous Brothers, "Unchained Melody."

5. "It's Too Late", words and music by Carole King and Toni Kathrine Stern. Performed by Carole King. Copyright, 1971. Published by Colgems EMI Music, Inc. Copyright administered by ASCAP.

6. Gary Puckett & The Union Gap, "Young Girl."

7. Simon and Garfunkel, "Cecilia."

professor and joining the crowd of faculty-student pairings that popped up on campus and became the talk of the faculty town circuit for years to come.

Anyway, as I said, I didn't sleep around. But many did. And I think along with that, there developed a certain cynicism about the lastingness of a love commitment. From Gordon Lightfoot's "If You Could Read My Mind" (" . . . the feeling's gone/And I just can't get it back"[8]) to Carole King's "It's Too Late," ("Something inside has died and I can't hide/And I just can't fake it"[9]). I'm reading Carly Simon's memoir that has recently come out, titled *Boys in the Trees*. Not only am I impressed with the large number of Who's Whos in the music business that she slept with, but if you remember, her first major hit was the song "That's the Way I Always Heard It Should Be." The first time I heard the lyrics—"the couples cling and claw/And drown in love's debris"[10]—I was stunned at the picture of marriage that the lyrics painted. The inevitable waning of love and affection, the empty smiles, the fakery, the quiet misery lasting over the years. And in the end, her seeming resignation to go ahead and marry because . . . well . . . because it was expected and . . . what the hell, why not? Just giving in and accepting the inevitable loss of love that goes along with it.

Yet through all of that '60s love madness, there was a search, and hunger for *communitas*, for a bonding and binding into some kind of communal love experience that seemed to always disappoint in the end. In his *The Republic of Rock*, Michael Kramer ends the work with the lines "Hey all you people, for goodness sake/Let's get to together, what does it take?"[11]

Reading Carly Simon's autobiography brought to mind Marcus Greil's *The History of Rock 'N' Roll in Ten Songs* that we looked at in an earlier chapter. Turning back to that work, although Greil focuses on the beginning and history of rock and roll as a specific music genre, I think his observation about music as the expression of the human spirit holds good for what we're talking about here. The human spirit he is referring to is an embodied expression of our free selves, breaching boundaries in our grasping for transcendence. A reviewer of Greil's book observes that "when the music was great and enduring, it was, in part, because the people making it lived with abandon."[12] And when we hear the songs again they evoke our early

8. Lightfoot, "If You Could Read My Mind."

9. King, "It's Too Late."

10. Written by Jacob Brackman and Carly Simon, performed by Carly Simon. Copyright 1970 by C'est Music and Maya Productions LTD and administered by BMG Rights Management US LLC.

11. Kramer, *The Republic of Rock*, 223.

12. Touré, "Greil Marcus's 'History of Rock 'n' Roll in Ten Songs,'" para. 8.

memories of the times and of the others we celebrated with in the youth of our lives.

Levitin makes the point more than once in his writing that music serves as what he calls an "honest signal"—awakening memories embodied deep within our brains, and the singer of lyrics expresses these personal truths in song. In other words, it's hard to fake the emotion-laden meaning. If you've never felt love, never felt betrayal, or loss, or rage, you just don't have it in you to express that kind of truth in song. In fact, apparently this is true not only in singing lyrics, but in other embodied expressions, such as a fake smile that masks the existential truth of felt meaning in a social interaction. In recent research by Iris Mauss and colleagues, they report that "positive emotional behavior that does not accurately reflect the person's experience may impede social connectedness and, in turn, psychological functioning."[13] These researchers report that such disconnection between expression and inner experience was found on six-month follow up to increase levels of depression and decrease a sense of well-being.

Which brings me back to an early memory of my own.

During my residency as a clinical psychologist at the Indiana University School of Medicine in Indianapolis, part of my training experience was a live-in weekend at a retreat center on the outskirts of the city. The purpose of the weekend was to train us budding psychologists and psychiatrists in how to run a group therapy treatment session. If I remember, there were twelve of us trainees, about equally divided by gender and our two disciplines.

Now you have to remember that this was the mid-70s, and we were still in the "tell it like it is, baby!" *zeitgeist*. Fritz Perls and other gurus of confrontational therapeutic gestalt methods were *au courant*, and this was going to be the approach used by the group trainers that weekend.

Well, there we were doing our group thing, and someone suggested that it might be a good idea if we all sat on the floor for this session. For some reason, I resisted sitting on the floor, so I became the only one still perched on my chair as the confrontational process began. Now you may know from personal experience that groups have a low tolerance for deviant behavior. So I became the target for group analysis. Finally, one of the guys who was a psychiatry resident decided that I was being uptight, and what I needed was someone to rub my neck.

I didn't want anyone to touch me, but as he approached and began massaging the back of my neck, the whole group fell silent and just watched. Finally, the guy quit and we all just sat there. The group leader then asked me how that was and I lied. I said, "Oh, that was fine." Now everyone knew that

---

13. Mauss et al., "Don't Hide Your Happiness!," abstract, 738.

I was lying and of course, being good gestalt participants, the whole group turned on me. At that point, one of the psychiatry residents announced that of all the women sitting in the room, I was the one he would least like to go to bed with.

Well, at that revelation, what did I do? I laughed. Yes, I laughed and that was the last straw. I realized late that I was now the target for animosity. So at that point, I committed the cowardly act of joining the rest of the group on the floor. Really. And that was that. And we moved on.

But that was the end of my participation in the weekend. I withdrew inside of myself and isolated myself from the group experience. On the last day, since it was a beautiful fall weekend, the group trainer had us sit in a circle outside on the lawn. She proposed that we each take a turn and tell the group what we learned during the weekend, how we benefitted from the whole experience. I knew that either I would lie again and say how wonderful and enlightening it had been, or I had to face another group confrontation. I remember watching as the circle's turn came closer to me, and when my turn was next, I simply stood up, gathered my notebook, headed for the house, packed my bag, threw it in my car, and drove away.

I had committed the unforgivable sin of walking out of a group before "closure" could be gained. The next day I had to face my clinical supervisor and I told him right up front what I had done. But he then laughed and said he had done the very same thing when he was a resident.

Actually, I did learn something important about myself that weekend. I learned that although many times in my life I have gone my own way, done it my way, bucked convention as we Boomers were want to do, nevertheless I have a pretty thin skin. That is, I was capable of "in your face," but I didn't have the armor that would shield me from hurt when others responded negatively to my independent ways.

Interestingly, I recently came across a report of a study that showed that the pain of social rejection is in fact real pain. That is, apparently the brain registers social rejection in the same region as physical pain—(to be technical, a region called the dorsal anterior cingulate and anterior insula neural centers). These researchers also found that such pain, registered experientially as hurt feelings (e.g., anxiety, depression, anger, jealousy, sadness)—at least some of which I experienced that weekend—could be mitigated by giving Tylenol. However the reviewer of this study also pointed out that chronic rejection over a long duration can have serious and long-lasting effects on both the brain and the psyche. One way or another one has to learn from the pain and deal with it in order to avoid those consequences.

So with that nod to our neurological equipment and our focus here on the love songs that awaken memories and stir our emotions, let's turn and go deeper into our marvelous brain function as we address the topic of love in all its manifestations.

Going Deeper

> The experience of being in love has been likened to an illness, an addiction, and even insanity. If you've ever fallen "madly" in love or been "insanely" jealous, you have a good idea why. Certainly, people have been known to become as obsessed with other people as an addict is with drugs. Love and addiction share a loss of reason, an absence of self-control, and an obsessive longing that must be satisfied.... Drug addicts may satisfy their need for intimacy by manipulating the biochemistry of bonding and attachment... think of how drug-addicted individuals so often become indifferent to other people.[14]

In an earlier chapter, we talked about how our human brains operate as a closed-loop system, regulating inner hemostatic processes such as the level of oxygen circulating through our blood stream and the level of potassium in our cells (although these regulated biochemical necessities are also affected by outer forces such as loss of pressure in an airplane or starvation). However, our spouse's level of blood oxygen does not affect our own.

But our brain is also more explicitly an open-loop system in the social realm. That is, we are greatly affected emotionally by others' emotional states. Cells such as mirror neurons cause us to mimic what we see others do—feeling others joy so we laugh; seeing others cry and becoming sad. Such cells "link us to each other. They appear to be an essential component of the social brain and an important mechanism of communication across the social synapse."[15] In fact, Daniel Goleman, in his classic work on emotional intelligence, has gone so far as to say that "failure to register another's feeling is a major deficit in emotional intelligence, and a tragic failing in what it means to be human."[16]

In his *The Neuroscience of Human Relationships*, Louis Cozolino makes the observation linking love and addiction quoted at the beginning of this section. We might want to debate whether he is actually describing human love or infatuation, and we'll look at the difference in the pages ahead. But certainly, if you have ever "fallen" head over heels in love with someone, you can grasp the truth of what he describes. That is, the biochemical linkage

---

14. Cozolino, *The Neuroscience of Human Relationships*, 115.
15. Root, "Wired Together," 34.
16. Goleman, *Emotional Intelligence*, 86.

between attachment to another and addiction to drugs is actually more than a metaphor.

In fact, as Cozolino goes into great detail to describe, the neurochemical systems affected by our relationships with others are the same as those affected by cocaine and heroin—accompanied by feelings of craving, dependence, and withdrawal when such intense attachments are lost. Although there is a clear evolutionary base for empathy and social behavior,[17] in our complex brains the neurochemical systems driving maternal behavior and pair bonding have become combined with evolved cognitive and emotional reward systems to create our current relationship patterns.

Cozolino notes that "neural networks involved in the regulation and release of motivational biochemicals are triggered from multiple brain regions involved in everything from primitive reproductive processes (thalamus), to fear and anxiety regulation (amygdala), to moral and aesthetic judgments (pre-frontal cortex)."[18] Undoubtedly what was happening in my brain during that new experience of kissing my first boyfriend—that warm, feel-good experience that I was bathed in that evening as I lay on my bed—was the release of these neurochemicals and consequent rush of hormones that couldn't be described but felt very good indeed. It was my first "heady" experience of this kind—again no pun intended.

Cozolino describes one study that scanned the brains of people who were deeply in love with someone, testing the hypothesis that when confronted with a picture of their loved one, the brain systems involved in positive feelings would be activated and brain centers responsible for negative emotional states and scanning of the physical environment for threat would be inactive. And this is exactly what the researchers found.

Cozolino suggests that the experience of love involves at least two processes: First, a decreased "activation of the fear systems, as demonstrated by the 'standing down' of the amygdala and the environmental processing of the posterior cingulate and other cortical areas."

"... Love turns off the alarm, cancels our insurance, and frees us from worry." And second, "love makes us happy by activating the brain's reward systems.... Love is a drug—in fact, a number of drugs (including endorphins and dopamine) resulting in similar patterns of brain activation as seen in taking cocaine." He also points out that evolution primarily preserved the negative emotion centers in our brain because natural selection was "more interested in keeping us alive than in making us happy."[19] Nevertheless, trust

---

17. de Waal, "The Antiquity of Empathy."
18. Cozolino, *The Neuroscience of Human Relationships*, 127.
19. Ibid., 401.

can be engendered and fear reduced in the service of social bonding that, overall and in the long run, has served our species very well over time.

But what does all this have to do with singing and love songs? A reminder here that in our early human ancestors the capacity to sing evolved before language and became established in the service of social bonding and care of offspring. As a form of social cognition, music became a form of communication to others at a distance. As psychologists Chris Loersch and Nathan Arbuckle note, "The pleasure we derive from listening to music results from its innate connection to the basic social drives that create our interconnected world."[20] Singing soothed the fear centers of our early, more primitive brain, and to this day we sing songs of love in celebration of the feelings that well up within.

As to Cozolino's "love rush" as addictive, songs that come to mind here are the Kingston Trio's "Scotch and Soda" ("jigger of gin, oh what a spell I'm in"[21]) and B. J. Thomas's "Hooked on a feeling/high on believing/that you're in love with me."[22] And we don't outgrow such a chemical rush. When my late husband—in the first days of our budding friendship—admitted to me that he loved me deeply, the effect of his admission was "seismic," as I later told him. My world was turned upside down and that "addictive" phase lasted actually quite a while—to the end of our relatively brief marriage, until the day Bud died.

Dan Levitin makes the careful and important distinction between that first rush of infatuation and the mature love that has weathered the ups and downs of life, undergirding long-term commitment to the other. He says that in general, the first neurochemical high that we described at the beginning of this section does tend to dissipate over time—he cites five to seven years as about right. But mature love lasts. He characterizes the initial, romantic love as "me-centered"—"hooked on a feeling"—versus true mature love as "other-centered." Perhaps in the end it is both—a matter of a shifting mixture over time, with elements of both attraction and commitment in the mix.

As noted at the beginning of this chapter, love is in fact many-faceted, ranging from parental love, love of friends, and love of ideals such as

---

20. Loersch and Arbuckle, "Unraveling the Mystery of Music," 777.

21. Written by Dave Guard and performed by The Kingston Trio. Copyright 1959/1961 by EMI Music Publishing Company, renewed 1987/1989 by Beechwood Music Corp. Administered by Sony/ATV Music Publishing LLC, 8 Music Square West, Nashville, TN 37203.

22. Written by James Mark, performed by B. J. Thomas. Copyright 1968 by Screen Gems-EMI Music Inc./Sony/ATV Music Publishing LLC, 8 Music Square West, Nashville, TN 37203.

freedom. But if we are talking about spousal love—love between partners that involves sexual expression—mature love is likely indeed a complex biological and social bonding process. Some researcher once noted that marital love remains strong if three elements are present: sharing the serious ups and down of life, sharing the daily trivia of ordinary living, and regular sexual engagement. Mature love is woven into our complex lives as we live them out over the years.

Levitin goes so far as to say that "love in its larger sense—the sweeping, selfless commitment to another person, group, or idea—is the most important cornerstone of a civilized society . . . essential for the establishment of what we think of today as human society, what we regard as our fundamental nature." As an example of such a love expressed in musical lyrics, Levitin cites Johnny Cash's song "I Walk the Line." It's both an "educational" warning for the singer himself (as well as others) to "toe the line," and to be true to his love commitment. But it is also an example of a "powerful love song, a song celebrating a commitment to something above the passing emotions of lust." Levitin says:

> Love songs, like all art, help us to articulate our feelings. They often use metaphorical language ("I'm on fire," "I will climb the highest mountain") to help us see our emotions from a different perspective. They stick in our heads to remind us, as the emotions ebb and flow, of what we once felt. And above all, they raise the feelings to the level of artistic expression—imbuing them with an elegance and sophistication that helps us strive for them even when the going gets tough.[23]

This is how we humans are wired. This is how we have evolved from our earliest ancestors. Our finest human tendencies for fidelity, altruism, and bonding with others enable us to commit to mature love in all its forms across our adult lifetimes. None of us probably love perfectly, but our capacity is there—inborn—and can be learned and moved nearer to perfection over time.

Even in cases of childhood neglect and abuse, where attachments are thwarted and early bonds with parents and then others are never formed, love attachments can be eventually learned. Many years ago, psychologist John Bowlby carried out research on infants who lost parents during war time. These babies failed to thrive and either didn't survive or became crippled emotionally, having never felt the comfort and security of maternal and paternal love.

---

23. Levitin, *The World in Six Songs*, 242.

But Cozolino says that "although there is consistency in attachment style from childhood into adulthood, many people show changes that reflect ongoing neural plasticity in attachment circuitry."[24] Such individuals can grow up to have secure relationships with others and forge strong bonds with their own children because they found someone who made them feel cherished and significant as individuals, interested in their "thoughts and feelings. Often it was a passion for some shared interest that connected them and provided a sense of belonging and accomplishment."[25]

Interestingly, Cozolino ends his discussion of growth potential, even in those deprived early on, by telling a story—or rather re-describing a very familiar story in our culture—Charles Dickens's portrayal of Ebenezer Scrooge in *The Christmas Carol*. Scrooge's capacity to love was awakened or revived by the visitation of his dead partner and three ghosts of Christmas past, present, and future. They "expose him to the kindnesses he had received from others in the past, the suffering and kindheartedness of those around him in the present, and the stark inevitability of his own death."[26] And Scrooge is transformed and becomes able to show love and kindness to others.

Cozolino points out that you could consider the work of therapists as embodying all three of Ebenezer's ghosts, exploring the past, testing the realities of the present, and imagining possible futures. Therapists and counselors take this journey with those who come for help because often their lives are ruled by fear and other negative input both within their brains and in their social surroundings—living Ebenezer's life in one way or another. And then many change their life stories for the better. And so can we all.

Interlude I: Meet Becky

Let me introduce my friend, Becky, to you. I have known her for seventeen years or so going back to when I was rector of St. Mark's Church in Richmond. So I didn't know her back in our youthful Boomer days. Therefore I will step back, and let her speak for herself as she reminisces about her early days and about the loves in her life as she weaves her Boomer story.

> I have been very blessed in life. Though my parents were very unhappy with each other and our family dysfunctional, I knew they both loved me; I owe them both a lot for that. As an only

---

24. Cozolino, *The Neuroscience of Human Relationships*, 410.
25. Ibid., 410.
26. Ibid., 411.

child, I spent a good deal of time alone, observing the world. I loved, and still do, being outdoors, walking, looking up at the sky, listening to the trees in the breeze. I was brought up in Sunday school and church, got my own grown-up Bible at eight, and personal spirituality rooted in me.

Social justice issues also became deeply embedded in me, at a young age and as an only child in an adult world. I witnessed hypocrisy in the Mississippi delta, where my paternal grandparents lived. The movie *Imitation of Life* was profound for me (sweet love hurting in a society of ugly discrimination). That probably sent me down my career path of clinical social work.

Trying to escape an overly dependent mother, I married—too young—a nice young man. We grew up, and he grew away—so that ended. I was devastated, yet could understand him and actually somewhat admired his ability to know what he needed and pursue it. A decade of "finding myself" ensued with the help of several girlfriends, who promoted such things. The Colorado mountains, a Grateful Dead concert, and hot springs were helpful.

I explored the world and relationships. I was very afraid of loving and committing again, yet afraid of being alone. Eventually I met my beloved, he taught me so much, was mature enough to love me in my immaturity, and allowed me the space to find myself and understand life. He brought it all together—understanding and claiming grace, self-acceptance, warts and all, as God accepts. It didn't hurt that he was so intelligent, handsome, romantic, and we loved so many of the same things!

The decades between my divorce and marriage to my beloved were so angst-ridden. Yet, no matter how depressed I got (personal journals remind me of how great was my confusion), there was always a little flame deep inside that I somehow knew would not go out. When I finally stopped clinging desperately and could risk being alone, I was able to maturely love.

My life with my beloved husband has been real, honest, loving, and full of joy. He's given me a ready-made family of adult children, grandchildren, and great-grandchildren. He has loved me and I have loved him, enhanced by a beautiful romance. I could not, and shall not, ask for more.

Although Becky's focus is of course on love in its variety of forms, she also reflects what we have seen throughout these chapters examining Boomer lives. An early, idealistic drive to make the world a better place, an unhappy moving out of a marriage that no longer suited one of the partners, and a struggle through the early years to story her life, and both find and create meaning beneath and throughout the hurt and pain that comes to all of us as we survive our past and grow through it.

We'll return to Becky as we examine our more mature years and look at what life yet holds for love and friendship.

THE NOW OF OUR LIVES: OUR SOULS AT NIGHT

It began with problems Leo was having in word finding. It became increasingly clear to at least me that this problem was not just the ordinary "tip of the tongue" search for a word that one couldn't retrieve, but a recurring and intrusive problem in word retrieval that was becoming worse over time. At about that time I flew out to California to visit my son and his family. My son Kev's wife Emily is a physician, and so I consulted with her about Leo's problem. She suggested that the cause might be a series of mini-strokes—undetected in themselves but resulting in the manifest cognitive deficit that concerned me.

Sometime after that visit, Leo experienced significant chest pains during a slightly uphill walk and doctors discovered a major cardiac blockage involving two main arteries in his heart. Two stents were inserted that helped with the blockage, but the cognitive deficits began to multiply. A geriatric neurologist prescribed some therapy or other to treat the onset of dementia, but Leo couldn't tolerate the meds—they triggered horrible nightmares. So he was taken off of all treatment except a minor anti-depressant and the dementia—likely vascularly based given his general cardiac disease—continued its downward spiral.

Thus, my beloved husband of thirty-plus years, my best friend, my colleague, my companion traveled from brilliant scholar—author of several books and multiple research reports, director of clinical training at Indiana University and chair of the Psychology Department at the University of Maryland Baltimore County—to someone who could not remember how to put on his sweater or tie his shoes or categorize even simple household items like spoons and forks. Here was my favorite conversation partner of decades, fading, fading, and finally gone as a whole, intact person.

I kept Leo at home with helpers as long as I could but finally I needed to look for a facility where I thought he would be safe and comfortable. After looking at a number of them, a friend recommended one nearby where her mother had been, and that is what I selected—thinking I could visit at least twice a day and be close to him when needed. I arranged for a private "studio" apartment on the Alzheimer's unit (euphemistically called the "memory" unit), decorated the living room area with plants and wall hangings, and prepared for the day of the move as best as I could.

Leo was aware enough of the pending move and resisted at first. And once he moved into the facility, the change after all these years was wrenching for me and unhappy for him. But within about two weeks, he "adjusted" to his surroundings and routines. Our physician gave the okay for our customary wine and cheese before the dinner hour, and so we resumed some kind of "normal" life for about six months. I also paid for the same private helper who had been in our home—a saint by the name of Rosalyn—to be with him during most of the day. When I couldn't be there, she was my eyes and ears overseeing his care. But his dementia grew worse, he became occasionally combative with staff, and he became unable to even recognize his youngest daughter when she visited. I created an album of family photos to spark his memory of loved ones, but his response was to try to chew on the album instead.

Unfortunately, even in many of the best of these places, staff turnover is frequent and chronic, and on Leo's unit, many of the "caregivers" were of pretty poor quality. And so it was that Rosalyn showed up one afternoon and found Leo in pain. No one had noticed that he hadn't voided in hours and once he was hospitalized, the diagnosis was acute renal failure. After two hospitalizations within a week's time, I had to find a nursing facility that could care for him—a really excellent one it turns out.

But within about a three-week period, he stopped eating and drinking and all systems began to shut down. The night before he died, I slept in a chair in his room—knowing that I was losing him and nothing could be done. The next morning the hospice nurse evaluated him and thought he might last through another day. Leo's daughter—the one he could no longer recognize—was in DC at a meeting, and we decided that she could wait to come down to Richmond until the meeting was over the next day. I went home to rest and while I tried to get a couple of hours sleep, Rosalyn called and said that he was gone.

This was both heartbreak and relief. Heartbreak because Leo had been my life for so many years, and in a profound sense, the one who shaped me in many ways—from my academic career, to my values, to my taste in visual art and music. Eighteen years older than me, in some sense he nurtured me into maturity on many levels. He was the center of my universe. So heartbreak.

And relief because the end was inevitable. The end began years earlier when he started sliding down the slope of vascularly based dementia with consequent loss of personality including the loss of a keen, sharp sense of humor. But I discovered again that you are never really ready, you never really expect that your loved one is actually going to die—until they do and then they are gone. I first discovered that sense of unreality when my dad was dying. I never *really* believed he would die until he did. And so with Leo. But there did follow a certain relief that his suffering—and to be honest, mine—was over.

But this was not, of course, the last love for me to lose to death. No. As I have noted in earlier chapters, Bud died of prostate cancer in 2013. In short, here is our love story.

Years before Leo died, Bud appeared on the periphery of my life. We first met when I was rector of St. Mark's in Richmond, and he showed up one Sunday in 1999 or so to give a series of lectures on miracles. He started attending St. Mark's on a regular basis (despite the fact that he was an eminent Scripture scholar on the Presbyterian seminary's faculty and was part of that denomination's clergy). Over time we became friends. In 2001 his wife, herself a biblical scholar of some renown, was diagnosed with pancreatic cancer and during her dying, I acted as her pastor—praying with them, supporting them on that last journey.

Sometime after Bud's wife died in 2002 and as Leo was beginning his downward course into dementia, Bud confessed that he had come to love me, and that he would wait for me as long as it took. Because he hoped someday that we might marry. And he did wait. For eight long years.

And so it came to be that after Leo died, Bud and I joined our lives together—even though as I said earlier, he had been diagnosed with prostate cancer about sixteen years before I knew him, and the PSA levels were always higher than they should be. The cancer cells were lurking in his body somewhere, but our hope was that the disease could be kept at bay.

We were married at St. John's in 2010 and the church was packed with family and friends. It was a joy-filled occasion despite all the sadness of our lost loves and past griefs. Our friend Edgar (Becky's husband by then) preached a wonderful sermon. At the reception later, many glasses of champagne were lifted in toasts to our hope and happiness. I have a wonderful photo on my refrigerator of one such toast—with sons and best friends gathered around our table.

Thus we began our life together. Our life together lasted two very good years—until around Thanksgiving of 2012 when Bud's oncologist suggested that he stop all treatment, enroll in hospice care, and that we enjoy whatever time we had left. In between our wedding and that call from the oncologist, Bud tried one medication after another, one treatment after another, from standard to experimental, hormonal to cytotoxic. He didn't want chemotherapy. He tried one dose and that was that.

I am reading Richard Lischer's *Stations of the Heart*, his memoir written as his son, Adam, was dying of metastatic melanoma. It is a very painful read for me because its pages bring back all the deaths in my own life, from my father's (who also died of metastatic melanoma), to Leo's of cardiac disease, to Bud's of metastatic prostate cancer that finally went everywhere in his body but his brain. About cancer "treatments" Lischer describes what he refers to as the "rhetoric of [medical] defeat," saying:

> It whittles hope down to size by means of a rational sequence of failures until the slim promontory on which the patient stands crumbles and the patient disappears. Standard treatments give way to newer therapies (no longer called treatments), which spawn innovative therapies, from which is selected the latest or most dangerous therapy, the failure of which necessitate an experimental drug whose only name is a government number. Eventually, the rhetoric shifts from quantifiable results, which, you must understand, vary from tumor to tumor, to the elusive "quality of life," which has already been ruined by the treatments themselves.[27]

And that is how it went. Bud knew he was dying. In fact, the summer before he died, we were at the Homestead, a resort in the mountains of western Virginia. And one morning at breakfast, he looked at me and said "I think I'm dying." And I said, "No!" As if my saying "no" would stop the process.

At any rate, after he stopped all "therapies" and enrolled in hospice, we still had a few good weeks left—through Christmas, including a couple of dinners out to celebrate our anniversary early. But shortly after the New Year in 2013, the bottom fell out, he became bedridden, and died the afternoon of January 28 at the age of eighty-five. I had cared for him at home, ground pain medicine into fine grain like salt, fed it to him in applesauce—with finally around-the-clock help so that I could sleep at night and care for him with others' help during the day. And then he was gone.

Acute grief reigned in my heart for the next year. Everywhere I drove, everywhere I went in Richmond, and everywhere I visited in our old haunts in the Poconos the following summer brought back vivid memories. Tears were my frequent companions and songs of the '40s that we would listen to on our travels brought him back to me and were both painful and comforting at the same time. Mark Oppenheimer, in a review of the book titled *Joy*—about the short, but happy marriage of Joy Gresham and C. S. Lewis—writes that the book reminded him "how love can befall us all."[28] And so it

27. Lischer, *Stations of the Heart*, 47.
28. Oppenheimer, "Joy," para. 10.

can at any age, even at eighty plus. Oppenheimer concludes that with that understanding, he felt better about life. And so do we all.

****

There are two issues worth noting at this point in our discussion of love. First, Somerset Maugham is reported to have said that "love is what happens to a man and woman who don't know each other." And my response to that is a resounding "No!" Infatuation yes, but love, no. I have known great love in my life with both Leo and Bud and both of them knew me very, very well—as I knew and understood them very well. We knew each other's faults and flaws as well as each other's loveable quirks and virtues.

Second, I wrote at the beginning of the last chapter that loss and love are really intertwined—you can't feel loss for something that you don't care deeply about—a person, a job, a friend, or favorite pet. Nevertheless, loss and love can be considered separately. So I have attempted to do that here. But my memories of the two greatest loves of my life that I have just described were refracted through the lens of loss. Let me just say again the obvious. When you are middle-aged and beyond, love and loss frequently if not almost always go together.

And there certainly are a spate of reports, memoirs, and novels about such love and loss that have appeared in print in recent years. But before turning to some examples from my own reading, let me just reiterate here what I have said before. As I have said time and again, music has evolutionary priority for our species. And as individuals, the music of our early years—the music of our youth when our brain in still maturing, pruning and rewiring neurons, and storing vivid memories in our midbrain neural centers—love songs, especially tunes with lyrics, are what we recall from our "back then" days. And we have looked at some of those songs earlier in this chapter.

But I think it is in the "now" of our Boomer lives as mature selves—still authoring the story of our lives as we make our way into middle age and beyond—that literature of one kind or another probably takes priority in terms of sense-making. Or at least I will assert that for me. Maybe in part because in my earlier years, with my professional scrambling and building a career in academia, I had little time for discretionary reading. My reading was all technical and driven by my research and grant-getting needs. It was only when I left academia that I discovered the joy and the wisdom that all kinds of good books generated. Reading became paramount to me as I continued to write my own life story. Hence, across all the chapters in this book, this is what I have considered—our music back then and our novels, biographies, poems, and yes, films in later years that provided the framework and the language for making sense of it all.

So let's consider here written words about love and loss. Not all of these books, reports, and memoirs are concerned with death, but all reflect a great devotion in the face of loss of one kind or another. For example, an article appeared a few years back in *The New York Times Magazine* about the incredible struggle waged by Peggy Battin—a bioethicist who had always argued for the right of the terminally ill to choose suicide—and her husband, Brooks, an academic who became a quadriplegic after a bicycle accident. Despite the fact that Brooks had always maintained that he would not want to live under such circumstances, the piece portrays not only their anguish but also the inability to let go of life and love for the other—as well as an overwhelmingly strong will to live on his part. At one point in the article, Brooks is quoted as saying "you can get used to anything."[29]

More recently, in her *One Hundred Names for Love*, Diane Ackerman describes the aftermath of her husband, the writer Paul West's massive and crippling stroke. West completely lost his ability for speaking, reading, or understanding spoken language, as well as his ability to perform any simple daily activity such as walking or feeding himself. Through constant daily care and coaching, Ackerman was able to assist West in recovering those lost abilities. Out of that loving care and process, Ackerman explains eloquently how the damaged brain can regroup, repair, and re-wire neurons to recover lost functions. The writer Abraham Verghese, in his review of Ackerman's book, says "this book . . . has renewed my faith in the redemptive power of love, the need to give and get it unstintingly, to hold nothing back, settle for nothing less, because when flesh and being and even life fall away, love endures. This book is proof."[30]

Considering love as many-splendored beyond romance, in his *The Risk Pool*, Richard Russo portrays one of the finest fictional descriptions of love between a grown son and his father as has appeared in fictional form. Set in a hardscrabble, blue-collar, upstate New York town, the story follows the growing-up years of Ned Hall, the son of two inadequate parents—a neurotic mother and a ne'er-do-well father named Sam. Despite Sam's lifetime of incredibly bad habits, in an offhand but endurable way he is devoted to his son, Ned, as they weave together a heart-warming, deep relationship over decades of mishap and disaster. As multiple reviewers of this novel

---

29. Henig, "A Life-or-Death Situation," para. 46.

30. Verghese, quoted in the front page of Ackerman, *One Hundred Names for Love*, n.p.

of Russo's point out, you know these people. You have met these people in their small-town everydayness. This fictional work speaks truth about our human condition and our capacity to love one another despite—as Leonard Cohen said—the cracks and flaws we all bear at our core.

And so do all really fine books, both fiction and nonfiction alike. While it is true, as some have asserted, that only living your own life can finally teach you about struggle and relationship and work and love, books can provide knowledge, convey strategies for dealing with life when it happens to you, and language to make sense of it all. To cite Paul Elie again, the reader finds herself "testing the work against one's own life and vice versa . . . . In the act of reading and writing, one stranger and another go forth to meet in an encounter of the profoundest sort . . . . We imitate our way to the truth, finding our lives—saving them—in the process. Then we pass it on."[31]

And so books have been my companion along the way of love and loss. Looking at my bookshelf now, these treasures remain to be reread again and again. Shortly after Bud died, Anita, our dear friend and matron-of-honor at our wedding, gave me Gail Godwin's *Evenings at Five*—a reference to a cocktail ritual that the widow named Christina had had over the years with her late husband Rudy. It is the tale of an ongoingness of a deep love, the "eternal quality of a romance completed."[32]

For some reason, one particular scene in Anne Tyler's *A Patchwork Planet* has been of major importance to me—both indelibly imprinting itself into my mind and working its way into a sermon. It's a dialogue between two characters, Martine and Barnaby, who work for a company that moves furniture and other heavy objects in the homes of elderly customers who can no longer carry out such tasks for themselves. And one day, Barnaby asks Martine if she ever thought of quitting because the job, essentially, was a sad one. And Martine answers in the negative. Then she gives Barnaby an example of why she wouldn't want to quit. She tells about taking a woman named Mrs. Gordoni to visit her elderly father in a nursing home because Mrs. Gordoni's car was in the shop. The father had suffered some kind of accident years before that damaged his brain, and he had absolutely no short-term, working memory. He couldn't remember from one moment to the next what had just transpired.

So this one day, Martine took Mrs. Gordoni to visit her father. And when the daughter stepped out of the room for a minute to speak to a nurse, the father leaned over to Martine and asked "Do you happen to be

---

31. Elie, *The Life You Save May Be Your Own*, xiii; 472.
32. Godwin, *Evenings at Five*, n.p.

acquainted with my daughter? She never visits!" And then this is the dialogue that has stayed with me:

> "See what I mean?" [Barnaby] said.
>
> "*That* kind of got me down."
>
> "Right."
>
> "But then you have to look on the other side of it," Martine said.
>
> "What other side, for God's sake?"
>
> "Well, it's kind of encouraging that Mrs. Gordoni still came, don't you think? She certainly didn't get *credit* for coming, beyond the very moment she was standing in her father's view. Just for that moment, her father was happy. Not one instant longer. But Mrs. Gordoni went even so, every day of the week."
>
> "Well," I said. Then I said, "Yeah, okay."[33]

Yeah, okay. Barnaby got it. And so did I. And so did the parishioners who heard that dialogue in some sermon of mine years ago. There was a truth embedded in that "Yeah, okay" that still brings tears to my eyes. Because it connotes a kind of genuine love for another that reaches the ideal of selflessness and self-sacrifice for another human being. Whatever else Mrs. Gordoni's motives were, nevertheless, she went. And gave her father joy in the process. Barnaby got it. And so do I.

Two other books that I want to mention here before going a bit deeper into what science may have to say about love in our current, older lives—one is fiction, the other a memoir. In *Our Souls at Night* (mentioned in the previous chapter), Kent Haruf—one of my very favorite writers who died this past year—wrote this, his last book before he died. It's about "old love"—love that developed between Addie Moore, an elderly widow, and Louis Waters, an equally elder widower. It's about the need for touch, the experience of sexuality in late life, and the developing affection between two old, lonely people who came to companion each other through the long nights. Their unconventional relationship comes to an end at the insistence of her family. But their love and companionship, albeit long distance by phone, remains to the end. "Just two old people talking in the dark."[34] It's a lovely, sad, and poignant picture of our need for love and companionship to the end of our days.

Finally, I want to mention Kay Redfield Jamison's *Nothing was the Same*. We met Jamison in the chapter on joyfulness, and now here she is

---

33. Tyler, *A Patchwork Planet*, 233–34.
34. Haruf, *Our Souls at Night*, 176.

talking about the death of her dear husband, Richard Wyatt, in 2002. Also referred to in the previous chapter on loss, this was another one of those hard books for me to read after Bud died. Jamison says "when he became ill and we knew he would die, he became my mentor in how to die with the grace by which he lived. What he could not teach me—no one could—was how to contend with the grief of losing him."[35]

And so also with the deaths of the loves in my life, both Leo and Bud. Different deaths because—despite the fact that they were both my mentors in some way—Leo had lost his reason by the time he was dying, but Bud had not. And Bud did, like Richard Wyatt, know that he was dying and did also die with great grace and dignity. Then also like Jamison, I had to find my own way out of grief. Like her, one saving grace was my writing, my work—both as distraction but also as giving purpose to my life.

Jamison also concluded that acute grief did fade, but the love did not. She quotes Graham Greene who observed that "'sometimes I think that the search for suffering and the remembrance of suffering are the only means we have to put ourselves in touch with the whole human condition . . . . Grief is at the heart of the human condition. Much is lost with death, but not everything. Life is not let loose of lightly, nor is love. There is a grace in death. There is life . . . . Love is altered but remains."[36]

With that, let's dig a little deeper here, and look at what some research has to tell us about love and storying our lives as we live them out in our middle-ageless years.

Going Deeper: "Let the River Run"

> We live amid narrative structures and narrative processes every hour of every day, enmeshed in countless storylines at once—those we spin around the experiences we remember, the world we inhabit, and the people we relate to, not to mention the storylines those people spin around *us*. And this says nothing of the stories we consume each day in newspapers and novels, or savor in movies, or swap in conversation—whose themes and scenes can haunt our thoughts for years.[37]

---

35. Jamison, *Nothing Was the Same*, 5.
36. Ibid., 182; 178.
37. Randall, *The Narrative Complexity of Ordinary Life*, vii.

"IMAGINE ME AND YOU..."

****

William Randall, in the quotation just given, pretty much covers the waterfront in terms of story—the stories we tell ourselves to make sense of our lives and the stories undoubtedly others spin about us—as well as the stories we immerse ourselves in from our surrounding culture in the form of books and films (as well as other art forms such as theater and poetry). In this current chapter we have already covered our brain on love, and have considered our learning love and gleaning wisdom from the songs we sing and the books we read. Here in this "going deeper" section, I'd like to say a bit more about Randall's first reference to the stories we spin, the creating of our storied lives as authors of our selves over time—in this case our own lives in love and friendship.

We have covered much of this basic ground in earlier chapters, and so I don't want to repeat myself here. In sum, we are storytelling animals as Jonathan Gottschall puts it. Our storytelling capacity is rooted in our evolutionary history, allowing the best storyteller in the tribe to gain attention and attract a likely mate, as well as help advance cooperation within the group which furthers its own survival ends. We have an inborn need to belong with others and as David Myers says "familiarity breeds liking, not contempt.... People who have people are not only the luckiest people alive, but also the happiest and healthiest."[38]

We story our lives and for most of us, at or near the center of the story are our loves and friendships. I began this chapter with the story of my first puppy love. And I started this section with my story of love and loss by death of the two men whose love helped shape my core self in our lives together—and who undoubtedly storied me in the process.

Here we are in our Boomer mid-lives still looking for love and holding our friends close as we weather the storms of life together. As Boomers we learned in our youth to move out of marriages that proved sterile or disappointing, and apparently we are still doing that even as post-middle age sets in. In one NPR "All Things Considered" segment, Ina Jaffe noted that as late as 1990, "fewer than 1 in 10 persons who got divorced was over the age of 50.... But today, 1 in 4 people getting divorced is 50 or older."[39] If you remember the biographical sketch provided by Dave in our chapter on religion, in his mid-fifties he moved out of a long-term, very unsatisfactory marriage into another relationship better suited to his values and needs. The trend continues.

38. Myers, *The American Paradox*, 193–94.
39. "Older Americans' Breakups."

Perhaps because of this upswing of late-life divorces, researchers have taken a look at what factors might play a role in keeping long-term relationships together. One finding reported in the recent literature has to do with the expression of gratitude in marital relationships and other intimate bonds. In one carefully done study, using both observational and longitudinal methods, the study authors report that "people who feel more appreciated by their romantic partners report being more appreciative of their partners"—more attentive to their partner's needs, more committed. The researchers say that outward expressions of gratitude within the relationship resulted in partners more "likely to remain in relationship over time."[40] Of course, as we saw in earlier chapters, the expression of gratitude has multiple benefits, including better mood, and in one study, better quality of sleep and healthier hearts after diagnosis of "asymptomatic Stage B heart failure."[41]

Back to authoring our stories of friendship and love. William Randall and his colleagues have written extensively about our storying in mid and later life. In his *The Narrative Complexity of Ordinary Life*, Randall—in a chapter devoted to friends and lovers—discusses at length what he calls the "intricate endeavor" of friendship. Of course we take for granted the stories that we weave about each other and that become part of the interpersonal world that we inhabit. But if you examine these mutual stories, they are complex, both shifting and rigid, with positive and negative aspects upon reflection.

On the positive side of friendship, those who are significant to us actually co-author our lives as we puzzle with them over ambiguous situations. We may describe distressful daily events to them and listen to their response, or simply "check in" and frequently touch base to at least in part get our bearings regarding ongoing messiness of our everyday lives. I have a dear friend named Karen—the "sister" to me whom I never had. We live in different states, see each other when we can, and check in with each other by phone at least every other day. We know each other's stories, and in the conversations we share, we somehow create a world between us that is unique to our pairing. Randall says, "You bring out a side of me no other person can.... If I didn't know you, not only would my life be less enjoyable, but I would be less 'me'—certainly a different me."[42] As Peter Berger and Thomas Luckmann cautioned many years ago, be careful who you talk to because a reality becomes created between you that shapes you as a person.

40. Gordon et al., "To Have and to Hold," 257.
41. "In Brief," 19.
42. Randall, *The Narrative Complexity of Ordinary Life*, 93.

But in addition to all this potential for the growth of the "me" in friendship, for Randall there also can be a negative potential in such mutual storying. All our friends who know us—those in the close, inner circle, and those in the outer regions of our lives—have their own story of us from the outside looking in. Some of these stories are probably fairer than others. Some of them are more rigid, some clinging to a version of our storied self that is no longer me. Randall says "apart from a minor amendment now and then, it's their story of me and they're sticking to it, however vigorously I protest that 'I'm not *like* that anymore!'"[43] But it's their story and they are sticking to it!

On the whole of course, the benefits of our co-authoring ourselves with good friends outweighs the negative risk of being misunderstood and storied in an unfair light. We indeed need each other to understand our sometimes troubling lives and the beauty of deep friendship—such as I experience with Karen, for example—is having a coauthor of the self as an anchor to rely on.

And then of course there is the romantic pairing that we all probably "fall into" from time to time. The kind of "love" that lights up the brain centers like an addiction, that rewards your experience with a high as addictive as drugs or excessive alcohol consumption. "Scotch and soda, jigger of gin, oh what a spell you've got me in."[44] Randall says "romance is nothing if not a narrative affair, fueled by fiction more than fact."[45] I suppose this is the kind of love that Somerset Maughan had in mind when he noted that love happens between two people who don't know each other well. So we make up a story and project the love object into the script that resides mainly in our imagination. When the other doesn't fulfill his or her part of the story then intrigue sets in which Randall refers to as "narrative intrigue." "The inability to get someone out of your mind corresponds to your ignorance of what the *real* story is."[46]

The first time that I heard Carly Simon sing "Let the River Run," I was swept up in that song's ecstasy. Although it was first written for the film *Working Girl* in 1988, I only found it last year. I heard it in my car on a CD given to me by a guy that I had become quite infatuated with. My friends saw him as really bad news. One kept saying something like "dump the jerk!" But I wouldn't listen to anyone, because I was really on that high, infatuated to the nth degree. Anyway, her lyrics in that song—like "It's asking

---

43. Ibid., 95.
44. The Kingston Trio, "Scotch and Soda."
45. Randall, *The Narrative Complexity of Ordinary Life*, 99.
46. Ibid., 100.

for the taking,/trembling, shaking"—played in my heart as I felt the ecstasy of the beat in my brain and body.[47]

And then when the story ends . . . which many romantic tales do and which that infatuation of mine most certainly did . . . a lost love can continue to haunt us afterwards. "What if? Maybe had I done . . . I shouldn't have sent that last text, if only I hadn't then . . ." But then, as Randall points out, although lost love can continue to haunt us, with the story forever incomplete with no satisfactory ending, nevertheless, we can also be enriched by its ending. "It enriches us because there can be more to be learned from a broken heart than a happy one; what not to do next time, what chances not to squander."[48] So we finish the story in any case, closing it off with—if not a happy ending—at least a wiser conclusion for its finish.

Finally, there is the story of mature love that develops and shapes us at our core. I have shared with you two of my great loves that filled my own life story with meaning, shaping me into the person I am now in a way that no other loves could have done. In a long-term relationship, we story each other's lives, and the story layers are complex indeed. There is my story of us, your story of us, as well as the story of our own individual lives. And this storying over the years is dynamic and shifting as we move through our lives together.

Randall points out the obvious. That we never know another—no matter how many years we live together—we never know another's story completely. The stories are mine, yours, and ours that we share. Our long-term intimate love relationship is a dynamic story filled by what we share and by what befalls us in our lives together. "If, as their two life stories become entwined as a couple story, through the sharing of common characters, events, and themes, each partner keeps alert to the depths of the other person's narrative, and is willing, in a sense, to read it—then, in theory, there's no end to what each can learn from the other."[49]

At this point, Randall introduces the topic of age in mature love. He points out that biographically speaking, we become more complex with age because our life story has simply accrued more characters, with more plots

---

47. Written by Carly Simon. Copyright 1989 by C'est Music and administered by BMG Rights Management US LLC. A note about "Let the River Run" by Carly Simon: I also heard in the lyrics concerning the New Jerusalem ("Wake the nation./Come, the New Jerusalem") a deeply religious meaning—an eschatological reference to the coming kingdom of God—God who will make all things new in the end. Thus in experiencing that song, its ecstatic words and rhythm meant to me both human love and God's love combined.

48. Randall, *The Narrative Complexity of Ordinary Life*, 101.

49. Ibid., 109–10.

and subplots developing over time. We add to the mix our memories of relationships—especially if the partner is now deceased. And sometimes the stories become considerably edited and created anew after one of the partners has died.

Doris Grumbach tells an amusing story about a couple who were known to fight bitterly over their long married years. After the husband died and the wife moved into a retirement community, she was overheard to say that there was "never a cross word between us."[50] Apparently the wife perfected and polished the story of their life together in a way that proved more satisfying to her current one than the past had been.

Age itself of course does become a significant factor in making and remaking the narratives of our lives, including meaning-making of past and present loves—those we are still within (even if the other has died) and those we have lost. In their *Storying Later Life*, Gary Kenyon, Ernst Bohlmeijer, and William Randall have edited a book about narrative and aging. In one of the chapters in that work, Randall comes back to the topic of growing older as an opportunity to reconfigure our stories and create deeper meaning in our lives.

In general, Randall argues that as we retire, as we lose by death a spouse or partner, as we lose friends one by one, typically we have more disposable time at hand to slow down and take stock of all that has been and to consider where we are at this point in life. Perhaps prompted by the fact that we are closer to death than before, such a reality often brings with it a philosophic perspective on our life as a whole. In such stock-taking, we have the opportunity to integrate painful or unresolved past episodes into our life narratives, finding some positive meaning such as growth and wisdom from losses, creating what McAdams refers to as "redemption stories"—redeeming the past pain and suffering and filling the present and future with meaningful purpose.[51]

Circling back to Carly Simon's memoir once more as we close out this section of going deeper in our current lives, Simon points out that her writing really began with her childhood and ended with her divorce from James Taylor in 1983. She notes that many relationships in her life since

---

50. Grumbach, "The View from 90," para 73.

51. Additional chapters in this edited book by Kenyon, Bohlmeijer, and Randall discuss interventions that enhance such restorying in later life. The authors describe practices such as reminiscence group therapy and life review therapy as effective means in enhancing the creation of new narratives in later life. For example, Kate de Medeiros, in her "Telling Stories: How Do Expressions of Self Differ in a Writing Group versus a Reminiscence Group?" describes how social context influences the stories that get created in a group setting.

have come and gone, "with most remaining solidly entrenched in the glad, grateful part of my memory." She ends with the following observation that seems fitting to use as closing thought in our discussion here. Simon says, "Over the years, I've learned something that has made my life easier, more honest and satisfying: I've stopped trying to stop loving."[52]

Finally on the next to last page Simon gives a fitting example of McAdams's redemption of past loss with present and future purpose and meaning. She says "I replace any unhappy, hurtful memories with those of music and joy and the perfect fourths and the shared genes and this house on the hill and the things scattered around the house that remind me that we are all ever only stewards of something larger than ourselves."

With that note, I'll turn to the final section of this chapter—the last in this book. And speak of the love of God that conveys ultimate meaning in my life and I believe in the world about us.

For the Love of God!

> God's [silent] abstention is only from human dialects. The holy voice utters its woe and glory in myriad musics, in signs and portents. Our own words are for us to speak, a way to ask and to answer.[53]

****

As I have said across these pages, God—transcendent Mystery—engages us as individuals at multiple points, from our brain synapses to our surrounding culture. To reiterate what Bruce Cockburn wrote, "the Divine infiltrates our being and manifests, as it must, through the electrochemical processes of our brain."[54] And in Peter Berger's classic work, *A Rumor of Angels*, he writes that within our surrounding cultural artifacts of art, poetry, and music, we see traces of God or "signals of transcendence." In my Judeo-Christian tradition, God is overflowing Love, spilling over into creation with life, hope, and sometimes even joyful ecstasy. For Christians, God is Love incarnate, manifested in God's Word made flesh—reflecting God's infinite and saving self with an assurance that in fact, despite all evidence to the contrary, all will be well at the end of it all.

52. Simon, *Boys in the Trees*, 369.
53. Denise Levertov, quoted in Wolfe, "The Harboring Silence," 6.
54. Cockburn, *Rumours of Glory*, 199.

Given the focus of this book on story, the story of our lives as we create ourselves in the stories we weave, and the focus here on love in its many-splendored form, this is not the place for theological exposition or argument or *apologia*. This is the place, at the end of this chapter, to think about how God—however we want to name this ultimate meaning in our lives—manifests God's self in our stories, how God comes to us in the stories we read and the stories we author.

In a piece written for *The Christian Century*, Richard Lischer reflected on the writing of St. Augustine, the fourth-century Bishop of Hippo who famously wrote his *Confessions*—the memoir of his early life and his coming to faith. And Lischer observes that Augustine "narrates the facts of his life as he remembers them, but what he's after is the meaning of it all."[55] In some sense, in writing this book—at least the memoir parts of it—I also have been telling my story as I remember it, both the past and the present. I suppose that is why I enjoy also writing my blog. I reflect on what is going on in my life and in the writing, and in the telling, I make some better sense of it all. In this chapter, I have tried to tell again and create deeper meaning of the loves in my life.

"I find that I want to slow down and listen for prayers that might be hiding in plain sight in any book." So says Stephanie Paulsell in an article about "Praying Jane Eyre."[56] There are some books, books of fiction, autobiographies like Augustine's, some profound poetry, that not only can speak truth or resonate with deep meaning in our lives, but also may convey something of transcendence in the reading. In the meeting of my life with the author's expression, emotions arise that signal some felt truth in my own life, some sense that "that's it!," some knowing that lies deeper than abstract language—indeed some "signal of transcendence."

And so we read, listening for those prayers in plain sight. Obvious examples for me are the writings of Marilynne Robinson, especially the figure of John Ames in *Gilead*. Ames is an elderly ordained clergyman with heart disease who also has a young wife and son. He senses that he doesn't have long to live and writes wisdom for his young son to absorb one day. At the very close of the book, Ames writes,

> It has seemed to me sometimes as though the Lord breathes on this poor gray ember of Creation and it turns to radiance—for a moment or a year or the span of a life. And then it sinks back into itself again, and to look at it no one would know it had anything to do with fire, or light.... But... wherever you turn your

55. Lischer, "Writing the Christian Life," para. 7.
56. Paulsell, "Praying Jane Eyre," 35.

eyes the world can shine like transfiguration. You don't have to bring a thing to it except a little willingness to see.[57]

At the very end of the book, Ames speaks of his impending death and burial. He observes that their little town is shrinking and in fact dying. But he says, "I love this town. I think sometimes of going into the ground here as a last wild gesture of love—I too will smolder away the time until the great and general incandescence."[58] In reading those words, there arises in me the sense of love beyond the grave, love and care continuing, and a deep hope again that in that end, all will truly be well for us and for those we love in God's renewed creation.

I have turned again of late to reading poetry, of slowing down enough to meet God in the poetics of some of my favorite writers. I have written at some length about some of those who I returned to over the years to nourish my soul—R. S. Thomas ("Why no! I never thought other than/That God is that great absence/In our lives, the empty silence/Within, the place where we go"), Denise Levertov ("Birds afloat in airs current,/sacred breath? No, not breath of God,/it seems, but God"), and Wendell Berry ("We travelers, walking to the sun, can't see/Ahead, but looking back the very light/That blinded us shows us the way we came").[59]

Most recently, I have added to my pantheon of favorites the poetry of my dear friend Isobel de Gruchy. She is indeed a profound and wonderful poet. Let me end this little excursion into meeting God's love through the written word with snippets from two of her works—one concerned with friendship and one concerned with old love.

In her recently published book of poems titled *Between Heaven and Earth*, Isobel has a lovely poem on "Friendship." "It is the conversation that can be put on hold, and resumed/as though there were no break./Friendship is the food that sustains the body,/the book that sustains the mind,/and the spirit that sustains the soul."[60] Lovely—and ripe with felt meaning. Finally, in an earlier book of hers, Isobel offers a poem in celebration of her and her husband John's golden wedding anniversary. The last stanza reads: "We have grown old together, you and I,/By God's grace and love, support,/Encouragement each for the other,/By the gift of children, grandchildren, friends/And we have been tested again by death,/But, because of all that has gone before/We have been able to walk on—together."[61]

57. Robinson, *Gilead*, 245.
58. Ibid., 247.
59. Levy, *Imagination and the Journey of Faith*, 57; 61; 59.
60. de Gruchy, *Between Heaven and Earth*, 44.
61. de Gruchy, *Walking On*, 13–14.

And so we tell our lives. We tell our lives in community because we are socially embedded creatures. In fact, most of our emotions make sense only in relation to other people. Ambition, fear, jealousy, mercy, anger, gratitude, and our focus here—friendship, and love—only have meaning within a communal context. Our emotional connection to others in community provides what David Heim calls a "school for the heart," a training ground for love and friendship, providing the stories that we draw from that create our deepest meanings in life—that "big picture" that McAdams talks about. In that community of love and friendship that surround us, we create and live out our "personal myth"—that "act of imagination that is a patterned integration of our remembered past, perceived present, and anticipated future."[62]

With that, let's turn back to our sketch of Becky, and listen in as she talks about her life now and in the years to come.

Interlude II: Becky Again

When we first encountered Becky, I mentioned that I didn't know her in our youth. But I did come to know her and we became dear friends over the past seventeen years or so when she and her Episcopal priest husband, Edgar, decided to make St. Mark's their worship home. During my time there, but especially after I left St. Mark's, Becky and Edgar became part of a very close circle of friends—we referred to the eight of us as "family"—celebrating each other's birthdays and other special occasions. We shared joy and sorrow over the years as death and life changes overtook our little "family." But let me stand back and again let Becky speak for herself as she reflects on her life story so far.

> About a year ago, a week or so after my beloved husband died, I was pacing my what seemed cavernous house, crying, talking to myself. Suddenly, I stopped in front of the mirror and stated, "I don't feel like a person anymore." I didn't know what that meant—but I knew it wasn't good.
>
> Well, I am now feeling like a "person" again. But what do I mean by that? I suppose the boundary around myself is healthier, distinct enough to allow and respect my sense of self, permeable enough to allow myself to be open to what's out there—people, experiences, the proverbial "what are you going to do with the rest of your life?"

---

62. McAdams, *The Stories We Live By*, 12.

I have grieved well, I believe, if that can be said of such a process. I have taken the advice of bereavement counselors and followed my instincts as to what to do or not to do at any given time. I now know I live best when I embrace the feelings, stare them directly down in their "deep dark eyes," and feel them to the max. I engage in conversation with myself and with my husband, which often feels indistinguishable from talking with God.

I enjoy time alone (maybe because I don't feel alone) more than I used to. I've always enjoyed people, and still do, but with greater self-respect and authenticity I believe. I seem to know and say what I think more readily. I am careful (in the literal sense of that word) of myself. I place high priority on daily physical exercise and eating well. I also please myself with a daily martini or wine, toasting my husband with a salute and a smile.

I am traveling to new and old places, taking long walks. I am working a couple of days a week—enjoying professional colleagues and hopefully being of help to patients and their families who are trying to manage the hospital experience. I engage with and treasure friends frequently—both long-standing and new. I meditate daily, which brings me a foretaste perhaps of the God I can only imagine, based on the love I have known and observed in this world. On my refrigerator door, I have posted two quotes: "A heart so full of love that there is no room for fear," and "How should I treat others? There are no others."

As to the future, I realize that chronology dictates a sense of my own mortality. Having been with my husband as he died, I fear my own [death] far less. I am also fortunate to feel financially secure.

I don't have specific expectations of the future—no grand plans or goals. I do know that every moment is precious to me. I want to experience new and old places, newly introduced and long-standing friends. I want to express my feelings more in poetry, drawing, dance. I want to keep working.

I have begun to allow more empty time and space. I now know I don't need to fill every moment as I used to. In fact, I need the empty space, where imagination and God can be discovered and known within me. I've always wanted to spend a whole year in Maine (a place I've dearly loved in summer). I feel the need to experience the tough seasons there as well as the sublime. I suppose there is this urge within me toward integrating the suffering and the joys of life; and finally understand the wholeness of God. I am so thankful for life, for God's love, for some God-given sensibility to be observant of it all. I look forward to growing more in consciously living out God's love until I no longer am a "person," but rather eternally indistinguishable from and one with God's Love.

Again, we see themes in Becky's sketch here that are common in our middle-ageless lives—from health zeal and self-care to a desire to still be productive in work and life. She has seemed to weather her grief at her husband's loss, finding some "redemption" in her past suffering. Becky certainly exhibits a continued path of growth and self-sufficiency, treasuring both friends and her own (and her "beloved's") company. She's a Boomer who is deeply religious, but one who also continues to explore new meaning and deeper understanding of God's Mystery in her life.

****

With that look into romantic and self-giving love and loss in our current lives through the eyes of Becky, we end this current chapter focusing on love in all its many manifestations. In fact with this discussion, we have now finished cycling through the great, universal, and existential themes of our existence: friendship, knowledge, joy, religion, comfort, and now love. To echo St. Paul's words, I do believe the greatest of these is love.

Thus we have addressed the topic of love in our lives—loves of our youth and loves in our more mature years that are frequently coupled with loss. As I have already observed in this writing, none of us loves perfectly. But when we love well, we reflect the highest pinnacle of human attainment. We learn how to love over a lifetime of watching it done well, being inspired to do likewise. Over a lifetime of drawing from our cultural menu of songs and stories, we struggle to make sense out of our deepest longings for others, transcending our own limits in this meaning-making process as we reach for friends, lovers, spouses, children and their children, and embracing ideals such as freedom and democracy—lifting us and others beyond mere subsistence to the realm of justice and peace.

But I do wonder about our future as storytelling animals, as Jonathan Gottschall so colorfully puts it. If in fact we create ourselves by authoring our own lives, creating and re-creating our life story as we move toward our ending, what happens when the culture no longer provides a full menu to draw from? What happens as our roots dry up that were once nurtured by religion's traditional myths and stories and hymn songs providing the Big Picture of ultimate meaning in our traditions? What happens when the written word becomes reduced to tweets and sound bites and images that flick across the screen? What happens when our songs express nothing but anger and violence and disjointed rhythms that jar the brain? What happens when we engage in world-making through interactive computer games and cease to engage with the everyday reality of our shared communal world outside our door? What then happens to our sense of self and our sense of a coherent life story over time?

We'll take a brief look at these questions in the epilogue to this book. But ever the optimist, I shall make every attempt to end on a hopeful note. Because ultimately, I believe we are drawn by a Purpose toward some ultimate end filled with love and hope and peace—characters in a story being told—playing our parts as best we can. Let's take one more pass at sense-making as we end this part of our journey together.

Epilogue
The Story of Our Lives and the Future of Fiction

These are undeniably nervous times for people who make a living through story. The publishing, film, and television businesses are going through a period of painful change. But the *essence* of story is not changing. The technology of storytelling has evolved from oral tales, to clay tablets, to hand-lettered manuscripts, to printed books, to movies, televisions, Kindles, and iPhones. This wreaks havoc on business models, but it doesn't fundamentally change story. Fiction is as it was and ever will be: Character + Predicament + Attempted Extrication.[1]

Jonathan Gottschall—the author of the quotation just given—and his book, *The Storytelling Animal*, is one of the major anchors that I have used for this writing. His is an important and accessible work about our human inborn capacity to tell stories and create our world in the process. But he and I parted ways when I got to his last chapter on the future of story, from which this citation was taken. What he says here is absolutely true. But I believe where he takes his final discussion is troubling to say the least. Let's look.

First, on the positive side, Gottschall points out that thousands of novels are published every year. Poetry has not died, folks still love the "small, intense stories poets tell"—including those found in the lyrics of the songs we sing. Video games have plots, even though the story lines are a little thin. Television is still a major deliverer of stories, and TV series such as *Downton Abbey* or *Mercy Street* have huge followings.

---

1. Gottschall, *The Storytelling Animal*, 186.

But Gottschall makes his point and then drives it into Neverland. He says "we were creatures of story before we had novels, and we will be creatures of story if sawed-off attention spans or technological advances ever render the novel obsolete. Story evolves. Like a biological organism, it continuously adapts itself to the demands of its environment."[2]

There is no doubt that we have moved into an Internet age, we have moved into a world of sound bites, small screen images, Facebook and Twitter. And there have been some studies carried out in recent years on, for example, the effects of video games on players' emotional, social, and motivational outcomes. Admittedly it is somewhat perilous to compare studies' outcomes, but perhaps a couple of examples will show that the results of such studies are quite mixed. For example, while one study carried out by Granic, Lobel, and Engels showed real social and emotional benefits of playing such games, another very well-done longitudinal study of long term effects of playing "risk-glorifying video games" done by Hull, Prescott, and Sargent showed an increase in "deviant behavior"—sensation seeking and rebelliousness.

I think we are all aware of the current danger of "self-radicalization" through the Internet—for example, the Boston Marathon bombers were incited to violence at least in part by such means, and the long outreach of Al Qaeda and other terrorist groups via their websites have recruited many to their radical cause. And rude, even aggressive tweets from Donald Trump to more compassionate messages from Pope Francis attract thousands if not millions of Twitter followers a day.

However, the effects of video games and the effects of social media on our political process and on wannabe terrorists and other radical groups are not the questions I am raising here. To reiterate, what I am asking is this: If we create ourselves by authoring our own lives, creating and re-creating our life story as we move toward our ending, what happens when the culture no longer provides a full menu to draw from?

Specifically, again I ask what happens when the roots dry up that were once nurtured by religion's traditional myths and stories and hymn songs providing a big picture of ultimate meaning to draw from in our historical traditions? What happens when many of our popular songs express nothing but anger and violence? What happens when we engage in world-making through interactive computer games such as MMORPGs (massively multiplayer online role-playing games) and cease to engage with the everyday reality of our shared communal world outside our door? What then happens to our sense of self and our sense of a coherent life story over time?

2. Ibid., 180.

As a psychologist trained in research methods, I appreciate the complexity of the questions I am asking and the difficulty of designing projects that would attempt to answer some of the questions raised. For instance, if you could identify a group of adolescents—when life stories begin to be pulled together into some kind of coherent whole—and somehow divide them into two matched groups made up of those who engage with the Internet very little and those who spend most of their waking hours on that Net, you might be able to follow them sufficiently to begin to unravel their life story-creating ability over time. But it would be hard to match the two groups because in today's culture, if you find any adolescents disengaged from the Internet world, then there would be a whole host of other aspects to their lives such as poverty or other deprivations that would impact the study findings.

And apparently the questions that I am here raising have not—to the best of my knowledge—been addressed within the scientific community. One researcher in the field of narrative psychology writes, "I've spent the last few days thinking about [your questions], and wish I had more to offer. Sadly, I know of no work that speaks directly to [them]."[3]

So we will close our discussion with some informed speculation. We have inherited our storytelling brains. Our human brains have evolved slowly over millennia, and likewise are slow to change. However, since both nature and nurture play roles in how our individual brains perform, the expression of our genetic makeup is affected by our surrounding culture. Our brains' neural networks are continually being rewired over our individual lifetimes as a result of our everyday experiences.

One of the other anchors in this writing has been Dan McAdams and his research on storytelling our lives. McAdams reminds us that from the cradle, we are actors on the world about us; from our early childhoods we are agents striving for goals influenced and shaped by our society; and from our adolescence we author our lives over the rest of our days. And we tell those stories in large part by drawing on the menu that our cultural world around us provides—songs, stories, symbols, conversations, and community traditions—to create a coherent sense of self with a past, present, and future world of meaning.

But here is the future culture that Gottschall winds up envisioning. It's a virtual world, distinct from the surrounding culture. He says that human attention is gradually "draining" into this virtual world. "Tens of millions of MMORPG devotees already spend an average of twenty to thirty hours per week absorbed in online adventures. According to a survey of thirty

---

3. Will Dunlop, UC-Riverside, personal communication.

thousand MMORPG players, about half all serious players form their most satisfying friendships in-game, and 20 percent consider MMORPG land to be their 'true home,' while Earth is 'merely a place they visit from time to time.'"[4] Like when they go to work or when they return home to visit the family before heading for the computer screen.

Now Boomers are probably not at much risk for such "draining," other than—as we have discussed in earlier chapters—having lost traditional communal roots and meaning-making stories that religious communities provide. And maybe not so much Gen Xers either—having been born before the current Internet world game craze—although they certainly know how to navigate that world as well. But I believe Boomers' grandchildren—the Millennials and beyond—are at risk because they may lack a broad and deep menu from which to draw as they immerse themselves in the next technological advance—losing the symbols of philosophical and theological meanings that undergird and give ultimate meaning to storied lives.

So the obvious. I would tell not only my sons but my grandsons and granddaughters to join a book club, read an actual newspaper (I realize that is quaint), talk to wise others—those who inspire you—over a cup of coffee or glass of wine, listen to the great music of our heritage, open your mind in silence to that transcendent being within whose ultimate story we pass our days—ideally within the context of some religious community. And live your human life to the fullest of your meaning-making capacity, storying it to the end of your days. Words of wisdom to live by and to pass on to those generations to come.

This is my wish for you as we now end this book journey that we have traveled together. May the fiction of your own life—that you continue to author—be coherent, hope-filled, wise, and forgiving, as you move toward the end of your own story in the years ahead. And so I hope that it shall be for us all.

---

4. Gottschall, *The Storytelling Animal*, 195.

Bibliography

Ackerman, Diane. *One Hundred Names for Love*. New York: W. W. Norton & Company, 2011.
Ahlstrom, Sydney. "The Radical Turn in Theology and Ethics: Why it Occurred in the 1960s." *The Annals of the American Academy of Political and Social Science* 387 (1970) 1–13.
Ammerman, Nancy. *Sacred Stories, Spiritual Tribes*. New York: Oxford University Press, 2014.
Attig, Thomas. "Relearning the World: Making and Finding Meanings." In *Meaning Reconstruction & the Experience of Loss*, edited by Robert Neimeyer, 33–54. Washington, DC: American Psychological Association, 2001.
The Beatles. "Eleanor Rigby." In *Revolver*. Capitol C4-46441, 1992, compact disc. Originally released in 1966.
———. "Help!" in *Help!* Parlophone CDP 7 46439 2, 1987, compact disc. Originally released in 1965.
Begbie, Jeremy. *Music, Modernity, and God: Essays in Listening*. Oxford: Oxford University Press, 2013.
Berger, Peter. *A Rumor of Angels*. Garden City, NY: Doubleday and Company, 1969.
Blum, Jason. "The Science of Consciousness and Mystical Experience: An Argument for Radical Empiricism." *Journal of the American Academy of Religion* 82:1 (2014) 150–73.
Boyd, Brian. *On the Origin of Stories: Evolution, Cognition, and Fiction*. Cambridge, MA: Harvard University Press, 2009.
Boyd, Malcolm. *Are You Running with Me, Jesus?* New York: Avon, 1965.
———. *The Underground Church*. New York: Sheed and Ward, 1968.
Brooks, David. *On Paradise Drive*. New York: Simon & Schuster, 2004.
Brown, Donald. *Human Universals*. Philadelphia: Temple University Press, 1991.
Bruni, Frank. "Gray Hair and Silver Linings." *New York Times*, November 9, 2014.
Cain, Susan. *Quiet: The Power of Introverts in a World that Can't Stop Talking*. New York: Broadway Paperbacks (Random House), 2013.
Church, Forrest. *Love & Death: My Journey through the Valley of the Shadow*. Boston: Beacon, 2009.
Cockburn, Bruce. "A Conversation with Bruce Cockburn." *Image* 84 (2015) 49–50.
Cockburn, Bruce (with Greg King). *Rumours of Glory*. San Francisco: HarperOne, 2014.
Cohen, Leonard. "Anthem." In *The Future*. Columbia CK 53226, 1992, compact disc.
———. "Hallelujah." In *Various Positions*. CK 66950, 1984, compact disc.

———. "Suzanne." In *Songs of Leonard Cohen*. Columbia CK 9533, 1990, compact disc. Originally released in 1967.

Cohn, Nate. "A Big Decline in Americans Identifying as Christian." *New York Times*, May 13, 2015.

Collins, Francis. *The Language of God: A Scientist Presents Evidence for Belief*. New York: Free, 2006.

Cowles, Gregory. "Oliver Sacks, Neurologist who Wrote about the Brain's Quirks, Dies at 82." *New York Times*, August 31, 2015.

Coyle, Bill. "Heart's Companion: Listening to Leonard Cohen." *Image* 79 (2013) 85–100.

Cozolino, Louis. *The Neuroscience of Human Relationships*. 2nd ed. New York: W. W. Norton and Company, 2014.

Currier, Joseph, et al. "Bereavement, Religion, and Post-Traumatic Growth: A Matched Control Group Investigation." *Psychology of Religion and Spirituality* 5 (2013) 69–72.

de Beauvoir, Simone. *The Coming of Age*. New York: W. W. Norton & Company, 1972.

de Gruchy, Isobel. *Between Heaven and Earth: Poems, Prayers, Pictures*. Eugene, OR: Resource, 2015.

———. *Walking On*. Hermanus, South Africa: Isobel de Gruchy, 2013.

de Gruchy, John. *Led into Mystery: Faith Seeking Answers in Life and Death*. London: SCM, 2013.

———. "Convocation Address." (Knox College, May 2014), http://www.knox.utoronto.ca/170th-convocation-address-the-rev-dr-john-de-gruchy/.

Denver, John. "Take Me Home, Country Roads." In *Poems, Prayers, and Promises*. RCA 5189-2-R, 1988, compact disc. Originally released in 1971.

de Waal, Frans. "The Antiquity of Empathy." *Science* 336 (2012) 874–76.

Diller, Vivian. "What Goes down Must Come Up." *The Huffington Post*, September 19, 2011. http://www.huffingtonpost, com/vivian-diller-phd/happiness-in-aging.

Douglas, Deborah. "Saved by Fiction." *The Christian Century*, October 17, 2012. http://www.christiancentury.org/archives/Vol129-Issue21.

Douthat, Ross. "All the Lonely People." *New York Times*, May 18, 2013.

Dubus, Andre. *Broken Vessels*. Boston: David R. Godine, 1991.

Dylan, Bob. "Like a Rolling Stone." In *Highway 61 Revisited*. Columbia CK 9189, 1988, compact disc. Originally released in 1965.

Edwards, Cliff. *Van Gogh and God: A Creative Spiritual Quest*. Chicago: Loyola University Press, 1989.

Ehrenreich, Barbara. *Dancing in the Streets: A History of Collective Joy*. New York: Henry Holt and Company, 2006.

Elie, Paul. *The Life You Save May Be Your Own: An American Pilgrimage*. New York: Farrar, Straus and Giroux, 2003.

Emmons, Robert. *Gratitude Works!: A 21-Day Program for Creating Emotional Prosperity*. San Francisco: Jossey Bass, 2013.

Emmons, Robert, and Michael McCullough. "Counting Blessings versus Burdens: An Experimental Investigation of Gratitude and Subjective Well-Being in Daily Life." *Journal of Personality and Social Psychology* 84 (2003) 277–389.

Emmons, Robert, and Michael McCullough, eds. *The Psychology of Gratitude*. New York: Oxford University Press, 2004.

Fate, Tom Montgomery. "The Presence of Absence." *Christian Century*, June 25, 2014, 30–31.

Follett, Ken. *Hornet Flight*. New York: Penguin, 2003.

Fox, Margalit. "Alice Herz-Sommer, who Found Peace in Chopin amid Holocaust, Dies at 110." *New York Times*, February 27, 2014.
Frankl, Viktor. *Man's Search for Meaning*. New York: Clarion Book, 1970.
Frederickson, Barbara. "Your Phone vs. Your Heart." *New York Times*, March 23, 2013.
Friedman, Howard, and Leslie Martin. *The Longevity Project: Surprising Discoveries for Health and Long Life from the Landmark Eight-Decade Study*. New York: Plume, 2012.
Gary Puckett & The Union Gap. "Young Girl." In *The Best of Gary Puckett & The Union Gap*. Hollywood HT-112, audio cassette, 1987. Originally released in 1968.
Gerrig, Richard. *Experiencing Narrative Worlds: On the Psychological Activities of Reading*. New Haven, CT: Westview, 1993.
Georges, Julie. "Music and Happiness." *Baby Boomer Bliss*. http://babyboomerbliss.net/music-and-happiness/.
Godwin, Gail. *Evenings at Five*. New York: Ballantine, 2004.
———. *Father Melancholy's Daughter*. New York: William Morrow and Company, 1991.
Goldstein, Elisha. "The Neuroscience of Happiness: An Interview with Rick Hanson." *PsychCentral* blog. http://blogs.psychcentral.com/mindfulness/2010/03/training-your-brain-for-the-better-an-interview-with-rick-hanson-ph-d/.
Goleman, Daniel. *Emotional Intelligence*. 10th anniversary ed. New York: Bantam, 2005.
Gone with the Wind. Directed by Victor Fleming. 1939. Burbank, CA: Warner Home Video, 2009. DVD.
Gordon, Annie, et al. "To Have and to Hold: Gratitude Promotes Relationship Maintenance in Intimate Bonds." *Journal of Personality and Social Psychology* 103 (2012) 257–74.
Gottschall, Jonathan. *The Storytelling Animal: How Stories Make us Human*. New York: Houghton Mifflin Harcourt, 2012.
Gottschall, Jonathan, and David Sloan Wilson, eds. *The Literary Animal: Evolution and the Nature of Narrative*. Evanston, IL: Northwestern University Press, 2005.
Granick, Isabela, et al. "The Benefits of Playing Video Games." *American Psychologist*, 69 (2014) 66–78.
Green, Joel, ed. *What About the Soul?: Neuroscience and Christian Anthropology*. Nashville: Abingdon, 2004.
Grumbach, Doris. "The View from 90." http://www.theamericanscholar.org/the-view-from-90.
Habermas, Tillman, and Susan Bluck. "Getting a Life; The Emergence of the Life Story in Adolescence." *Psychological Bulletin* 126 (2000) 748–69.
Haidt, Jonathan. "Elevation and the Positive Psychology of Morality." In *Flourishing: Positive Psychology and the Life Well Lived*, edited by Corey L. M. Keyes and Jonathan Haidt, 275–289. Washington, DC: American Psychological Association, 2003.
Haidt, Jonathan, and Craig Joseph. *The Happiness Hypothesis: Finding Modern Truth in Ancient Wisdom*. New York: Basic, 2006.
———. "Intuitive Ethics: How Innately Prepared Intuitions Generate Culturally Variable Virtues." *Daedalus* Fall (2004) 55–66.
Hamilton, Gabrielle. "Gabrielle Hamilton." *New York Times*, November 23, 2014.
Hanson, Rick (with Richard Mendius). *Buddha's Brain: The Practical Neuroscience of Happiness, Love, & Wisdom*. Oakland, CA: New Harbinger, 2009.

Harris, Paul. *The Work of the Imagination: Understanding Children's Worlds*. Oxford: Blackwell, 2000.

Harris, Richard. "MacArthur Park." In *A Tramp Shining*. MCA MCAD-10780, 1993, compact disc. Originally released in 1968.

Haruf, Kent. *Plainsong*. New York: Alfred A. Knopf, 1999.

———. *Our Souls at Night*. New York: Alfred A. Knopf, 2015.

Havermas, Tilmann, and Susan Bluck. "Getting a Life: The Emergence of the Life Story in Adolescence." *Psychological Bulletin*, 126 (2000) 748–69.

Heilbrun, Carolyn. *The Last Gift of Time: Life Beyond Sixty*. New York: Ballantine, 1997.

Heintzelman, Samantha, and Laura King. "Life is Pretty Meaningful." *American Psychologist* 69 (2014) 561–74.

Henig, Robin. "A Life-or-Death Situation." *The New York Times Magazine*, July 13, 2013, 27–33, 42, 50.

Henslin, Earl. *This is Your Brain on Joy: A Revolutionary Program for Balancing Mood, Restoring Brain Health, and Nurturing Spiritual Growth*. Nashville: Thomas Nelson, 2008.

Hillesum, Etty. *An Interrupted Life: The Diaries, 1941–1943, and Letters from Westerbork*. New York: Henry Holt and Company, 1996.

Hopkin, Mary. "Those Were the Days." In *Postcard*. Apple Records TOCP-67566, 2005, compact disc. Originally released in 1977.

Howe, Neil, and William Strauss. *Generations: The History of America's Future, 1584 to 2069*. New York: William Morrow, 1991.

Hudson, Robert, and Judith Gonyea. "Baby Boomers and the Shifting Political Construction of Old Age." *The Gerontologist* 52 (2012) 272–82.

Hull, Jay, et al. "A Longitudinal Study of Risk-Glorifying Video Games and Behavioral Deviance." *Journal of Personality and Social Psychology* 107 (2014) 300–325.

"In Brief." Monitor on Psychology, June (2015) 19.

Jamison, Kay Redfield. *Exuberance: The Passion for Life*. New York: Vintage, 2005.

———. *Nothing Was the Same*. New York: Alfred A. Knopf, 2009.

Jones, Landon. *Great Expectations: America and the Baby Boom Generation*. New York: Coward, McCann and Geoghegan, 1980.

Kenyon, Gary, Ernst Bohlmeijer, and William Randall. *Storying Later Life: Issues, Investigations, and Interventions in Narrative Gerontology*. New York: Oxford University Press, 2011.

Kidd, D., and E. Castano. "Reading Literary Fiction Improves Theory of Mind." *Science*, October 3, 2013, 377–80.

Kim, Hee Jung, et al. "Culture and Social Support." *American Psychologist* 63 (2008) 518–26.

Kimmelman, Michael. "The Urban Home Away from Home." *New York Times*, January 29, 2014.

King, Carole. "It's Too Late." In *Tapestry*. Ode Records EK 34946, 1986. Originally released in 1971.

King, Ursula. "The Zest for Life: A Contemporary Exploration." In *From Teilhard to Omega: Co-creating an Unfinished Universe*, edited by Ilia Delio, 184–202. Maryknoll, NY: Orbis, 2012.

King, Laura, and Joshua Hicks. "Whatever Happened to 'What Might Have Been'?" *American Psychologist* 62 (2007) 625–36.

The Kingston Trio. "Scotch and Soda." In *The Kingston Trio*. Capitol T 996, 1958, LP.

Klinenberg, Eric. *Going Solo*. New York: Penguin, 2012.

Kramer, Michael. *The Republic of Rock: Music and Citizenship in the Sixties Counterculture*. New York: Oxford University Press, 2013.
Lamott, Anne. *Help, Thanks, Wow*. New York: Penguin, 2012.
Le Doux, Joseph. *Synaptic Self: How Our Brains Become Who We Are*. New York: Penguin, 2003.
Lehrer, Jonah. *Proust was a Neuroscientist*. Boston: Houghton Mifflin, 2007.
Leithart, Peter. *Gratitude: An Intellectual History*. Waco, TX: Baylor University Press, 2014.
Levitin, Daniel. *This is Your Brain on Music: The Science of a Human Obsession*. New York: Plume (Penguin Group), 2007.
———. *The World in Six Songs: How the Musical Brain Created Human Nature*. New York: Dutton, 2008.
Levy, Sandra M. "Primitive Symbolic Consciousness and the Death Penalty in American Culture." *Anglican Theological Review* 83 (19) 717–34.
———. *Imagination and the Journey of Faith*. Grand Rapids: Eerdmans, 2008.
Levy-Achtemeier, Sandra M. "A Taste of Heaven: God of the Synapse." http://www.sandralevy.net/Blog/tabid/112/ArticleID/21/ArtMID/501/Default.aspx.
———. *Flourishing Life*. Eugene, OR: Cascade, 2012.
Light, Alan. *The Holy or the Broken: Leonard Cohen, Jeff Buckley and the Unlikely Ascent of "Hallelujah."* New York: Atria, 2012.
Lightfoot, Gordon. "If You Could Read My Mind." In *Sit Down, Young Stranger*. Reprise Records 6392-2, 1987, compact disc. Originally released in 1969.
Lin, I-Fin, and Susan Brown. "Unmarried Boomers Confront Old Age: A National Portrait." *The Gerontologist* 52 (2012) 153–65.
Lipsitz, George. "Who'll Stop the Rain?" In *The Sixties: From Memory to History*, edited by David Farber, 206–34. Chapel Hill, NC: The University of North Carolina Press, 1994.
Lischer, Richard. *Stations of the Heart*. New York: Vintage, 2013.
———. "Writing the Christian Life." *The Christian Century*, August, 24, 2015, 22–25, 27.
Loersch, Chris, and Nathan Arbuckle. "Unraveling the Mystery of Music: Music as an Evolved Group Process." *Journal of Personality and Social Psychology* 105 (2013) 777-98.
Lynch, Thomas. "How We Come to Be the Ones We Are." In *The Good Funeral: Death, Grief, and the Community of Care*, edited by Thomas G. Long and Thomas Lynch, 3–30. Louisville: Westminster John Knox, 2013.
MacDermot, Galt, et al. *Hair—Vocal Selections (Broadway Version): Piano/Vocal/Chords*. Van Nuys, CA: Alfred Music, 2009.
MacKay, Hugh. *Generations: Baby Boomers, Their Parents & Their Children*. Sydney: Pan Macmillan Australia Pty Ltd, 1997.
Mar, R., et al. "Exploring the Link between Reading Fiction and Empathy: Ruling out Individual Differences and Examining Outcomes." *Communications*, 34:4 (2009) 407–28.
Maranz Henig, Robin. "A Life-or-Death Situation." *New York Times*, July 17, 2013.
Mauss, Iris, et al. "Don't Hide Your Happiness! Positive Emotion Dissociation, Social Connectedness, and Psychological Functioning." *Journal of Personality and Social Psychology* 100 (2011) 738–48.
McAdams, Dan. "The Psychological Self as Actor, Agent, and Author." *Perspectives on Psychological Science* 8 (2013) 272–95.

———. *The Stories We Live By.* New York: Guilford, 1993.
———. *The Redemptive Self.* New York: Oxford University Press, 2006
McAdams, Dan, et al. "Family Metaphors and Moral Intuitions: How Conservatives and Liberals Narrate Their Lives." *Journal of Personality and Social Psychology* 95 (2008) 978–90.
McAdams, Dan, Ruth Josselson, and Amia Lieblich, eds. *Identity and Story: Creating Self in Narrative.* Washington, DC: American Psychological Association, 2007.
McEwan, Ian. "Literature, Science, and Human Nature." In *The Literary Animal,* edited by Jonathan Gottschall and David Sloan Wilson, 5–19. Evanston, IL: Northwestern University Press, 2005.
McGilchrist, Iain. *The Master and His Emissary: The Divided Brain and the Making of the Western World.* New Haven, CT: Yale University Press, 2009.
McIntosh, Daniel, et al. "Religion's Role in Adjustment to a Negative Life Event: Coping with the Loss of a Child." *Journal of Personality and Social Psychology* 65 (1993) 812–21.
McNeill, William H. *Keeping Together in Time: Dance and Drill in Human History.* Cambridge, MA: Harvard University Press, 1995.
Merton, Thomas. *The Seven Storey Mountain.* New York: Harcourt, Brace and Co., 1948.
Miles, Jack. *Christ: A Crisis in the Life of God.* New York: Alfred A. Knopf, 2001.
Miller, William. *Dorothy Day: A Biography.* San Francisco: Harper & Row, 1982.
Mithin, Stephen. *The Singing Neanderthals.* Cambridge, MA: Harvard University Press, 2006.
Myers, David. *The American Paradox: Spiritual Hunger in an Age of Plenty.* New Haven, CT: Yale Nota Bene, 2001.
Nader, Ralph. "Pete Seeger—"Character, Personality, Intuition and Focus." *The Huffington Post,* April 2, 2014. http://www.huffingtonpost.com/ralph-nader/pete-seeger-ralph-nader_b_4705622.html.
Neimeyer, Robert. "The Language of Loss: Grief Therapy as a Process of Meaning Reconstruction." In *Meaning Reconstruction & the Experience of Loss,* edited by Robert Neimeyer, 261–92. Washington, DC: American Psychological Association, 2001.
Newberg, Andrew. *Principles of Neurotheology.* London: Ashgate, 2010.
Newburg, Andrew, and Mark Waldman. *How God Changes Your Brain.* New York: Ballantine, 2009.
Novotney, Amy. "Music as Medicine." *Monitor on Psychology* (2013) 46–49.
"Older Americans' Breakups Are Causing a 'Graying' Divorce Trend." *All Things Considered.* NPR. February 24, 2014.
Oliver, Mary. "And Bob Dylan Too." In *A Thousand Mornings: Poems,* 27–28. New York: Penguin, 2013.
Oppenheimer, Mark. "Examining the Growth of 'Spiritual but Not Religious.'" *New York Times,* July 19, 2014.
———. "Joy: Poet, Seeker, and the Woman who Captivated C.S. Lewis." Review of *Joy: Poet, Seeker, and the Woman who Captivated C.S. Lewis* by Abigail Santamaria. *New York Times,* August 7, 2015, Sunday Book Review.
O'Rourke, Meghan. "Deadlines." *New York Times,* July 7, 2013.
Pals, Jennifer. "Constructing the 'Springboard Effect': Causal Connections, Self-making, and Growth within the Life Story." In *Identity and Story,* edited by Dan McAdams et al., 175–99. Washington, DC: American Psychological Association, 2007.

BIBLIOGRAPHY

Partridge, Christopher. *The Lyre of Orpheus: Popular Music, The Sacred, & The Profane*. New York: Oxford University Press, 2014.

Paulsell, Stephanie. "Praying Jane Eyre." *The Christian Century*, May 14, 2014, 35.

Prejean, Helen. *Dead Man Walking*. New York: Vintage, 1994.

Quindlen, Anna. *Lots of Candles, Plenty of Cake: A Memoir of a Woman's Life*. New York: Random House, 2012.

Raab, Lawrence. "My Life before I Knew It." In *A Probable World*, 57. New York: Penguin, 2000.

Ramachandran, V. S. *The Tell-Tale Brain: A Neuroscientist's Quest for What Makes us Human*. New York: W. W. Norton & Company, 2011.

Randall, William. *The Narrative Complexity of Ordinary Life: Tales from the Coffee Shop*. New York: Oxford University Press, 2015.

Rauch, Jonathan. "The Real Roots of Midlife Crisis." *The Atlantic*, December 2014, 88–95.

Reuter-Lorenz, Patricia A, and Denise C. Park. "Human Neuroscience and the Aging mind, A New Look at Old Problems." *Journal of Gerontology: Psychological Sciences* 65B (2010) 405–15.

The Righteous Brothers. "Unchained Melody." In *Just Once in My Life*. Philles Records PHLP-4008, 1965, LP.

Robinson, Marilynne. *Gilead*. New York: Farrar, Straus, & Giroux, 2004.

Root, Andrew. "Wired Together: How Our Brains Are Connected." *The Christian Century*, April 3, 2013, 32–34.

Roof, Wade Clark. *Spiritual Marketplace: Baby Boomers and the Remaking of American Religion*. Princeton, NJ: Princeton University Press, 1999.

Rosengren, Karl, et al., eds. *Imagining the Impossible: Magical, Scientific, and Religious Thinking in Children*. Cambridge, MA: Cambridge University Press, 2000.

Rosenthal, Peggy. "An Apprenticeship in Affliction." *Image* Spring (2012) 83.

Roth, Erin, et al. "Baby Boomers in an Active Adult Retirement Community: Comity Interrupted." *The Gerontologist* 52:2 (2012) 189–98.

Sacks, Oliver. "The Joy of Old Age. (No Kidding)." *New York Times*, July 6, 2013.

———. "My Own Life." *New York Times*, February 19, 2015.

Sander, Ellen. *Trips: Rock Life in the Sixties*. New York: Scribner, 1973.

Seeger, Pete. "Which Side Are You On?" In *Pete Seeger's Greatest Hits*. Columbia CK 65711, 2002, compact disc. Originally released in 1967.

Shallcroix, Amanda, et al. "Getting Better with Age: the Relationship between Age, Acceptance, and Negative Affect." *Journal of Personality and Social Psychology* 104 (2013) 734–49.

Shaw, Luci. *God in the Dark: Through Grief and Beyond*. Grand Rapids: Zondervan, 1993.

Simon, Carly. *Boys in the Trees*. New York: Flatiron, 2015.

———. "Let the River Run." In *Working Girl (Original Soundtrack Album)*. Arista ARCD-8593, 1989, compact disc.

———. "That's the Way I Always Heard It Should Be." In *Carly Simon*. Elektra 74082–2, 1988, compact disc. Originally released in 1971.

Simon and Garfunkel. "America." In *Bookends*. Columbia CK 9529, 1985, compact disc. Originally released in 1968.

———. "Cecilia." In *Bridge over Troubled Water*. Columbia CK 53444, 1993, compact disc. Originally released in 1969.

255

BIBLIOGRAPHY

———. "The Dangling Conversation." In *Parsley, Sage, Rosemary, and Thyme*. Columbia CK 66001, 2001, compact disc. Originally released in 1966.

———. "The Sound of Silence." In *Sounds of Silence*. Columbia CK 9269, 1989, compact disc. Originally released in 1966.

Smith, J. W., and A. Clurman. *Generation Ageless: How Baby Boomers Are Changing the Way We Live Today . . . and They're Just Getting Started*. New York: Harper Collins, 2007.

Taverner, Royette, and Teena Willoughby. "Adolescent Turning Points: The Association between Meaning-Making and Psychological Well-Being." *Developmental Psychology* 48 (2012) 1058–68.

Thomas, B. J. "Hooked on a Feeling." In *On My Way*. Scepter Records SPS570, 1968, LP.

Torres, Stacy. "Old McDonald's." *New York Times*, January 22, 2014.

Touré. "Greil Marcus's 'History of Rock 'n' Roll in Ten Songs.'" Review of *History of Rock 'n' Roll in Ten Songs* by Greil Marcus. *New York Times*, December 7, 2014, Sunday Book Review.

Trimble, Michael. *The Soul in the Brain: The Cerebral Basis of Language, Art, and Belief*. Baltimore: Johns Hopkins University Press, 2007.

The Turtles. "Happy Together." In *Happy Together*. Sundazed Music SC 6037, 1994, compact disc. Originally released in 1967.

Tyler, Anne. *A Patchwork Planet*. New York: Alfred A. Knopf, 1998.

Villiamy, Ed. "Terezin: Music from a Nazi Ghetto." *The Guardian*, April 5, 2013. https://www.theguardian.com/music/2013/apr/05/terezin-nazi-camp-music-eva-clarke.

Viorst, Judith. *Necessary Losses*. New York: Free, 1986.

Visser, Margaret. *The Gift of Thanks: The Roots and Rituals of Gratitude*. New York: Houghton Mifflin Harcourt, 2009.

Volf, Miroslav. "What is the Difference between Joy and Happiness?" *Big Questions Online*. https://www.bigquestionsonline.com/2014/10/21/what-difference-between-joy-happiness/.

Weir, Kirsten. "Mission Possible." *Monitor on Psychology* October (2013) 42–45.

Wells, Samuel. "Thanks for What?" *Christian Century* January 8, 2014, 35.

Wiman, Christian. *My Bright Abyss*. New York: Farrar, Straus and Giroux, 2013.

Wiman, Christian, and Matt Fitzgerald. "Embrace and Abandonment: A Pastor and a Poet Talk about God." *Christian Century* June 25, 2014, 22–27.

Wolfe, Gregory. "The Harboring Silence." *Image* 86 (2015) 6.

Wolpe, David. *The Healer of Shattered Hearts*. New York: Penguin, 1991.

Zunshine, Lisa. *Why We Read Fiction: Theory of Mind and the Novel*. Columbus, OH: Ohio State University Press, 2006.

www.ingramcontent.com/pod-product-compliance
Lightning Source LLC
Chambersburg PA
CBHW030613230426
43661CB00053B/1972